ELENA FERRANTE'S KEY WORDS

Tiziana de Rogatis

ELENA FERRANTE'S KEY WORDS

*Translated from the Italian
by Will Schutt*

Europa
editions

Europa Editions
214 West 29th Street
New York, N.Y. 10001
www.europaeditions.com
info@europaeditions.com

Copyright © 2018 by Edizioni e/o
First Publication 2019 by Europa Editions

Translation by Will Schutt
Original title: *Elena Ferrante. Parole chiave*
Translation copyright © 2019 by Europa Editions

Prior to publication this book was peer reviewed by two anonymous reviewers.

Library of Congress Cataloging in Publication Data is available
ISBN 978-1-60945-563-7

de Rogatis, Tiziana
Elena Ferrante's Key Words

Book design by Emanuele Ragnisco
www.mekkanografici.com

Cover image: Alfons Mucha, *Lottery of the Union of Southwestern Moravia*
(poster, detail, 1912) © Mucha Trust / Bridgeman Images

Prepress by Grafica Punto Print—Rome

Printed in the USA

CONTENTS

For Rosetta Gervasio, my brilliant friend

ELENA FERRANTE'S KEY WORDS

NOTE

Works by Elena Ferrante cited in this essay are listed in parentheses as follows:

ban—*The Beach at Night*
doa—*The Days of Abandonment*
fer—Cited material appeared in the *Guardian* and elsewhere
fr—*Frantumaglia*
ld—*The Lost Daughter*
mbf—*My Brilliant Friend*
slc—*The Story of the Lost Child*
snn—*The Story of a New Name*
tl—*Troubling Love*
tlts—*Those Who Leave and Those Who Stay*

For all other works, the author's last name and, where applicable, a page number are given.
Please see the bibliography at the end of the book for a complete list of references and further information about how the cited works have been used.

1. Elena Ferrante's Readers Around the World

How do we pick up the thread of a discussion to talk about the women friends in America who celebrated purchasing the quartet together? How do we unspool it to reach the reader in Leeds, England, for whom Elena Ferrante's Naples is reminiscent of Glasgow and, in general, every city on the margins of the neoliberal economy? How can we stretch that thread all the way to Australia, where a British reader who emigrated forty years ago finds in *The Neapolitan Novels* the same violence she knew in the tiny Northumbrian village where she was born? How do we untangle the skein in China, where a male student from Nanking University points out the arc of the Italian Communist Party embedded in the quartet, while a female student from Fudan University, in Shanghai, sees *smarginatura* (a term that Ferrante employs to describe the dissolution of boundaries) as a reaction against the forms of arrogance endured by women? Why not finally intertwine the thread of memory with that of emotion by recalling the reader who, again in Leeds, stood up at the end of a talk on "Ferrante Fever" and, in a loud, stentorian voice, said, "Tell Elena Ferrante to keep writing! Tell her we want to read her stories here in Yorkshire!" However far apart on the world map, these distant and distinct voices are united by a passion for this author's work. I have heard them at talks and readings that I have given about *The Neapolitan Novels* over the past two years. Their chorus suggests that, thanks to Ferrante's writing, Naples and Italy generally have given us a repertoire of stories about our globalized ultra-modernity: a classic for our times.

Because we now live in a local and global web, Elena and Lila—two little girls who represent our hopes and fears for the future, who show us that frightened rootedness is the most painful form of displacement—speak to us; in our lives, too, those who leave *are* those who stay. For readers, the quartet excites dark impulses, unresolved questions, and tangled emotions about the major transformations taking place today, by way of an almost provocative depiction of Naples and its particular (social, cultural, political) makeup, which flies in the face of modern order. Strange, perhaps even exoticized by readers in certain passages, the city is also familiar, a kindred spirit, a sister, because it is part of European history and embodies a crisis of progress, the shadow line where today's globalized West has lost its way. The appeal of this locally rooted yet cosmopolitan story lies in its volcanic metamorphosis of lives and time. There is something excessive and elusive about the quartet, which is why this "epic story of a great friendship" (Benini) is much more than a love story and far less than a conventional oath of loyalty. This large historical tableau is actually—in Ferrante's own words—an investigation into the lives of its figures and their sufferings, a countermelody to the rhetoric of country, progress, revolution, even feminism.

To shed light on the meaning of this metamorphosis, I have mapped out the themes found in the author's complete works. Indeed, I have conceived of this book as an Ariadne's thread of key words, which, like signal lights, can indicate the many twists and turns of Ferrante's writing and help us navigate the labyrinth of her international success: a success that originated in Italy, has been nurtured in America by readers and critics— James Wood deserves special mention—and eventually led to the book's publication in forty-eight countries, where it has reached more than ten million readers worldwide (including a million three hundred thousand in Italy and three million in the US). Ferrante's translator Ann Goldstein is also to thank for the spread of "Ferrante Fever" across the US. Goldstein has participated in many public talks about *The Neapolitan Novels* and presents, together with the invisible author, a model of creative female partnership that mirrors the literary partnership of Elena and Lila at the heart of the quartet (Milkova[1]).

2. The Chapters in This Book

Elena Ferrante's Key Words targets the same varied cross-section of readers who in every corner of the world have found *The Neapolitan Novels* meaningful. I will also discuss the quartet in the context of the author's first three novels—*Troubling Love* (1992), *The Days of Abandonment* (2002), *The Lost Daughter* (2006)—the fable *The Beach at Night* (2007), and the essays, letters, and interviews collected in *Frantumaglia* (2003–2016). Like the quartet, these creative and critical works revolve around a new form of female identity made visible by a common set of themes and images. Lurking behind Elena and Lila are Delia, Olga, and Leda, the main characters of *Troubling Love*, *The Days of Abandonment*, and *The Lost Daughter*, respectively. These five women are bound by a common narrative about female subjectivity and its ability to dismantle itself and be reborn from *frantumaglia*, a traumatic experience in which reality is shattered, an experience closely linked to the *smarginatura* that governs *The Neapolitan Novels* both formally and thematically. It is no coincidence that both terms are neologisms, one of them semantic (*smarginatura*; see 3.2); their novelty suggests the need to rename the world from a new point of view. Given that "the narrative choices . . . can all be traced back to the changing condition of women at the center of the narrative" (fr 276), the two friends' metamorphosis and/or *smarginatura* can be linked to the metamorphosis and/or *smarginatura* of the books' forms and themes.

Chapters Two and Three ("Female Friendship" and "*Smarginatura, Frantumaglia*, Surveillance: Between Mothers and Daughters") explain how Ferrante's entire body of work has given voice to crucial features of female difference, a historical, existential, and biological otherness that rebalances the scales and rewords what we have inherited from the age-old repertoire of the male imagination. While reckoning with that repertoire's tendency to classify emerging female subjectivity as a deviation from (male) standards, the difference depicted in the quartet has shifted its center of gravity. Chapters Two and Three retrace the signs of such otherness in the practice of female friendship, in its controversial and baffling forms, in a *troubling* dimension of love and abandonment, in *frantumaglia, smarginatura*, and a new kind of surveillance, in the hidden channel connecting all these emotions and experiences, in the combative but foundational relationship between mothers and daughters, and in motherhood as both frame and cage of public life, its successes as well as its failures. These are "fragments with the most varied historical and biological origins . . . fickle agglomerations that maintain a fragile equilibrium, that are inconsistent and complex, that can't be reduced to a fixed framework" (fr 217).

But difference is also a point of view, a means of constructing new categories of perception through which to rewrite contexts that are only apparently unrelated: literary forms as bilingualism, urban spaces as hubs of Italian and European history. Beginning with this difference, Chapter One, "A Brilliant Popular Narrative," analyzes the narrative mechanism of *The Neapolitan Novels* and the novelty of this engaging and innovative story, which cannot be dismissed as commercial literature. The final four chapters ("Naples, the Urban Labyrinth"; "Two Languages, Emigration, and Schooling"; "Violence, Imagery,

Disappearances"; and "History and Stories") dwell on the long time frame of the quartet and the fragments of history that emerge from it: Naples as a border city, a labyrinth both in and outside the straitjacket of modernity; the conflict and cross-pollination between standard language and dialect; the emancipation of new female and bilingual voices; national identity as a tale of emigration; school as a formative and alienating experience for a "second-class" woman; the language of male violence and its blend of physical and symbolic domination; the dissipation of history from the 1950s through the first decade of the new millennium.

3. Alienation and Inclusion

These key words in Ferrante form the lexicon of a story about women caught between emancipation and marginalization, a story both intimate and social, which can paint both the big picture and its cracks. In the quartet, gender—that is, the historically and culturally determined role of women—provides the lens that allows us to take in an entire historical-social landscape and is, crucially, what makes the scenario interesting to millions of readers worldwide. As Ferrante points out, this large historical tableau emerges from the perspective of "alienation-inclusion" that gives the plot its structure (fr 283). Elena and Lila—the first the daughter of a porter at the city hall, the latter the daughter of a shoemaker—represent a lower-class, female point of view that is historically subordinate to the logic of male power and its various hierarchies. Yet thanks to the events of the 1950s to '70s—from the social mobility of the Italian economic miracle to the transformation of civil society and feminism—this is a point of view that can become inclusive and central by virtue of its roots in these very margins. The female "margin" is not relegated to the private realm—that inner, domestic gynaeceum and home-*cum*-prison—but, rather, is inevitably internalized and recreated by Elena and Lila as they break free of its moldy confines; though they manage to fight back bravely, they are often embarrassed and humiliated in public spaces. Ultimately, the marginalized novel becomes a coming-of-age (and deviating-from-the-norm) story within which Elena and her writing career emerge as a clear subgenre: the *Künstlerroman*, or "artist's novel."

The narrative encompasses all the historical inequalities of female identity and depicts the contradictions inherent in a self that is torn between her centrality to the creative act and her historically subaltern role. To quote a popular feminist slogan, to which the entire perspective of *The Neapolitan Novels* cycle is indebted, "The personal is political." These four words speak to "what we are made of" (fr 332), insofar as women's bodies are shaped—in public spaces even before domestic ones—by a type of subordination rooted in an ancient symbolic order that produces structural inequality between men and women. In the quartet, the subplots about human destiny reveal their strata of power and violence through women's lives while at the same time giving rise to an inclusive female mode, which has succeeded in turning the personal into the political, beginning with one woman's moral and immoral relationship with another. Therein lies the ultimate meaning of *The Neapolitan Novels*' polyphony, of the narrative mechanism that shapes the story from the echo of Lila's words in Elena's and from their "splendid and shadowy" (slc 451; see 1.5) friendship, forged from emancipation and power.

4. Ferrante in the #MeToo Era

Among the reasons for Elena Ferrante's international success, three others are worth mentioning, all of them connected.

First, Ferrante revisits our idea of brilliance or "*genio*" (Setti[1] 111), a concept traditionally attributed to men, and locates it chiefly in the friendship between the two main characters (thereby breaking the stereotype that women are incapable of forming bonds; of, as they say in Naples, "*non tenere a genio*"; Brogi[1]). Second, she portrays Elena and Lila as two women who are extremely intense and vivid *because* they are problematic and embody, each in her own way, ambiguities and contradictions. Just think of Elena's opportunism, Lila's notorious "spite," and the mixture of nobility and misery that defines their friendship. Last, Ferrante fashions from their story a parable of survival, not of victimhood. The pathos of the victim is actually exorcized by the two friends' complexity and by their fictional representation as women who, on the one hand, have had to suffer the physical and symbolic violence of male domination (sometimes deluding themselves into thinking they can manipulate and control it), but, on the other hand, have also sought, at various stages in their lives, to develop creative forms of resistance. The survival of Elena and Lila is not just a creative form of struggle against the status quo but also a painful reflection on the colonized parts of their own imagination.

The years that preceded and then saw the explosion of the #MeToo phenomenon and the issue of violence against women (as a normalized practice that pervades all social classes and countries) are the same that, not coincidentally, saw the widening of all forms of inequality, gender inequality chief among them (Danna). Enter Ferrante, whose writing has provided our international consciousness with a female ethic of survival and an indirect response to the attempts to dismiss #MeToo as a victims' movement. In the quartet, surviving means recognizing our disenfranchised female past in our daughters' emancipated present, acknowledging the violent line of matricide in the maternal family tree, processing the legacy of male domination through a controversial but solid model of friendship, and building a new capacity for self-assertion and creativity on victims' understandable fragility and contradictions (see Chapters 2, 3 and 6).

I use the word survival here in its broadest sense, one that welcomes, first, feminist debate about processing abuse—which had already started in the 1970s—as well as the philosophical and cultural model that can explain the extraordinary anthropological, temporal, and spatial density of the quartet. Elena and Lila's marginalization is, to borrow the art historian Didi-Huberman's metaphor, an "imprint," the reemergence of a mark that some people consider outmoded and obsolete, but which resurfaces in the world at another point in history. From the perspective of #MeToo, this "imprint" has reemerged today, in the era of globalization, when "nothing has faded, everything is here in the present" (fr 366), a painful period in which the archaic and the ultra-modern, regression and progress, coexist. At the same time, survival is the ability to form a new social imaginary by overwriting the old, at times erasing old signs instead of adding new ones, even renaming the old images from a female perspective: the pictures (see Chapter 6) through which Ferrante's protagonists reformulate images of male domination have a subversive power analogous to the abuse stories of #MeToo, where the victim, by the very act of telling her story, becomes a survivor.

5. Who's Afraid of Elena Ferrante?

The quartet indirectly challenges the circumscribed place assigned to women writers by certain publishers, journalists, and academics in Italy. Golden cage or ghetto, in either case it's regarded as "a by-product, good only as a pastime for women" (fr 316). On the other hand, the ability to create a female viewpoint that is simultaneously specific and choral, sentimental and political, in the large historical tableau that is *The Neapolitan Novels* represents a break from this cage and ghetto, a challenge to the "different standards of *credibility* in fiction" (Brogi[2]) still applied to female and male writing. So, who's afraid of Elena Ferrante? Many critical responses to the quartet are, at their root, reactions against the way the novel trespasses beyond the confines traditionally staked out for women writers, against the way it challenges literary hierarchies (in particular, the double standards for men and women writers), and against the point of view from which the stories are told—reactions that are purely reflexive, muddled when not downright hysterical, and at times embarrassingly poorly argued.

It may be interesting to compare such reactions to those that greeted the release of Elsa Morante's *History*, in 1974. One of the most important Italian novels of the second half of the twentieth century has often been described as, for example, a sentimental, mawkish *romanzone*, or romance novel. Not surprisingly, in both cases the dispute is over two women writers whose revisions of history became widely popular. Both novels were born of a twofold ambition: to describe the violent and/or chance refractions of major world events, personal lives, and their vulnerable differences over a very long period of time, and to engage—albeit using different strategies—as many readers as possible in this flow of time. The comparison reveals the similarity between the most intransigent critiques of Ferrante and the no less extreme critiques aimed at Morante, showing how each advances two overlapping lines of criticism: The first concerns gender and the way a portion of the Italian cultural world is closed off to women writers and the anti-hierarchical viewpoint through which they construct the world. The second, aesthetic, has to do with the persistence in Italian literature of an occasionally fussy experimental cult that rejects style or its (in appearance only) opposite—the highbrow cult that identifies literary artistry in elegant and refined prose (a taste that is widespread to this day and which, several decades ago, dismissed the writing of Svevo and Pirandello as ugly). Both hardline approaches to style promote elitist taste and label as mediocre and/or slavish to market logic all forms and genres of writing that, on the one hand, express a complexity that originates in the world of the novel and not in stylistic or ideological presuppositions, and, on the other, attempt to engage a wider audience.

6. Belying Our Expectations About Identity

Earlier I spoke of the viewpoint of women writers. I think this is an essential issue for Ferrante precisely because (and not in spite) of her decision not to reveal her true identity. Indeed, there's something which no financial prying, no statistical analysis, no invasion of privacy, and no shadow of marital or patriarchal support can ever take away from her or us, her female and male readers. In a country like Italy, where male journalists, publishers, and professors consistently undermine women writers and their visibility, Elena Ferrante has chosen to stand with those women. If we were to take the many far-fetched rumors to their extreme, we might go so far as to say that Ferrante is both man and woman, transvestite and/or transgender, heterosexual and homosexual, a single living being, a couple, a threesome, a collective. We cannot know her true identity with absolute certainty, but one thing we do know is that during her two decades of writing in seclusion—from her first novel, *Troubling Love* (1992), to the publication and success of the first volume of the quartet, *My Brilliant Friend* (2011)—she chose to make herself less prominent, not more. Not only in her novels but also in the many interviews and letters included in *Frantumaglia*, Ferrante has chosen to fashion the world from a woman's point of view. On the literary, social, and communicative (pronominal, syntactical, linguistic) plane, she has asserted and demonstrated that a woman's perspective is decisive. Nobody will ever be able to take that away from her, or us.

In countless interviews, Ferrante has provided reasons for her absence from the public stage, reasons connected to an idea of authorship as utterly disentangled from the empirical individual: "The author is the sum of the expressive strategies that shape an invented world, a concrete world that is populated by people and events" (fr 355). Her desire to highlight the truthfulness of fiction has also drawn sharp reactions from critics who see her choice to conceal her identity as a marketing ploy to increase sales. In certain corners of Italian culture, there seems to be a link between success and betrayal, a kind of moral equivalence according to which good sales correspond to a work's lack of literary merit, to its being dumbed down for commercial appeal. All we need to do is read the first seventy pages of *Frantumaglia* to understand that Ferrante's decision to remain anonymous dates back to her earliest publications, when she was a niche author who could never have imagined her future success—that it was a decision made to safeguard her creative independence: "I prefer that the corner for writing remain a hidden place, with no surveillance or urgency of any type" (fr 85).

This strategy of self-protection is confirmed by the surprising dynamic of her interrupted correspondence. In the years that followed the publication of *Troubling Love* and up until *The Days of Abandonment* (2002), some of her replies to letters and interviews—later included in the first edition of *Frantumaglia* (2003)—were either never sent or variously sabotaged before being released to the public (fr 47, 51, 57, 69, 74). Such reserve is truly alien to today's rampant narcissism and in no way corresponds to the conspiracy theories that dismiss Ferrante's writing as the product of a marketing team. Moreover, her decision is motivated by an oft-repeated polemic against a need manufactured by the media to "[invent] protagonists while ignoring the quality of the work" (fr 255). Ferrante responds to this manufactured need with her "experiment," which directly brings into play the freedom of the reader. "My experiment," she writes, "is intended to call attention to the original unity of author and text and to the self-sufficiency of the reader, who can get all he needs from that unity" (fr 299). If curiosity about the author—on the wave of her success and despite her intentions—sometimes fuels readers' desire for autobiography, that is due to a paradoxical and currently widespread need among readers to approach narratives that are fictional by nature as if they were authentic experiences that speak directly about real life. Rather than a cynical marketing ploy, this powerful fantasy surrounding memoir (where fictional events are constantly attributed to the author's life in a kind of never-ending autobiography) is symptomatic of our present-day hunger for reality, and should give us pause. If anything, there is in Ferrante a powerful determination to reshuffle the deck and belie established expectations.

With its blend of the critical and the conversational (see 3.6), *Frantumaglia* shows how the writer intended to cast doubts on the confessionalism of autobiography by forming over time a liminal "I," free to reveal itself in secret. "Writing is a free act," she says, "by means of which, to use an oxymoron, one secretly opens oneself" (fr 178). At the same time, she eludes the expectations linked to so-called women's writing. The (almost paranoid) complaints about her anonymity actually reveal another cultural presumption, one that demands that an artist bare her soul, rubber-stamp the truthfulness of the feelings and experiences that she writes about, put herself on display and dish about her family, her marriage, and her divorce, providing readers with a photo album of herself then and now, in group pictures or by herself, at cocktail parties and on book tours, especially if the artist in question is a woman. In other words, if she is, by certain conventions (conventions pertaining to a part of Italian culture, naturally), the best spokesperson for the cult of sentiment, private confession, the humble life of feelings.

And, if the writer in question has for decades drawn inspiration from a historically marginalized place, like the outskirts of a city, and a city like Naples, at that—a sort of aggregate of the collective unconscious of Italy and of Naples—then biography becomes paramount. Because only if your birth certificate proves you were *really* born and raised in that marginal world can you guarantee that the purity of Naples (in keeping with a certain Neapolitan essentialism) will not be peddled on the market or, on the contrary, that your literary voice is sufficiently charged with exotic intensity (in keeping with the country's rampant paternalistic condescension toward the city). Naturally, Ferrante is not the only one who has to contend with such expectations; in many ways, it is an international issue that has increasingly imposed standards of authenticity on marginalized corners throughout literature, the very corners to which women and ethnic or postcolonial writers are traditionally relegated (including, to a certain extent, the literature of the Italian South; Huggan 155, 163). If Ferrante makes these expectations particularly clear to us, it is because her choice has sabotaged them, forcing us all to reconsider their presumed naturalness and the ideologies lurking behind them.

I wonder how a biting, unsettling tale like *My Brilliant Friend* has been embraced let alone grasped by so many readers, female and male, to the point that the quartet has become one of the most well-regarded works of contemporary world literature. Perhaps it is because nowadays we all need fiction that conveys the symbolic power of the margins of our time, that drags us through layers of time and the forms of social domination up to the present, that shows us the connection between the particular and the universal, as the world's best writers do: those who subscribe—whether or not they are aware of it—to "rooted cosmopolitanism" (Beck 19). Perhaps today all of us need the social and gender-based backwardness of our contemporary moment to be revealed to us not in the guise of a philosophical idea or essay but in the guise of a story. Perhaps what we need, ultimately, is a story based on a human event, universally felt and universally experienced, an event finally visible in literary form and in our social imaginary: the friendship between two women.

Many friends, both female and male, have accompanied me on this journey through the world of Ferrante, helping me interpret new horizons of our contemporary imagination, thanks to their research, attention, and advice. Although I alone bear responsibility for the contents of this book, my deepest thanks go to the following people and institutions:

Alessio Baldini, Anna Baldini, Francesco Barbieri, Laura Benedetti, Giuseppe Bonifacino, Maurizio Braucci, Daniela Brogi, Stefano Brugnolo, Carlo Caruso, Richard Carvalho, Domitilla Cataldi, Pietro Cataldi, Luigi Cinque, Stefano Cracolici, Chiara De Caprio, Francesco de Cristofaro, Marina de Rogatis, Anna Di Toro, Raffaele Donnarumma, Monica Farnetti, Enrica Ferrara, Eva Ferri, Cristiana Franco, Pierantonio Frare, Massimo Fusillo, Immacolata Giacci, Alessandra Ginzburg, Adalgisa Giorgio, Ann Goldstein, Marina Guglielmi, Simon Hackett and St. Mary's College, University of Durham, the Institute of Advanced Study (IAS) at the University of Durham, Helena Janeczek, Jhumpa Lahiri, Viola Lo Moro and the women behind the Tuba bookshop, Stefania Lucamante, Alberto Manai and the Italian Cultural Institute at Shanghai, Silvia Manfredo, Simona Micali, Stiliana

Milkova and Oberlin College, Mauro Moretti, Mariella Muscariello, Massimo Palermo, Valerio Petrarca, Emanuela Piemontese, Stefania Rimini, Maria Rizzarelli, Olivia Santovetti, Niccolò Scaffai, Will Schutt, Ottavio Sellitti, Nadia Setti, Maria Sica and the Italian Cultural Institute at Stockholm, Michele Sisto, Silvia Sommaruga, Elena Spandri, Adriana Sulikova and the Italian Cultural Institute at Bratislava, Serena Todesco, Désirée Trankaer, Andrea Villarini, Sergio Zatti, Katrin Wehling-Giorgi and the School of Modern Languages and Cultures, University of Durham.

1. Ferrante Fever

I just was captured by it." "I was . . . shoveling the books quickly." So say Elizabeth Strout and Jonathan Franzen, two of the most important American writers today, in the film *Ferrante Fever* (2017), and their words have been echoed by more than seven million readers around the world who have found themselves stricken by the need to devour all four volumes of *The Neapolitan Novels*. "Ferrante Fever" isn't an isolated case. Although the phrase originated in a New York bookshop in 2015, and is a playful pop reference to "Saturday Night Fever," it also alludes to the kind of pandemic that fiction has long inspired. *Werther-Fieber* was the term used to describe the international wave of hysteria surrounding the publication of Goethe's novel *The Sorrows of Young Werther* (and its translations) in 1774, which caused copycat suicides, was subsequently banned, and spawned less traumatic phenomena, including pilgrimages to the supposed site of Werther's grave, Werther-inspired male fashion, and the sale of promotional items. Then there are the Janeites, a term coined in 1894 (although the phenomenon began much earlier) to describe the many readers so crazy about Jane Austen's work that they exhibited their familiarity with the author by affectionally referring to her by her first name. Another novel that caused a mass epidemic was Wilkie Collins's *The Woman in White*. From 1859 to 1860 readers flocked to England's bookshops to buy the magazine in which the novel appeared in serial form. Ferrante, too, might subscribe to the credo with which Collins educated his friend Charles Dickens in the rhythms of the sensational: "Make 'em cry, make 'em laugh, make 'em wait."

In short, the taste and the techniques for enthralling readers by producing hair-raising states of alarm begin with the novel—the inclusive, popular hybrid genre par excellence. As Carlo Emilio Gadda pointed out upon rereading Alessandro Manzoni, the novel by its very nature opens itself to various readers and various readings as it seeks to address both "lowbrow" and "highbrow" audiences (Brogi[3] 221). In our day, when tastes are far less classist and hierarchical, the novel also addresses a highbrow audience that wants to be lowbrow and is willing to be transported by an entertaining, tautly paced, plot-driven book that also happens to be the vehicle of a complex vision. Paradoxically, the novel, precisely because of its hybrid roots, has a history of driving critics to make labored distinctions based on a phobic need to separate high and low. It's enough to read the introduction of Peter Brooks's magisterial *Melodramatic Imagination*, of 1976, to realize how shocking the idea was that the classic novelists of the nineteenth and twentieth century, such as Balzac, Conrad, Dickens, Dostoevsky, James, Lawrence, and Proust, recycled melodrama and popular modes of entertainment.

Ferrante is a master of intertwining high and low; that alone is a rare skill in a writer. Nevertheless, though the quartet can look like a "sensation novel," though it moves at breakneck speed, it is not a recipe devised to incite, and then satisfy, readers' superficial cravings. Quite the contrary: it is both a brilliant and a popular narrative. With *The Neapolitan Novels*, the author—concise, experimental, and refined in her previous three novels—had the courage and creative intelligence to inject the stuff of entertainment and popular literature into a complex, uncommercial form. Not coincidentally, Elsa Morante employed the same strategy, starting with her novel

Menzogna e sortilegio (*Lying and Witchcraft*, translated as *House of Liars*). Proudly embracing the restrictions still encumbering women's writing, she stationed herself on the edge of tradition—the very place to which these restrictions intended to relegate her—and then, from that marginalized position, carved out a new center. The moment these writers situate their material in the margins and recreate it in an original key, they reckon with their own delegitimization, not by internalizing it but, on the contrary, by transforming it into a position of otherness that strengthens their own authorial "I."

In this light, you could apply to the quartet an apt critical term that has been used to describe the hybrid form of Morante's first novel: hyper-genre (Porciani 89). In both cases, we are confronted with a work that blurs the line between the novel and the anti-novel. In the quartet the epic of a new female subjectivity coincides with the fragmentation of History, the serial novel and melodrama bump up against the doubling effect of the story within the story, and the airy symmetry of the structure is broken down by problematic, incongruent characters and their destinies (cf. 7.2). For Ferrante, "resorting to low sources," rummaging through the "cellar of writing," and reckoning with "a fund of pleasure that for years [she] repressed in the name of Literature" (fr 64) means drawing on subgenres, like thrillers, serial novels, the Neapolitan *sceneggiata*, even photo romances—that is to say, marginalized genres—to create her own work. Such a strategy seeks to imbue writing with the emotional energy of plot, bypassing the most experimental twentieth-century models, and, at the same time, to rewrite and transform the "great foundational novels" (fr 269), with their dramatic turns of events, reversals of fortune, and multiple storylines.

2. The *Smarginatura* of the Plot

The writing of *The Neapolitan Novels* erects and dismantles barriers simultaneously. On the one hand, it employs order and cohesion to ensure that the events develop from a careful and engaging application of the principle of unity in difference, and, on the other, it sets in motion a series of twists to disrupt that order and infuse the narrative world with "signs of first-hand knowledge of terror" (fr 373). The story grew primarily out of "a sort of chaos to depart from, an obscurity to illuminate" (fr 322): the morass of interiority is the subject at the center of the canvas. Aware of the disorienting effect that her work might have, the author herself asks that the reader "confront himself" (fr 325). "The fate of a story that tends toward truth" (fr 331) depends on readers' willingness to set aside their unfulfilled expectations and open themselves up to the new possibilities within the same work. In fact, unlike serial novels or thrillers, the quartet encourages readers' involvement only to frustrate it. The episodic nature of commercial literature is sabotaged: loose ends aren't tied up (on the contrary, they suggest that the plot will thicken); the identities of murderers and kidnappers aren't revealed; disappearances go unaccounted for; the conspicuous yet natural death of Gigliola isn't explained until 805 pages later (after the third paragraph of *Those Who Leave and Those Who Stay* we have to wait until the end of *The Story of a Lost Child* to learn more; slc 460); Lila's apparently most intimate experience, *smarginatura*, is actually suffered by Elena long before her (cf. 3.2); even the expectations created by the title of the first volume are upset (it is Lila who calls Elena her "brilliant friend" and not the other way around; mbf 312). Likewise, the expectations of a coming-of-age or romance novel are introduced only to remain unfulfilled: public and private ambitions and erotic and sentimental chimeras are tried and tested to the very end, yet they are drained of meaning and progressively abandoned at the edges of the narrative.

One of the "low sources" that Ferrante plumbs is the Neapolitan *sceneggiata*, a popular form of musical drama, from which she takes a weighty, compelling plot full of surprising twists, especially at the close of many of the chapters into which, for that very reason, each section is divided. This variant of melodrama is the most cumbersome genre in popular Neapolitan culture: a staging, in song and speech, of primary emotions and their physical gestures, about the battle between good and evil, a form that gives life a dramatic boost. But here the over-the-top scenario is embedded in a sophisticated narrative, following a longstanding tradition of the best of Neapolitan experimentalism, which strives to include popular culture in literature. Ferrante uses melodramatic, stereotypical tropes—passion, honor, murder: the reality of the *rione*—to tell a far more complex story. In her hands, the stock characters of the *sceneggiata* (*"issa, esso e 'o malamente"; "'o zappatore ca nun s' 'a scorda 'a mamma"; "i figli ca so' piezz e' core"; "'a malafemmena"*[1]) become problematic. Take the mobster Michele, for instance. He's the one male character who, for all 1,630 pages, manages to love and declare his love—a love that is violent, sophisticated, and cerebral—for a woman, i.e., Lila (tlts 207-8 and 301-4). Or Elena, who, though frequently accused by her own family of having betrayed her origins (snn 328; tlts 47)—in melodramatic tones that appear closely linked to the *sceneggiata* "Zappatore," or "Digger" (Donnarumma[1] 144)—finds greater meaning in her acknowledgment of her mother and heritage than in her own artistic career.

These are just a few of the quartet's compositional strategies that "emphasize instability" by reducing "the techniques that

---

[1] "Heroine, Hero, and Villain"; "The Digger Who Can't Forget Mamma"; "Children Are a Piece of the Heart"; "The Bad Woman."

present events as incontrovertible milestones" (fr 368). *Smarginatura* is much more than a perceptual experience of Lila's invoked at various stages of the narrative (cf. 3.2); it is a breakdown of the structure and coherence—well before the contents—of the drama. To dissolve the barriers of the narrative means to insert a counterforce into the flow of the plot that disrupts the story's linear progression. The experience of breaking down reality is closely related to *frantumaglia*, another key word in Ferrante's poetics, which describes "the part of us that escapes any reduction to words or other shapes, and that in moments of crisis dissolves the entire order within which it seemed to us we were stably inserted" (fr 312). Form is the first thing that psychic disorder corrodes, the principal form that governs human experience: chronology. As we'll see (cf. 3.6), this experience is central to the quartet, as it is to Ferrante's first three novels, yet it is also a carefully calculated mode in her nonfiction.

3. A Plastic Prose Style

The signature of Ferrante's poetics lies in the plasticity of her prose, which enables her to remain anchored in the real world, with its objective, opaque, and trite features, and also reveal, epiphanically, its metaphorical depth. In various interviews, the author equates "narrative order" with writing that "is clear and honest," with "the events of everyday life" and the compelling story they make (fr 234). It may sound like a simple or simplistic formula, and some critics and readers in Italy have seen it as such, but it is not. Because by "events" she means, chiefly, the web of relations connecting individuals in a drama of intrapsychic and social correspondences. The "events" of the quartet are the polyphonic system that constantly weaves together Elena's point of view with Lila's (cf. 1.4

and 2.6); they form the delicate, porous wall separating the public "I" from the disorder of *frantumaglia*. When Ferrante claims that her writing is guided by feeling, she has in mind not romantic confession but the complicated, polyphonic syntax of human relations. Only writing, not life or memory, can fabricate a story, sacrificing when necessary order (the façade of verisimilitude) for the disorder of the interior world (fr 240, 308).

Writing is about searching for "the right tone" (fr 310), it is an expressive tool that can guide an event toward its murkier, more resistant center, because writing is rooted in a preverbal realm, where words fail us. For example, we witness a burst of unrestrained emotion when, at the end of one chapter, Elena bitterly sums up her first two pregnancies. Until that moment she had sought to show Lila and herself only the cheerful side of those experiences; now she says, "I was for the second time pregnant and yet empty" (tlts 260). With brutal clarity, her words capture the truth that until that moment she had denied, in the repressed depths of an individual whose right to exist is denied by her own biology. Not by chance, the metaphors Ferrante uses to reflect upon her style are deliberately anti-aesthetic. Style is the search for literary truth, which is often at a remove from, if not antithetical to, formal elegance. It is the "unpleasantness" of a process that she likens to butchering eels, to the relentless pursuit of a goal. "When I write," she says in one interview, "it's as if I were butchering eels. I pay little attention to the unpleasantness of the operation and use the plot and characters as a tight net to pull up from the depths of my experience everything that is alive and writhing, including what I myself have driven away as far as possible because it seemed unbearable" (fr 226). In the quartet, such murky depths often emerge in the form of dialect, which rarely appears in direct transcription yet is far more diffuse than one might think (cf. 5.3). The incursions of dialect into the Italian

fabric are in any case always *meaningful* and aimed at an anti-
melodic use of Neapolitan, which is perceived as a language of
violence. When Elena inquires after Lila, recently married to
Stefano, Pinuccia replies, *"Si sta imparando"* ("She's learning,"
or, translating the locution literally, "She has made herself
learned") (snn 30). Her devastating answer signals to a reader
that the code of male oppression belongs to the culture and is
chiefly absorbed by its victims: women (cf. 4.4.). As Elena will
discover immediately afterward, the evidence of this form of
reeducation is Lila's face, disfigured by her husband.

My Brilliant Friend opens coolly with the investigation into
Lila's disappearance: "This morning Rino telephoned. I
thought he wanted money again and I was ready to say no"
(mbf 19). But the moment Elena begins to describe the *rione*
of her childhood and the descent into Don Achille's cellar, the
tone quickly shifts, and her narration sounds like a scary fairy
tale (Brogi[1]). "When you haven't been in the world long,"
Elena says, "it's hard to comprehend what disasters are at the
origin of a sense of disaster: maybe you don't even feel the
need to" (mbf 29). The depiction of Naples in the opening
pages is real because it is anti-realistically distorted by Lila and
Elena's childlike fears and overlapping points of view. Leave it
to fiction, which, "when it works, is more charged with truth"
(fr 351), to construct a fabulist perspective: "Don Achille, for
example, was not only in his apartment on the top floor but
also down below, a spider among spiders, a rat among rats, a
shape that assumed all shapes" (mbf 31). The quartet operates
on such shaky ground; the writing starts out clear-eyed and
guarded only to plunge readers into the dark depths of an
emotion and pull them out again.

Ferrante honed this technique in her first three novels.
Troubling Love begins just as coolly, with the news that the
birthday of Delia, the novel's narrator and main character,
coincided with the death of her mother. The location is stated

with unflappable precision: "My mother drowned on the night of May 23rd, my birthday, in the sea at a place called Spaccavento, a few miles from Minturno" (tl 11). Here, too, a few pages later the emotion of the narrative takes a rapid plunge: the mother's funeral, the outbreak of physical symptoms connected with grief, the descent into the city of Naples, and the investigation into the mother's death. Ferrante has called attention to the importance of her novels' openings, the ritual value of the first words that she looks for "as a magic formula that can open the only true door to the story" (fr 321). This initial, searching tone is actually the start of an increasingly violent descent to the emotional heart of the novel. "I tend," Ferrante says, "toward an expansive sentence that has a cold tone but at the same time exposes a magma of unbearable heat" (fr 269). Its purpose is to probe the intersection of "reality, hyperreality, and vision" (Scarinci), after which the writing becomes progressively more insistent on opening up the pores of the world being described.

Another representative example is the portrayal of Elena's mother, where an examination of the effects of poverty on a woman from the lower classes intersects with the expressive charge of her young daughter's hatred.

> Sometimes I heard her angrily crushing with her heel the cockroaches that came through the front door, and I imagined her with furious eyes, as when she got mad at me.
> Certainly she wasn't happy; the household chores wore her down, and there was never enough money. (mbf 45)

This psychosocial realism produces a fairy-tale-like cross between Morante and Anna Maria Ortese. That is to say, it is similar to the transfigurative techniques ushered in by *Menzogna e sortilegio*—which defied the neorealist fashion of the day—and later revived in Ortese's *The Sea Doesn't Bathe Naples*. As mentioned earlier, the entire structure of *Menzogna e sortilegio* has many things in common with *The Neapolitan Novels*: in Morante's work, too, the realist narrative, like a great nineteenth-century novel, prone to flatten time into a straight line of fulfilled destinies, becomes fragmented and dispersed by an element of the magical-fabulist (famously so in the chapter openings). In this light, you can begin to talk about a magical realism of the Italian Meridione, embodied by these two novels and rooted in the interplay between the false bottom of reality and the false bottom of the writing. This stylistic "double register" (fr 274) enables the author to track both her characters' thoughts and their wildest emotions, to build a fictional artifice and to immerse us in the characters' lives, to combine a fragmented, unreliable narrator and engage with the—always dual, always polyphonic—truth. The writing encompasses "a register and its shadow, given [the writing's] clarifying urgency and symbolic density, analytical lucidity and subtext, communicative transparency and violent vividness" (Manetti[1]).

Such duality produces a flexible cognitive experience, one that can reconcile high and low. For example, the double register can shuttle between interrogating the mechanics of male violence and delving into the darkest emotions of the two main characters—victims of that same violence—thus avoiding the risk of a politically edifying or pathetically moralizing fiction. Such is the case with one exemplary image with which Elena seals the fate of the young married woman, a role Lila is confined to: "[T]he condition of wife had enclosed her in a sort of glass container, like a sailboat sailing with sails unfurled in an inaccessible place, without the sea" (snn 57). The image is an objective correlative that operates on both an emotional and intellectual level. On the one hand, it connects the elegant and unattainable ("inaccessible") beauty of the boat to the desire for status that drove Lila to marry, shutting herself up in a cage of expensive clothes, brand-name accessories, a nice home. On the other, it associates her with the claustrophobia of imprisoned freedom, of the constricted body, like a sailboat that doesn't move though its sails are "unfurled": and thus with the false movement of marriage. While on the former, more superficial level Elena, the "friend with glasses and pimples" (snn 46), feels envy toward her friend by way of detached rational judgment, on the latter, far more profound level she empathizes with her friend's imprisonment.

4. The Metamorphosis of Time

The Neapolitan Novels present a kaleidoscope of social classes and contexts, a richness of representation rare in the contemporary Italian novel. With its chorus of characters, Elena and Lila's coming-of-age story weaves together the *rione* and its lower-class families, high school and the Scuola Normale Superiore di Pisa, the petit-bourgeois world of Maestra Oliviero and the bourgeois world of Elena's professors, the intellectual aristocracy of the Airota family and Franco Mari, Bruno Soccavo's factory and its laborers, the publishing milieu in Milan and the rotating cast at Mariarosa's communal apartment, sites of protest and feminist activism. As is typical of novels, the quartet keeps generating multiple *stories* that strive to come together to form a complete, unified whole. Three of the four titles[2] in the quartet emphasize the word "story," as do many chapter headings in individual volumes ("The Story of Don Achille," "The Story of the Shoes," "The Story of Bad Blood"), and these are placed in relation to the cycles of life ("Childhood," "Adolescence," "Youth," "Middle Time," "Maturity," "Old Age").

---

[2] The original title of *Those Who Leave and Those Who Stay* is *Storia di chi fugge e di chi resta*, i.e., *The Story of Those Who Leave and Those Who Stay*. (translator's note)

The narrative span of social ascent and descent is balanced by the device of "recognition," which is to say, "the reappearance in the present of people connected to the past"; the character arcs tell "the story of a repetition compulsion in which, while the scenery changes, the same substance returns" (Donnarumma[1] 139–40). However, this additional cohesive element in the narrative world is actually produced by a blurring—or *smarginatura*—of lives, by the breakdown of the form that the "I" has attempted to give its destiny. The case of Nino is emblematic: increasingly demonstrating his affinity with his womanizing father, he grows into "a big ruddy man with thinning hair who was constantly celebrating himself" (slc 470). In the quartet, physical distortion speaks to the bitter triumph of heritage over the hopes and ambitions of individuals, a "tangle of existence as it concerns both individual lives and the life of generations" (fr 333).

Another central force of the narrative is similarly blurred: exile (cf. 5.1). This recurring theme is apparently constructed from a series of contrasts between Elena and Lila, between those who leave and those who stay: they occupy different spaces (Lila can live only in the *rione*/Elena has to distance herself from it), speak different idioms (dialect/Italian; cf. 5), and embody different symbols (attachment/displacement). Yet taken in its entirety, the narrative strategy rejects the false dichotomy of rootedness vs. exile, authentic *napoletanità* vs. emigration, regional identity vs. national identity. Because those who leave *are* those who stay, and vice versa. Those who leave, like Elena, return to live in the neighborhood—in Elena's case, for thirteen years—though not without atoning for having abandoned their origins. Those who stay in Naples, like Lila, live in exile from the city, uprooted by *smarginatura*. In turn, with the disappearance of Lila, the city itself is exiled: Naples and its geography are no longer a key element of the novel (the endless research into Naples that

Lila had undertaken during the last twenty years of her life disappears along with her). Naples is a place of belonging and of estrangement. Like the mother figure, it is "the unloved beloved" (fer[1]), a place that inspires in its daughter both love and detachment— in both cases ferocious. In short, behind this contrast lies the mystery of their two destinies' otherness, shaped by "a careful calibration of stereotype and dissolving boundaries" (fr 369).

The kaleidoscope of characters and stories that fills the pages of the quartet is an abundance surrounded by a void. Although, as I pointed out earlier, the structure of the novel aims to chart an entire biological and existential cycle, the first part of Volume One ("Eliminating All the Traces") and the epilogue of Volume Four ("Restitution") break the circle and frustrate our expectations for a linear story by anticipating the end at the beginning. (Indeed, "Eliminating All the Traces" immediately tells us that Lila has disappeared.) This void is reported at the outset of both volumes with the discovery of Lila's radical plan to disappear: before leaving, she cuts herself out of the family photographs and, by returning the dolls, definitively flames out in the final chapter. Lila's last ritualistic gesture leaves her friend holding the thread that had connected them, the same one that they had begun to unwind sixty years earlier, stealing from each other these two emblems of a childhood world beset by violence and the absence of motherly love, and throwing them into the cellar (cf. 1 and 2). The two dolls are "the one trace left of those who have truly experienced the destabilizing effects of *smarginatura*" (Fusillo 153). The annulment of the childhood initiation ritual is a melancholy balance that affects both friends, "formed, deformed, reformed" by their friendship (snn 456). Elena's social ascent progressively dissolves, allowing the feelings of solitude and inadequacy that have always beset her to emerge explicitly during the years in Turin. Commenting on her friend's actions, she herself bitterly observes, "Real life, when it has passed, inclines toward obscurity, not clarity" (slc 473). The image recalls the vivid metaphor in Eugenio Montale's poem "The Balcony," where a female ghost leans out into the dark to gather a flicker of meaning:

> The life that shimmers
> you alone can see.
> You lean out to it
> from this unlit window.

In Ferrante's hands the darkening shimmer is situated at the end of a downward spiral in recent Italian history, conjured in the last part of *The Story of the Lost Child*. Existential drama is grafted onto the political drama, as the final chapter evokes "the flimsiness of a shattered 'I' that powerfully echoes the shattering of an entire country" (Crispino).

As a title, "Restitution" also recalls the power of chronology to reverse course, to flow backward, restoring only fragments and detritus. One of the most interesting aspects of the quartet is its ability to represent the metamorphosis of time, where chronological constriction and expansion, order and chaos, linearity and geology all intertwine and clash. This metamorphosis is in sync with our current anthropological need for storytelling, a need that has led to many noteworthy international TV series (the quartet has already been made into a series, directed by Saverio Costanzo) and, in Italy, to the film *The Best of Youth* (Donnarumma[1] 147). On the other hand, the plastic and inclusive tension of the quartet as a hyper-genre brings it into dialogue with *In Search of Lost Time* and the vertiginous experience of the reader as she passes through the continuity and the transformations of time in Proust's world text (Fusillo 149).

The family saga that emerges out of the tangle of Elena and Lila's stories contains a double temporality. The Naples of *The*

Neapolitan Novels is a world in which the ancient and the ultra-modern exist side by side and mingle, complicating and diluting linear time, obliterating any stable notion of history and its major events. Indeed, Naples defies progress. It is "the great European metropolis where faith in technology, in science, in economic development . . . was revealed, most clearly and far in advance, to be completely without foundation" (slc 337). The *rione* is both primitive and cutting-edge. There, the ferocious, cyclical logic of violence ("We were a chain of shadows who had always been on the stage with the same burden of love, hatred, desire, and violence"; tlts 291) meets the rhythm of commercial and technological transformation (the establishment of the first computer company in Italy—Enzo and Lila's Basic Sight—and the farseeing financial speculations of the Solaras).

Further, the old world underlies the family novel of mother-daughter conflicts and identification: the mother figure tells the age-old story of female subordination, which the underclass poverty of the *rione* keeps intact and glaringly brings to light (cf. 3.3). This mix of the old and the ultramodern blocks mothers and daughters from seeing the source of the stereotype, from seeing themselves as belonging to the march of progress, which would do away with such backwardness and draw a clear line between the two time frames and the two worlds. In *The Neapolitan Novels*, the old world is instead the backbeat of the present day, a fault line drawn with lucid objectivity, with neutral disenchantment.

5. Polyphony

Another centrifugal force in *The Neapolitan Novels* that blends with the centripetal form of the traditional novel is the polyphonic, dual narrative, thanks to which Elena's narrative voice overlaps with that of her friend. At the center of the story there is a "*relational subjectivity*, always ongoing, always narrated" (Cavarero[1] 4).

> [Lila] has managed to insert herself into this extremely long chain of words to modify my text, to purposely supply the missing links, to unhook others without letting it show, to say of me more than I want, more than I'm able to say. (slc 24)

The writing of the novel itself stems from a desire to fill, as if by magic, the hole left by Lila's mysterious disappearance:

> I wish she were here, that's why I'm writing. I want her to erase, add, collaborate in our story by spilling into it, according to her whim, the things she knows, what she said or thought . . . (tlts 105)

Polyphony, too, is decisive in turning the narrative into a hyper-genre. If it's true that "we are the destabilizing collisions that we suffer or cause," if the constituent parts of our "I" are found in the cracks produced by the ordinary traumas of our relationships and not in the apparent stability of the edifice, inscribing the other's presence in the story produces "interpenetration, turmoil, and also, to be precise, an incongruous mixture of expressive registers, codes, and genres" (fr 368).

The dual narrative voice is the result of the novel's focus on Lila's thoughts, which emerge from the various forms of documentary material that she left behind. Elena leans on the authority of the eight notebooks her friend sends her in 1966 (snn 15–18) and continually refers to them; Lila's long confession fuels the writing of the years between 1967 and 1969 (tlts 103–172); and Elena's third child, Imma, attests to Lila's passion for Naples around the mid 1990s (slc 436–443). Every volume in the cycle opens with a framing prologue whose function is occasionally reiterated in the course of the narrative, and which serves to give voice to the absent friend, a voice that has been silenced in part because Elena herself destroyed those intense, evocative notebooks—a source of envy and competitiveness—and now must recreate them from memory. The narrative voice proceeds by affirmations, revisions, restarts, and negations, ventriloquizing the friend and decoding her mysterious inner self. Elena's discourse constantly becomes blurred as she abdicates her own individuality and her dominion over the narrative of events (cf. 2.6). The technique is a way of exorcising envy and anticipating emotions: thanks to the notebooks, the narrative voice centers on Lila and her (still buried) feelings, as well as on their effect on Elena. They are sisters and strangers, guardians and rivals, establishing a symbiotic competition—now euphoric, now distressing—in which, however, each of them, the one telling the story and the one whose story is being told, lives and imposes her right to live.

The structure allows for reversals (Elena's story is, actually, also narrated by Lila) and a very fluid focus, while the narrator becomes detached from herself—and the reader from the narrator. For example, when Elena tells the story of her friend's honeymoon and rape, the entire focus is on Lila, which is authorized by the written record that the latter entrusted to Elena in 1966, six years after her wedding. "I begin to tell the story of her honeymoon, not only as she told it to me," says Elena, "but as I read it later in her notebooks" (snn 31). From this perspective, it's undeniable that Stefano turned into a monster. Yet a few pages on, another perspective emerges to suggest that the same character is meekly, tormentedly human. I'm referring to Elena's meeting with Stefano a few months after the wedding, when the young woman appears incredibly willing—despite the visible signs and full report of the abuse Lila has endured—to believe in Stefano's kindness and good sense and to be taken in by his request to talk ("What pleased me was the importance he attached to me"; snn 86) to the point that she even conceals the meeting from her friend. The gap between these two episodes is created by Lila's truth, a truth that Elena's narrative "I" does not fully disclose until she reads the notebooks and, in 2010, writes the story of their life, yet which this same easily manipulated narrator tends to overlook in her conversation with Stefano, owing to her competitiveness and ambivalence.

The "oscillation" (fr 276) between their two points of view makes Elena an unreliable narrator and Lila a mystery. On the one hand, Lila is always and overtly spiteful; the adjective dogs her for the entire story, as do the details of her "small" eyes, like "cracks" (narrowed, that is, in anger), a kind of formulaic epithet that also links her to a "witch" (capable of murdering her own children in her uterus by sheer will) and later to a "madwoman" (following the loss of Tina). On the other hand, the clearest and most searing gestures of tenderness in their friendship come from Lila herself. For instance, it is Lila who, enveloped in the nauseating smell of cured meats at the Soccavo factory, her hands mangled from stripping meat, eagerly takes Elena's hand and kisses it when Elena comes to announce that her first book is going to be published (snn 463). The discourse that the underlying narrative mechanism makes easily legible, ordinary because based on opposites, is contradicted by the polyphony. As Ferrante points out, "The structure of the narrative is such that neither Lila nor Elena can ever be definitively locked within a formula that makes one the opposite of the other" (fr 358).

Intertwined, the two voices produce in the text an ever-present ambiguity, which muddies the waters of the narration and makes both characters problematic; neither can be reduced to a fictional "type." The pleasure of reading the work lies not only in this weave but in something both more concrete and more elegant: the reader becomes enthralled by the narrative mechanism of their friendship. From this perspective, we are moved by the exposure to an extremely ordinary relationship, one that male and female readers alike have experienced (Cavarero[2]

117), and by the impossibility of solving the mystery of the two friends, by the feeling that we are caught in a web of ambivalences that the relationship and the story have simultaneously woven.

Female polyphony is also a response, grounded in form, to two varieties of male monologism: that of violence against the women in the *rione* and that of intellectual autism. Whether journalists or academics, all the men in the novel with a hint of intellectual ambition or capacity can turn women into objects, even elevated objects, of their discourse, yet they are never able to recognize women as conceptual, creative, and existential subjects in their own right. Elena and Lila's polyphony is an ambivalent, spoken form. It alone can bring to life a female point of view capable of naming the ferocity that women are subjected to without relegating them to the stereotypical role of victim, without making their narrative pathetic or weepy. Historically represented—and perceived by women themselves—as invisible and silent, or at best gregarious and second-class, the female point of view cannot position itself at the center of the narrative in an immediate and unconscious manner. It reaches the center by way of a complex construction, a premise and a framework that strengthen their raison d'être through doubling. Only an exceptional circumstance can justify their centrality: death, disappearance, absence.

In this sense, the quartet can be linked to two very different storytelling models. The first comes from television. In *Desperate Housewives*, a dead woman, a ghost, posthumously narrates the equally ghostlike obsessions of her living friends and the middle-class subdivision they reside in. The second comes from literature. I again refer to *Menzogna e sortilegio*, Elsa Morante's first novel, in which, just as in *The Neapolitan Novels*, Elisa's narrating "I" identifies itself as the writing "I," whose point of view is animated and sustained—here, too, in an ambivalent and antagonist sense—by the fake letters of her dead mother, Anna. Like Lila, Anna is compared to a wicked witch; her actions and powers of seduction equated with exorcism and witchcraft. Therefore, the evil presences of Anna and Lila give the two narratives an energy that, though ambiguous, has a contagious, redemptive force that drives the two women close to them (Elisa and Elena) to give voice to a gender that has been silenced for millennia.

6. The Story Within a Story

The story within a story is the hinge on which the quartet swings between form and its dissolution. On the one hand, the plot settles into a coherent and definite direction—its stated purpose to magically conjure up Lila by evoking the world of her and Elena's friendship—while, on the other, it strays into a labyrinth of minor chronicles and a surfeit of details, where meaning is lost and Elena's motivation for writing—to resurrect her friend and find a coherent and meaningful universe around her—recedes into the distance. In either case, the story's metanarrative qualities—part of the experimental novel tradition—exposes the complexity of the quartet's narrative strategies (Santovetti[1] 506).

Let's look first at the metanarrative features that create story and then at those that dissolve it. From the very first pages of the novel there is a book within the book and a sisterhood within the sisterhood. The money gained from Don Achille after the expedition to the cellar—the two origin myths of Elena and Lila's friendship—is used to buy Louisa May Alcott's novel *Little Women*. Significantly, their worship of the book is not exhausted by child's play but, rather, is audaciously linked to social prestige and what this prestige represents symbolically: money. At this point, at Lila's urging, they plan to write a novel that will make them rich. For a brief period from third grade to fifth (cf. 4.5), this metanarrative feature doubles both girls' independent space and their bond. Like the heroines of Alcott's novel, they will be sisters. Like Jo (the tellingly masculine sister), they will become writers. For Elena, this is the first step toward "the exhausting conquest of female authorship" (Gambaro[1] 159), solidified in part by the connection between her name and the pseudonym assumed by the author of *The Neapolitan Novels*, a name that is, in turn, also at the center of a series of symbolic associations with the world of myth. The "figural connection between literature and money" (Gambaro[1] 161) recurs frequently in the course of the novel, as a cross between economic instability and the search for solutions—more or less brilliant—to constant financial troubles. Emblematic, in this sense, is the recovery of the typescript rejected by both Adele and Lila in 1973 and resubmitted eight years later by the publisher's then firm deadline (cf. 3.8). The path of the book will branch out into various illusions and digressions that give shape not only to the fragility of female agency but to its perseverance and con- tradictions; Elena's hopes that her new status as a bourgeois wife can free her from having to hold a job and ensure her an independent creative space are immediately dashed when she becomes pregnant and reverts to the role of homemaker. Her plan to write a feminist essay about "men who fabricate women" (tlts 361) stems from her desire to "make a good impression on Nino" (slc 80; Santovetti 182), the man who will turn out to be one of the most industrious manufacturers of "female automatons" (tlts 354).

In the portrait of the artist as a young and adult woman that is *The Neapolitan Novels*, there is never a clear line between domestic space and the space of public success; instead, the two converge, however tensely. On the one hand, the form and content of Elena's writing are determined by the impossibility of imbuing her authorial voice with the central, liberated characteristics typical of men's writing. On the other hand, free of these limitations, her writing acquires a remarkably prehensile and inclusive force. Female authorship is a frame that can transform into a prison at a moment's notice; it is an omnivorous drive that engulfs all other desires and experiences. To the various forms of existential chess, we must add Elena's perpetual sense of inadequacy and her euphoric exhibitionism, which emerges during her literary speaking engagements, another detour in the story within the story. Her book tours, the web of malign and benign comments, the self-censorship and misrepresentations of herself that Elena engages in during debates, the praise and criticism her books receive, the translations and strange cover designs chosen by foreign publishers—this universe takes up a considerable amount of space in the story. As a result, Elena becomes fundamentally bewildered: page by page, her feelings of inadequacy progressively diminish until they disappear altogether, yet she experiences public affirmation with "a mixture of pride and fear, a dart of pleasure that ended in anguish" (tlts 53). This whole constellation of experiences and reflections on her writing strengthens and drives the plot forward, situating it within a very meaningful argument about the uneven roles and destinies of the two sexes.

This age-old inequality, internalized by men as much as by women, causes the female artist to be socially and existentially vulnerable, prone to collapse into and reemerge from *frantumaglia* (cf. 3.6), which systematically smothers and fans female ambition. Elena's constant metanarrative references to cementing her identity as a writer are "fabricated by and immersed in the temporal, social, and psychic conditions of muted female life that we are compelled to understand in reading the work: interruptions, blockage, long censorship, derision, self-hatred, internalized repression" (Blau DuPlessis 103). The quartet joins a relatively recent group of novels about the development of women artists in which the artistic object "can be made only through an immersion in personal vulnerability, in a breakdown, or a breakthrough, as in Gilman, Lessing, and Atwood, or as an articulation of long-repressed grief or love, usually the experiences of a daughter in relation to parents, as in Woolf and Olsen" (Blau DuPlessis 103). The quartet puts an important spin on this twentieth-century model, however. In its case, both vulnerability and its resolution, as well as continual crisis and creative inspiration, are produced by female friendship. As we'll see in the next chapter, this is a practice that lies both inside and outside the logic of patriarchy.

The plot is also revived by the triangular dynamic that activates the book and yet again attempts to show the novelty of the female role in the world of culture and its symbolic hierarchies. For example, the book of Beckett's plays is totally absorbed into the dynamic of "reciprocal theft" (Tortorici) between the two friends, that is, the act of appropriation with which the story begins: the act of throwing the dolls into the cellar. Lila may steal Nino away from Elena on Ischia during the summer of 1960 by talking about the book that Elena loaned her, but a few months later those same brilliant remarks about *Happy Days* and *All That Fall* (snn 212, 221–2) are the buoy that Elena clings to during her oral entrance exam at the Normale (snn 326). Similar payoffs involving books inspire Elena to commit other intellectual thefts. For instance, Elena counters Lila's social ascent after her engagement to Stefano by appropriating her friend's arguments about the fourth book of the *Aeneid*. These thefts accelerate the decline of their childhood plan to become writers, which unites the girls, and then separates them, just two years later, when Lila is prohibited from going to middle school (Gambaro[2] 174).

The utopia of creative sisterhood that began with *Little Women* comes to an end in another symbolic exchange connected to a book: *The Blue Fairy*, the story Lila writes as a child and, fourteen years later, burns in the courtyard of the Soccavo factory after receiving it from Elena, who has come to share the news of the publication of her first novel (cf. 2.6). Lila's gesture is even more significant if you consider that, for Elena, Lila's "childish pages" are "the secret heart" of her own novel. "Anyone who wanted to know what gave it warmth," she confesses, "and what the origin was of the strong but invisible thread that joined the sentences, would have had to go back to that child's packet, ten notebook pages, the rusty pin, the brightly colored cover, the title, and not even a signature" (snn 455).

The Blue Fairy confirms Lila's brilliance and seals her fate: marginalization from—and defeat at the hands of—the scholastic institution. Even if her story springs from the friends' original pact to write together, it is composed without Elena, who is busy taking private Latin lessons in order to matriculate to middle school, a preparatory class that Lila doesn't attend because she cannot continue her studies. Lila's defeat is further confirmed by the classism of Maestra Oliviero, who will refuse to comment on the little girl's work because, once Lila is excluded from continuing her education, she becomes a "pleb" (cf. 4.3). In short, the "book" lies at the center of a three-way exchange, which on the one hand defines both the text and what it symbolically incarnates, i.e., the complex process of cultural emancipation pursued by a group doubly subaltern in class and gender, a sort of ambiguous object heralding experience and transformation as well as envy, inequality, and conformity. On the other hand, the triangular dynamic significantly tightens the threads of the plot, helped along by the contrast between Elena's academic and institutional career and Lila's path from worker to autodidact in the growing field of computer science.

The story within the story is not only a centripetal but a centrifugal force that tends to break up the order of the narrative and divert it from the stated intention to breathe life into a coherent world evoked by devotion and friendship toward Lila. A tense complementarity between life and writing takes shape. Life keeps evading Elena's ability to represent it or capture it in a tidy order. With the writing of her second novel (not published until many years later), both the impotence of her fiction and the elusive, mercurial quality associated with Lila become clear. Asked by her friend to weigh in on the manuscript, Lila derides it on the very basis of its "mask" of fastidious realism: "The disgusting face of things alone was not enough for writing a novel: without imagination it would seem not a true face but a mask" (tlts 274). On many occasions, confronted by Elena's need to "paste one fact to another with words" (slc 262), she will reiterate, provocatively, that "meaning" is nothing more than a "line of black markings that look like insect shit" (slc 431).

The ideal model isn't contained in Lila's writing alone, in the famous eight notebooks that Elena receives in 1966, which hide some nearly imperceptible artifice behind their naturalness (snn 18), but actually emanates from her voice. "I should write the way she speaks," Elena says, "leave abysses, construct bridges and not finish them, force the reader to establish the flow" (slc 169). If life is elusive, fiction still has the deadly power to destroy it, engulfing not only the stages of Elena and her daughters' lives but the relationship with which the quartet begins ("Giving dates to the events that concerned me, and my daughters, cost me a lot, and I forced them into the writing, which took me more and more time"; slc 335). The two protagonists' friendship breaks off in 2007, following the publication of the story "A Friendship," which, though bearing "all the necessary disguises" (slc 465), is inspired by the loss of the dolls and the child Tina (Santovetti[2] 187).

The symbolic power of this text is underscored by the fact that it is the only one of Elena's works mentioned by name in the quartet. With this short text—the germ of the same narrative cycle composed just four years later—Elena breaks her silence about the event and the *rione* in general, which Lila had imposed on her two years before. Elena's breach will cause Lila to react peremptorily and refuse to see her again. Where had I gone wrong? Elena wonders. But her innocence proves feigned, given that the question is followed by an examination of her own seductive designs: "I had deliberately exaggerated the moment when [the dolls] disappeared into the darkness of the cellar, I had accentuated the trauma of the loss, and to intensify the emotional effects I had used the fact that one of the dolls and the lost child had the same name" (slc 465). So Elena's writing appears inadequate, not only on an aesthetic plane but on an ethical one, too, because, as Ferrante, speaking of the connection between autobiography and art, says, writing is "illicit appropriation . . . a dragnet that carries everything along with it: expressions and figures of speech, postures, feelings, thoughts, body, troubles" (fr 357). At this late stage in the quartet, Elena's list retroactively reveals to the reader how unreliable a narrator Elena is: racked with envy, reticent, insecure, she lashes out against Lila, the very figure her narrative promises to render truthfully and mold into the "enduring form" of the story (slc 371).

Even if Elena's unreliability doesn't fully emerge until the last volume, it's a fine thematic thread that gradually thickens over the course of the entire narrative cycle, one that should be linked to her relationship with Lila. In fact, Lila is the source of perfect style, a style that extends toward life so boldly as to lead to her self-elimination: her "self-destruction *in an image*" (snn 123), the enlargement of her photo (cf. 6), the burning of *The Blue Fairy*, and her actual disappearance, which she carries out like an "aesthetic project" (slc 455). Consequently, Elena's writing, "dissatisfied with itself" (fr 286), originates in this "secret competition" with her friend. Her clash with this abstract ideal materializes in childhood with *The Blue Fairy*, then with the letters and notebooks given to her by Lila, and crystalizes with her anguish about the book on Naples, the book that Elena imagines her friend had written as an adult and in old age, the book that bears the brilliance of an autodidact, and which would have revealed the mediocrity of Elena's entire writing career once and for all.

Truly decisive is the ghostly, totalizing form of this creative imbalance: an obsession that grips the reader no less than Elena, given that this narrative device was conceived precisely to prevent confirming Lila's ghostly myth. In the entire quartet we find not one line written by Lila. In a work as firmly metanarrative as this, there is never room for the other person's writing. "Lila," Ferrante says, "can only be Elena's tale: outside that tale she would probably be unable to define herself" (fr 360). This "model of Lila" functions to dissolve "the model of Elena" (Micali) on a poetic as well as an existential plane. In 1983, as the two friends go to work on an article against the Solara brothers—their last creative collaboration—Lila fetches from one of her mysterious hiding places "the red book," the famous notebooks in which Manuela Solara recorded the loans and proceeds of the family's secret business. Magically haloed in memory, the book ("a secret document at the heart of bloody adventures") appears on the table in all its squalor: a pile of "very ordinary dirty notebooks with the lower right edge raised like a wave" (slc 310). Studying them, Elena gauges the gap between the fiction of memory and the authentic fiction that aspires not to the truthful transcription of manners and milieus, but to literary truth. This reality once removed, true but often shy of verisimilitude, reveals the anti-conventional, anti-stereotypical nucleus hidden within immediate reality "when it captures the confusions of existences, the making and unmaking of beliefs, the way fragments from varying sources collide in the world in our heads" (fr 344). In a flash she realizes that Lila was right about her second novel: "My book —even though it was having so much success—really was bad, and this was because it was well organized, because it was written with obsessive care, because I hadn't been able to imitate the disjointed, unaesthetic, illogical, shapeless banality of things" (slc 310–311). Elena glimpses in those creased pages the polarity of two narratives, one nesting inside the other, as in a matryoshka doll, leading to opposite outcomes: for Lila, erasure; for Elena, endless multiplication. Elena Ferrante's writing contains both.

Chapter Two
Female Friendship

1. Female Friendship as Practice of Difference

F emale friendship has until now been significantly under-represented. In *A Room of One's Own* Virginia Woolf remarks on how female friends in Racine and the Greek tragedies were "confidantes," and then mothers and daughters, while up through Jane Austen's day "all the great women of fiction were . . . not only seen by the other sex, but seen only in relation to the other sex" (Woolf 98). In the nineteenth-century Victorian novel the bond between two women friends becomes more visible, thus more frequently dramatized, yet their stories still revolve around a male character. Though a recurring element in the plot, the friendship between two women remains secondary to the romantic triangle, to a competition for the same love interest—crucial, sure, but still part of the marriage plot (Buchanan 78). In many storylines, for example, both friends love the same man, but one of the two withdraws from the competition. If on the one hand their bond is considered "a relationship that generates plot," on the other it is never "its primary agent, subject, or object" (Marcus 79).

This explains Woolf's excitement when, in a novel by Mary Carmichael, she reads that "Chloe liked Olivia." "And then it struck me," writes Woolf, "how immense a change was there. Chloe liked Olivia perhaps for the first time in literature" (Woolf 97). Alas, Woolf's excitement is, like the novel in question, fictitious: Mary Carmichael is an author Woolf invents, evidently just as unreal and as unrealized, in 1929, the year *A Room of One's Own* was released, as the possibility that a relationship between two women could be the main storyline and most engrossing element of suspense in a narrative. We have to wait for Doris Lessing's *The Golden Notebook*, published in 1962, to see how a female friendship—in this case, between Anna and Molly, "free women," as they are christened by the title of the sub-novel—constitutes "an immense force for dismantling patriarchal structures" (Audet 215–216). Another book from the 1960s that occupies an important place is Christa Wolf's *The Quest for Christa T.*, the first-person account of a female friend who reconstructs the brief and intense life of a young woman in search of existential authenticity in the increasingly rigid cultural climate of East Germany.

Just how powerful the theme of female friendship is was clear from the release of the first volume of *The Neapolitan Novels* (Benedetti[1] 173–175). The quartet marks a breakthrough in the representation of something many women experience but still don't single out as key to their development: friendship with members of their own sex. Indeed, the story's main characters are two women friends, Lila and Elena; its main focus their lives and bond, from their childhood on the humble outskirts of Naples to their adulthood, from 1950 to 2010, or from the ages of six to sixty-six. Yet also crucial is the way the content of the quartet determines its form. The main narration becomes polyphonic, dual, accommodating within Elena's voice the voice of the *other*—of the missing friend whom Elena conjures (cf. 1.4, 2.4, and 2.6). One of the most pervasive stereotypes about women is that they don't know how to be friends, which is to say they don't know how to establish a loyal, transparent relationship free of murky feelings like jealousy and envy. *The Neapolitan Novels* breaks this stereotype by placing the two women's intense yet fiery friendship at the heart of the story.

Elena and Lila's friendship develops in an unsettling manner, as a *practice of difference*. Theirs is not the classic ethos of the reciprocal, loyal bond between two equals: this kind of self-determination is a male privilege, one historically predicated on, and inevitably a complement of, male dominance. As subaltern women, placed on the lowest rung of society from their adolescence, the two friends personify the gender and social disparity on which their pact is forged. That she isn't interested in bringing together two individuals who represent disembodied and self-governing entities is a fact Ferrante alerts us to: "Exploring the disorderliness of female friendship meant learning to set aside every literary idealization and every temptation to instruct" (fr 293).

The noun the writer uses, "disorderliness," is highly significant: it suggests the contrast between male friendship and female—order versus chaos, rules versus entropy. There appears to be a radical split between the classical ethics of friendship, ruled, according to Aristotle, by a dialectic of disinterested affinity and political opportunism, and Derrida's postmodern ethics, which deconstructs the idea of friendship as the recognition of a likeminded individual and calls for a new "politics of friendship" inspired by the pursuit of otherness. Yet in reality, beyond the content of their arguments, the classical philosopher and contemporary deconstructionist convey, by way of Cicero, Seneca, and all the epic and modern narratives of this emotional connection, a shared vision: a stable syntax, grammar, and set of rules aimed at defining what friendship is and how it is practiced and preserved. The male pact has held in check the inevitable ambivalences—rivalry, betrayal, ordinary disappointment—that a bond so complex, a cross between public alliance and private confession, can generate. For centuries these unavoidable dynamics have been policed by a code of behavior that extends beyond national borders. If that is how friendship has played out in the West, then we can easily understand how this pseudo-universalism masks an underlying male aspiration to govern. It is an ethos that, in theory at least, frees those men who recognize and practice it, making them social extroverts and brotherly allies.

Because for centuries a woman could not inhabit the public space reserved for man as a political and social animal, female friendships are more vulnerable, more lawless, more exposed to the destablizing effects of structural ambivalences that the centuries-old male code of behavior seeks to contain and revise. Therefore, the elective affinity between women is "disorderly," a profoundly intense experience unmediated by tradition, geneaology, or clearly-drawn boundaries between public and private life. Female friendship is the "rudimentary map" (fr 346) for a spiritual landscape yet to be explored, delineated, and defined. In this case, gender difference leaves invisible traces (invisible due to a lack of clear semantic footprints) as soon as it silently deviates from the norm: this difference has been generated and continues to be generated by centuries of domination. Such a difference means that female bonds still rest on a dearth of pacts and rituals: "Friendship between women has been left without rules. Male rules haven't been imposed on it, and it's still a territory with fragile codes where love (in [Italian] the word 'friendship'—*amicizia*—is related to love, *amare*), by its nature, carries with it everything, lofty sentiments and base impulses" (fr 240).

In *The Neapolitan Novels* Ferrante dramatizes the terrible mix of envy and elective recognition that inevitably characterizes any friendship between two women, between two dominated subjects attempting to achieve emancipation. The success of the quartet is also due to its acceptance of that bit of truth lurking underneath the stereotype of imperfect female friendship, as well as in its portrayal of imperfection as a component—and not the defining feature—of such foundational bonds, which, while rocky, can hardly be called insignificant.

In many interviews Ferrante has underscored the need to catalog the forces at work in the "inevitable cohort of bad feelings" produced by the bond of female friendship (fr 240). What counts is the basic tone: "Competition between women is good only if it does not prevail; that is to say if it coexists with affinity, affection, with a real sense of being mutually indispensable, with sudden peaks of solidarity in spite of envy, jealousy, and the whole inevitable cohort of bad feelings" (fr 359). In fact, while arrogating to themselves the same rights that male friends enjoy, Elena and Lila experience their friendship as a blend of transcendence and immanence. Love and resentment, fits of passion and self-centeredness, confessions and secrets, cohabitation and separation: all intertwine over the course of their tempestuous relationship.

One example of their torturous coexistence is the scene in which Elena helps Lila prepare for her wedding. Sixteen yet already deeply marked by the destinies determined by their class and gender, both girls sense Lila's marriage will have a traumatic effect on their relationship. Pain, solidarity, hope, fear, jealousy—Elena is beset by a morass of conflicting feelings about their imminent separation:

> I had a confusion of feelings and thoughts: embrace her, weep with her, kiss her, pull her hair, laugh, pretend to sexual experience and instruct her in a learned voice, distancing her with words just at the moment of greatest closeness. But in the end there was only the hostile thought that I was washing her, from her hair to the soles of her feet, early in the morning, just so that Stefano could sully her in the course of the night. (mbf 313)

The bond between Elena and Lila is unstable because its dynamic is, by design and necessity, unchecked by proper or exemplary behavior. "It's a shortcut," remarks Ferrante, "to set aside what is formidable about women, to imagine us merely as organisms with good feelings, skilled masters of gentility" (fr 151). Depicting the ambivalence of their bond as historically and psychologically determined, *The Neapolitan Novels* refuse to reduce the experience of female friendship to the conventional, and instead invest it with profound symbolic meaning. For, as the writer emphasizes, "We have to learn . . . to speak with pride of our complexity, of how in itself it informs our citizenship, whether in joy or in rage" (fr 152).

2. Female Friendship as Creativity

"We held each other by the hand and entered" (mbf 75): the impactful first-person plural launches the two girls out to the seaside, far from the *rione*. Even before this, heading out to face the "ogre" Don Achille, they consecrate their adventure with the same physical act: "[W]hen I reached her she gave me her hand. This gesture changed everything between us forever" (mbf 29). Clasping hands is the initiation rite that defines Elena and Lila's friendship as, primarily, a pact of solidarity, an oath to transform their lives and to "[break] the long chain of illiterates" (snn 450). There are several watershed moments in their public and social pact: their search for the dolls, their trip to the sea, their purchase of *Little Women*, the writing of *The Blue Fairy*, the designing of the shoes, Lila's relationship with Stefano, the acquisition of schoolbooks for Elena, the collagework done to the enlarged photograph of Lila, Elena's articles condemning the Soccavo factory and the Solara brothers. Creativity also penetrates the traditional sphere of motherhood and is renewed as a result of their expecting daughters (Tina and Imma) at the same time, and the new alliance that shared experience produces. At the gynecologist they "liked sitting next to each other . . . separate from the other pregnant women, whom [they] observed ironically" (slc 157). Their ventures into the world and genealogy—into the domain of the past and present—overlap when they collaborate on the article against the Solaras, their writing mirroring their daughters' games:

> We sat down at the kitchen table, while Tina and Imma chattered softly, moving dolls, horses, and carriages . . . It was a long time since we had undertaken something together . . . Our heads collided—for the last time, now that I think of it—one against the other, and merged until they were one. (slc 310–312)

This scene, in which motherhood, writing, and play converge, is particularly significant. Far more than in the male ritual, friendship is, in this case, the projection of an intimate bond onto the screen of the world. The very structure of the story thereby breaks another stereotype about female friendship, which our collective imagination often relegates to the suffocating realm of "societies of consolation" (Raymond XIV), and reinfuses their bond with creative energy.

The epic and domestic quality of the quartet in fact depends on its construction of the friendship plot, which—like a flotation device—immediately returns the intimate story to the neat surface of reality and makes the women "generators of meaning, language, children, history." (Clark) The two friends' connection creates a porousness between the interior sphere and the social, which then permeate one another in an endless series of refractions. Whether one friend is interrogating the other—now anguished, now euphoric, now simply syntonic—or interfering in or making a speculative or actual judgment about the other's life, "each manages to enter the form of the other, which continues to act, as an form of autonomous life, beyond the bounds of the physical presence that produced it" (Lagioia 364). The dolls, *Little Women*, *The Blue Fairy*, the shoes: all are symbols of the transformative power of friendship, thanks to which the violence of the *rione* morphs into a game that in turn produces an object-talisman, a means of exorcising the ferocious logic of adults and the violence of men.

In addition to being a talisman, the object is like Osip Mandelstam's description of amber: a thick resin trapping a potentially living fossil. In fact, each of these creations contains a violent nucleus, neutralized and rendered aesthetic by their friendship, yet which could spring to life again at any moment. It is no coincidence that two of these objects, the dolls Tina and Nu, bookend the long narrative, first disappearing and then, fifty-six years later, mysteriously reappearing. The dolls evoke the beginning and end of magical time (the plunge into and reemergence from the morass of Naples) as well as the summation of an entirely female narrative in which a doll symbolizes the cycle of womanhood, encompassing friend, daughter, and mother, a sort of "composite body of all Ferrante's Neapolitan mothers and daughters" (Milkova[2] 98). Tina and Nu are synchronous objects that stand out as a dysphoric and painful variant of the female twin archetype identified by Jung when he stated that "every mother contains her daughter in herself and every daughter her mother" (Jung[1] 188). Hence, the dolls can also be considered reversible hybrids, part of a magic spell of transformations and equivalencies that appears throughout Ferrante's work (indeed, both *The Lost Daughter* and the story "The Beach at Night" place these symbolic dolls at the center of their stories).

At the same time, the dolls function as creative objects that (before and after they disappear) usher in a new stage of the girls' lives, enabling them to deal with traumatic violence in a mediated and autonomous way, to work through the experience they have repressed, and, gradually, to come to terms with it. "The mind's dreams have ended up at their feet" (mbf 314): such are Lila's words when she puts on her wedding shoes, the shoes that she dreamed up when still a little girl and that, the first time she sees them "made real," stir up "a violent emotion, as if a fairy had appeared and made a wish" (mbf 304). The whole arc of the quartet can be read as the story of the progressive disintegration of the friends' magical childhood pact. The treasure chest becomes the cash register at Stefano's grocery ("Money for her was that drawer, the treasure chest of childhood that opened and offered its wealth"; snn 109). The blue fairy rematerializes as the kind, anonymous female professor with blue hair who opens the door to the Pisa Normale for Elena. The clamor of sociopolitical awareness inspired by the article attacking the Solaras is what remains of the great war that Lila wanted to wage against them. And so, in a relentless countermelody, the "cheap and ugly" (slc 473) dolls reappear at the end of the quartet in their true form.

3. Projective Identification

To understand how original Ferrante's approach to friendship is, it may be useful to compare her work to *Sex and the City*, another contemporary tale of female companionship. The story of Elena and Lila breaks the very taboo that the four New Yorkers' friendship is founded on: desiring and seducing their friend's man. Even a TV show that pushed the envelope by depicting liberated and libertine women stopped short of this transgression. In fact, the story's development hinges on respecting it.

In contrast, the arc of *The Neapolitan Novels* reaches a narrative climax, as it were, when, during the summer of 1961, in Ischia, seventeen-year-old Lila has an intense love affair with Nino, the man Elena has loved since childhood. To get back at Lila for humiliating her, Elena decides to lose her virginity to Nino's father, Donato Sarratore, on the beach of the Maronti. The parallel erotic scenes are a major twist that serves to broach a complex subject: that the dynamic of Lila and Elena's relationship revolves around addition and subtraction, gain and loss, fulfillment and hollowness. This constant breaking of boundaries and their appearances is so intense that, beside Lila, "solid" Elena feels "sodden, earth too soaked with water":

[As] we were returning . . . after our violations, I couldn't get away from the usual confused sense of disparity, the impression— recurrent in our story—that I was losing something and she was gaining . . . Everything in the world was in precarious balance, pure risk, and those who didn't agree to take the risk wasted away in a corner, without getting to know life. I understood suddenly why I hadn't had Nino, why Lila had had him. I wasn't capable of entrusting myself to true feelings. I didn't know how to be drawn beyond the limits. I didn't possess that emotional power that had driven Lila to do all she could to enjoy that day and that night. I stayed behind, waiting . . . I also realized that at the Maronti, in Barano, I had left nothing, not even that new self that had been revealed. I had taken everything with me, and so I didn't feel the urgency, which I read in Lila's eyes, in her half-closed mouth, in her clenched fists, to go back, to be reunited with the person I had had to leave. And if on the surface my condition might seem more solid, more compact, here instead, beside Lila, I felt sodden, earth too soaked with water. (snn 296, 288–9, 294)

The "confused sense of disparity" that Elena feels as she gauges the difference, in terms of passion, between their respective "violations" (their sexual experiences with father and son) becomes clear six years later, when Elena reads Lila's notebooks (which Lila entrusts to her in 1966, and which an envious Elena will throw into the Arno; cf. 1.5). Reading Lila's account of the night she first made love to Nino, Elena understands that the "disparity" stems from her own conformity, her incapacity to expose herself to the same risks of total passion recounted in those pages. She recognizes "in [Lila's] fulfillment the reverse of [her] emptiness":

Fortunately I didn't read her notebooks until later. There were pages and pages about that day and night with Nino, and what those pages said was exactly what I hadn't had and couldn't say. Lila wrote not even a word about sexual pleasures . . . She talked instead about love and she did so in a surprising way . . . Nino . . . had snatched her away from death . . . He had restored her capacity to feel. He had above all brought back to life her sense of herself . . . This, more or less. Her words were very beautiful, mine are only a summary. If she had confided it to me then . . . I would have suffered even more, because I would have recognized in her fulfillment the reverse of my emptiness. (snn 295-296)

The competition for Nino definitively exposes the supportive *and* competitive foundation of Elena and Lila's friendship, a foundation that will last for about twenty years, sometimes emerging explicitly, and sometimes implicitly. Yet the competition never completely jeopardizes the bond between them. Ferrante herself explains how their relationship functions: "The many events of the lives of Elena and Lila [show] how one draws strength from the other . . . not only in the sense that they help each other but also in the sense that they ransack each other, stealing feeling and intelligence, depriving each other of energy" (fr 233). It is interesting to learn that "one draws strength from the other" not only thanks to their supportiveness and mutual respect but also thanks to their rivalry, which leads them to appropriate from one another, at a cost, dolls and men, writing and future plans.

What the two friends experience, intensely and frequently, is "projective identification": the reciprocal need to bring "aspects of oneself to bear on the life of the other" (Jesurum). Very early on, for example, Lila invests Elena with the status of "brilliant friend," thus holding Elena responsible for distinguishing herself at school and in the creative arts. By giving her this title, Lila is asking Elena to fulfill her own true potential (Maksimowicz 219): "I *want* you to do better, it's what I want most, because who am I if you aren't great, who am I?" (tlts 273). At her lowest moments Elena feels that this projective identification has bled her dry and dominated the darkest corners of her interior life: "All our lives she had told a story of redemption that was *hers*, using *my* living body and *my* existence" (slc 473); "As usual [Lila] was taking on the job of sticking a pin in my heart not to stop it but to make it beat harder" (slc 94).

For her part, at just six years old, Elena assigns Lila the function of a militant, creative pioneer. Lila will be the one to beat a path through uncharted and hazardous territory, while her friend will trail behind, trying to keep up with her, "at her pace": "I had decided that I had to model myself on that girl, never let her out of my sight, even if she got annoyed and chased me away" (mbf 46). By taking this supporting role—to compensate for her "demotion" (mbf 46) after their teacher discovers Lila's precocious reading and writing skills—Elena implicitly renounces her own creative gifts, yet she will thereafter blame this decision on Lila. In addition to irreversibly compromising her future vocation as a writer, Elena's refusal to occupy the freeing (and threatening and self-destructive) spaces of creativity is the real reason she does not name her own *smarginatura*, which she experiences long before her friend (mbf 57) but never acknowledges (except to deny it, for example after the earthquake of 1980; slc 171) (cf. 3.2). Mutual outsiders, both Lila and Elena are nomads in search of a "marvelous land" (mbf 164) to inhabit. They constantly invest people, places, and things with the status of *Heimat* (homeland): a space they are able to identify only because they seek it together, yet which only one of the two can occupy, provided, however, she doesn't let the other in.

Electing to acknowledge one another as friends involves both in an initial project, but, inevitably, one of the two is later excluded. Elena feels that her education is a gift from Lila, that its prospects are made desirable by Lila. Nevertheless, all of Elena's scholastic achievements are shown to leave Lila out, making her feel even more excluded from the privilege that she "had lost forever" (mbf 259): the privilege of being admitted to middle school and receiving an education. "As soon as I could," says Elena, "cautiously, I pointed out to her that I would go to middle school and she would not" (mbf 81). Once Elena enrolls in a classical high school, Lila tries to narrow the gap by teaching herself Greek in the months leading up to the start of school. In response, Elena attempts to distance herself from Lila and nurses the desire to erase her "like a drawing from the blackboard" (mbf 142). But the shock of her destructive impulse scares Elena, prompting, on the contrary, a renewed sense of attachment ("I immediately went to find her") and subordination. Elena accepts being introduced to the classical language by her friend, while her repressed anger breaks out across her face:

> I let her teach me how to do the quadrille. I let her show me how many Italian words she could write in the Greek alphabet. She wanted me to learn the alphabet before I went to school, and she forced me to write and read it. I got even more pimples. (mbf 142)

In an effort to compete with Elena, Lila comes up with a plan to design shoes, a plan apparently born out of a pact with her brother Rino. Lila's creative, entrepreneurial endeavor is a way for her to compensate for being excluded from school: "It was most of all, she said suddenly, a way of showing you that I could do something well even if I had stopped going to school" (snn 143). On the heels of this competitive rupture come the rites of youthful seduction, as Lila's beauty blossoms and permanently establishes her erotic power and her superiority to Elena:

> . . . I had bigger breasts . . . Gigliola was a dazzling blonde . . . Carmela had beautiful eyes . . . But there was nothing to be done: something had begun to emanate from Lila's mobile body that the males sense, an energy that dazed them, like the swelling sound of beauty arriving. (mbf 143)

Desire takes the form of one girl trying to outpace the other. Besides the timeline of events, this constant chase, first in the field of knowledge and later in the triangles of seduction, is what really marks time in the quartet ("I couldn't," declares

Elena, "spend my time following her or discovering that she was following me, either way feeling diminished"; mbf 142).

Very quickly both girls' exclusions crystallize into social roles. That is how Lila, apparently shielded by her new status as the fiancée of a wealthy man, reverses her loss at school and her drop in cultural stock:

> . . . [She] with a few hurried but good-humored remarks cut off any possible conversation and went on to show me Stefano's presents . . . while the things that I loved . . . slumped in a corner, deprived of their meaning. (mbf 261–2)

In this instance, Elena is the one barred from the new land that the two conquer together (both defended Lila's right to choose her own fiancé and nurtured the illusion that Stefano was a good man who could free her from the *rione*). Even trying on Lila's engagement gifts as a joke makes Elena feel inadequate (and thus unsuited to the occasion). "I tried on the dresses and jewelry; I almost immediately noticed that they would never suit me as they did her; and I was depressed" (mbf 262).

In the course of the friends' childhood and adolescence, the formative experiences of women are collectively perceived as mutilations, whereby receiving an education implies giving up beauty and passion (Elena's fate), and acquiring beauty and seductive power precludes receiving an education (Lila's fate): "[What] I lacked she had, and vice versa, in a continuous game of exchanges and reversals that, now happily, now painfully, made us indispensable to each other" (mbf 259). Projective identification gives structure and meaning to such mutilations, which cease being "natural" to the structurally castrated female condition the moment one or the other friend endures them as a domination or theft: "It was as if, because of an evil spell, the joy or sorrow of one required the sorrow or joy of the other" (mbf 257). The rivalry and competitive anxiety produced by the two friends' fantasies of superiority and expropriation enable them to gain partial freedom from the gender inequality and violence both are subjected to. The original model of this exclusion and projection dynamic is the premature termination of Lila's scholastic career (ended by her parents in the fifth grade), about which Elena feels torn. On the one hand, young Elena gets a foretaste of what school is like when she no longer has to endure comparisons to her friend and be deprived of the teachers' attention. On the other, Lila's absence immediately drains learning of all intensity. Eliminating Lila means impoverishing the desire for knowledge itself:

> I soon had to observe that, since Lila had stopped pushing me, anticipating me in my studies and my reading, school . . . had stopped being a kind of adventure and had become only a thing that I knew how to do well and was much praised for. (mbf 187)

When, in 1959, her fifteen-year-old friend informs her of her wedding date—the following fifth of March, nine months later—Elena is gearing up to take her oral exams. Their divergent fates make increasingly clear "the meaninglessness of school":

> The concreteness of that date made concrete the crossroads that would separate our lives. And, what was worse, I took it for granted that her fate would be better than mine. I felt more strongly than ever the meaninglessness of school, I knew clearly that I had embarked on that path years earlier only to seem enviable to Lila. And now instead books had no importance for her. I stopped preparing for my exams, I didn't sleep that night. (mbf 275–6)

4. Primary Envy

A foundational scene in the quartet occurs in the first forty pages of *My Brilliant Friend*, when the girls go looking for the dolls that fell into Don Achille's cellar. The loss seals their friendship under the sign of "reciprocal theft." Lila steals Elena's doll and throws it into the cellar, then Elena immediately retaliates, stating, "What you do, I do" (mbf 54). Years later, on Lila's wedding night, Elena repeats this formula word for word: "I wanted to be penetrated, I wanted to tell Lila when she returned: I'm not a virgin either, what you do I do, you can't leave me behind" (snn 27).

Ferrante boils down the plot of the quartet to little more than a sentence, telling us that these same dolls and their link to Tina, the girl who disappears in 1984, are central to the story: "[their] friendship . . . begins with the treacherous game of the dolls and ends with the loss of a daughter" (fr 280). Looming over both events—one a fairy tale, the other a tragedy—is the shadow of loss and the other's hand in that loss. First, young Lila rashly drops the doll into the dark cellar and triggers in her friend an archetypal form of anguish, the sense of "falling forever" and "going to pieces" (Winnicott 18) that one feels when deprived of the mother's holding environment. Elena reacts to this anguish by replicating Lila's gesture and joining her in the search for the dolls, but—in so doing—she herself "fades into the recesses of Lila's unreflective shadow" (Maksimowicz 212). Then there is the far more crushing loss of Tina ("The grief couldn't coagulate around anything"; slc 339), for which Lila suspects her friend is indirectly responsible. "They thought they were stealing your daughter and instead they stole mine" (slc 449), she says, believing the Camorra had been looking to get even with Elena for her second novel and had mistaken Tina for Imma after the publication of a beautiful photo of Elena with Tina wrongly identified Elena as the girl's mother.

"If I ran away," writes Elena, recalling one of the many playground battles during which she discovered her need to fight by her friend's side, "I would leave with her something of mine that she would never give back"; "[already] then there was something that kept me from abandoning her" (mbf 34). This pair of sentences displays how Elena wavers between mutual love and envy, a sense of irreparable loss compensated by a power play. Elena feels that Lila's heartfelt request that she come study in her home-cum-prison now that Lila is the wife of a grocer ("What's the point?" "To know that you're there"; snn 46) confirms her fate as "the friend with glasses and pimples" (snn 46) and, more importantly, Lila's sense of triumph, her final victory in this win-or-lose game ("She really wanted me fixed in the role of someone who spends her life with books, while she . . . took everything, granted everything"; snn 93). To exist means to take something away from the other; a gain for one is a loss for the other:

> And [Lila's] life continuously appears in mine, in the words that I've uttered, in which there's often an echo of hers, in a particular gesture that is an adaptation of a gesture of hers, in my less which is such because of her *more*, in my *more* which is the yielding to the force of her less. (snn 337)

Fueling this escalation of loss and gain is "primary envy" (Klein[1]), an emotion that reactivates the archetypal origin story that every human being experiences with their mother. In the very first stages of life, the mother figure is perceived as "the feeding breast" who—from the newborn's sweeping perspective—never provides all the nutrition she needs. The newborn's sense of helplessness and frustration before this maternal power causes them to feel intense predatory desires (to varying degrees, depending on their inner resources, their mother's capacity to handle them, and their environment) and, subsequently, a profound sense of guilt and persecution directed at the mother (Klein[1]).

In Elena and Lila's friendship, the presence of one has for the other a similarly nourishing, guilt-inducing, and punishing power; however, they are constantly rescued from this feeling by their ability to *remain connected* through their mutual fantasy of desire, guilt, and paranoia. Their relationship engages the reader too, because it is embodied in the quartet's polyphonic and interpersonal form, in a circular development that dissolves the boundaries of the narrating voice and generates a story about the narrator *through* the story of her friend (cf. 1.5). One recurring strategy is that of overhearing Lila's thoughts and the internal, utterly aphasic echo that Lila's thoughts stimulate in Elena: "I didn't answer, prevented by a strong emotion" (snn 143). The interior life is simultaneously sealed off and trespassed upon, because it hinges on the possibility of "hearing the mad sound of the brain of one echo in the mad sound of the brain of the other" (snn 466).

The boundaries of the relationship can be dissolved to arrive at the realm of the erotic, at the edge of every intensity and experimentation of the body and mind, conveying a need for an inclusive, totalizing intimacy. Boundary-crossing is a constant in Lila and Elena's friendship; it carries on into their adult lives. But there is one symbolic phase, marking the end of adolescence and the transition into adulthood, when boundary-crossing is most clearly manifest. It occurs during the aforementioned scene, as Elena helps Lila prepare for her wedding and wedding night. She contemplates the beauty of Lila's naked body with a surprising sense of desire and shame. Finally, obliquely, with a hat tip to Sappho, a series of rhythmic clauses discloses a third emotion: jealousy.

> [It] forces you . . . to rest your gaze on the childish shoulders, on the breasts and stiffly cold nipples, on the narrow hips and the tense buttocks, on the black sex, on the long legs, on the tender knees, on the curved ankles, on the elegant feet; and to act as if it's nothing, when instead everything is there . . . and your heart is agitated, your veins inflamed. (mbf 313)

Sentimental, romantic, passionate—the various adjectives that psychology applies to friendship reveal "the difficulty of encapsulating in a formula behavior that eludes definition and often representation too" (Benedetti[1] 184).

5. Symbiosis and Otherness

Everything about Elena and Lila is characterized by symbiosis. Born a few days apart, bearing two-syllable alliterative nicknames (Lenù and Lina; or, as only her friend calls her, Lila), they have opposite physical traits and, more importantly, personalities. From the age of six their two temperaments are, as a result of their relationship, rigidly sorted into hypo- and hyper-aggressive ("We made a pact when we were children," Lila declares, "I'm the wicked one"; tlts 144) and later they are unveiled to be apparent, spontaneous complements to one another. Elena puts it this way: "I fair, she dark, I calm, she anxious, I likable, she malicious, the two of us opposite and united" (slc 157). In a few rare sequences in the narrative, the two protagonists' friendship is defined by a balance of opposites, by a divided energy that only when combined manages to give shape to the world: "I, I and Lila, we two with that capacity that together—only together—we had to seize the mass of colors, sounds, things, and people, and express it and give it power" (mbf 138). Yet they are depicted most frequently as asymmetric complements, formed from the start by Elena's submissiveness and low self-esteem, hinging on a dynamic of fullness and emptiness:

> I was blind, she a falcon; I had an opaque pupil, she narrowed her eyes, with darting glances that saw more; I clung to her arm, among the shadows, she guided me with a stern gaze. (mbf 257)

> I was becoming, as the months ran by, a sloppy, disheveled, spectacled girl bent over tattered books that gave off a moldy odor, volumes bought at great sacrifice at the secondhand store . . . She went around on Stefano's arm in the clothes of an actress or a princess, her hair styled like a diva's. (mbf 265)

*

Their two daughters are also connected by the proximity of their birthdays and by their names: Tina, besides being the name of Elena's doll, is a common diminutive of Imma (Immacolata). An analogous symbiosis also determines how they are depicted; Lila's supremacy extends to Tina and Elena's inferiority to Imma:

> Bitterly I compared the daughter of Nino and me to the daughter of Lila and Enzo. Tina seemed prettier, healthier than Imma: she was the sweet fruit of a solid relationship . . . Tina says "Mamma" clearly, all the syllables, Imma doesn't do that yet and is almost a month older. I felt at a loss and sad. (slc 243–44)

> . . . Imma had been making me anxious: when I compared her with Tina I was sure she was suffering from some developmental problem. (slc 256)

> Although my daughter was pretty, and intelligent, beside Tina she turned dull, her virtues vanished, and she felt this deeply. (slc 321)

Symbiosis may be the underlying pulse, yet the story also develops from the disintegration of boundaries, a disintegration spurred, on the one hand, by Lila's entropic and centrifugal force, and, on the other, by Elena's inner emptiness. While Lila tends to perceive outer boundaries as unstable (cf. 3.2.), Elena is regularly pained by her lack of an inner nucleus. She feels empty ("I'm made of nothing"; snn 29–30), dissipated by her continual efforts to mimic others' words and postures. In both cases the boundary between inside and outside blurs. Lila lives in fear of explosion, contagion, a transitive energy that dissolves external forms before arriving at her own ("[S]he had deposited that sensation of threat, the anguish over the difficult choice she had, making one of [the pots] explode like a sign, as if its shape had decided abruptly to cede"; mbf 231). Elena lives in fear of implosion, internal breakdown, the slippage of an empty form (" . . . I made no attempt to find a form for my emotions . . . The island faded, lost itself in some secret corner of my head"; mbf 243).

Elena insists on pointing out her own stability during Lila's breakdown after the earthquake of 1980 (" . . . in me fear could not put down roots, and even the lava, the fiery stream of melting matter . . . the fear it provoked in me, settled in my mind in orderly sentences, in harmonious images"; slc 179). But she is merely being defensive. Well before her friend, Elena has experienced *smarginatura*; the ground has given way underneath her since she was ten years old, though she doesn't know it or want to define it (cf. 3.2). Hence her friend takes the form of a "demanding ghost" (mbf 97), chillingly revealing not only Elena's metaphysical absence, but also, and especially, Lila's own: an unbridgeable estrangement that, despite their symbiotic tension, cannot be chalked up to a mirror image (Brogi[1]) or a "secret voice" (fr 277). That narcissistic function will be supplied by Nino, who, while described as exceptionally effeminate ("a fragility opposed to virile strength"; snn 60; "an insignificant limp agglomerate of effeminate flesh and bone, too long and breakable"; 363–64), is most often depicted as the male equivalent of the socially ambitious Elena. Not by coincidence, Ferrante has called attention to the inherent vacillation between the two friends and therefore in the overarching structure of the story. Regularly "disappointing" (fr 269) expectations and straying from the original premise of complementary characters, the quartet prohibits us from reading the friends as doubles or enigmatic twins. On the contrary, the enigma is produced by the way in which the pace of the story dissolves and breaks down, constantly reminding us of the failure of their symbiosis: "When Lila's pace becomes unsustainable, the reader grabs onto Lenù. But if Lenù falls apart, then the reader relies on Lila" (fr 277).

6. Distortion and Recognition

As with all symbiotic relationships, Elena and Lila bond in order to compensate for a void: friendship makes up for their original flawed relationships with their mothers, depicted in the quartet as links in a genealogical chain of female debasement materialized and perpetuated in the *rione* by the loveless and negligent relationships between mothers and daughters (cf. 3). To borrow the title and subject of Ferrante's first novel, Elena and Lila's relationship is as *troubling* (Brogi[1]) as their past relationships with their mothers (cf. 3). Elena's tale betrays her infantile need to replace her mother's limp gait with the surefooted and determined gait of young Lila, the repulsive body of the former with the agile and energetic body of the latter. "I devoted myself to studying and to many things that were difficult, alien to me," she says, "just so I could keep pace with that terrible, dazzling girl" (mbf 47; Benedetti[1] 177). "My mother," Elena recalls, "was diminished almost to nothing, and yet she had been truly burdensome, weighing on me, making me feel like a worm under a rock, protected and crushed" (slc 221).

But if her bond with her mother is only depicted as invasive, then her friendship with Lila can only take the form of a more vital variant of this punishing relationship. The diabolical element of their bond is unveiled by the first volume's epigraph from *Faust*, which eulogizes humankind's debt to the evil spirit, "the comrade . . . who works, excites, and must create, as Devil": "[T]here was no way to feel that things were settled; every fixed point of our relationship sooner or later turned out to be provisional; something shifted in her head that unbalanced her and unbalanced me" (tlts 226). Also diabolical are the numerous variations of the first reciprocal theft of the dolls. Elena, for example, slowly paints a portrait of herself as a thief of other people's brilliance, passing off Lila's insights as her own at critical moments in her academic career. Her aping of Lila's "fluid and engaging [writing] style" (mbf 276), her discourse on Dido and the city (mbf 161, 187–89), her arguments against Catholic metaphysics (mbf 261, 296), her use of the book by Beckett (snn 221, 326), and her manner of defending herself against the racist attacks of the girls from the Normale (snn 333)—these are only a few examples of a dynamic, at times real and fictitious, that will come to define Elena's literary vocation. Beginning with her first novel, the creative act is for Elena a faint, subtle rewriting of her friend's words. *The Blue Fairy*, the letter, the notebooks, even Lila's secret book about Naples and the loss of her daughter are the sources of Elena's translation and betrayal (Falkoff), an act as haunted and obsessive as it is impossible for the reader to verify, because the reader will never be able to read a snippet of Lila's texts, only Elena's impressions of them (in the case of the secret book, not even those). "I was added to her," says Elena, "and I felt mutilated as soon as I removed myself. Not an idea, without Lila" (tlts 282–83). The "addition" produces a vacuum, an immense void that stems from her feelings of persecution, which, at their most extreme, lead her to secretly want to erase her friend from existence (mbf 142), to "diminish her in order not to feel her loss" (snn 31), literally to see her dead (tlts 227, 261, 339).

Distortion and recognition form the knot that gives the two friends' identity an ebb and flow like movement (Lucamante[1] 319). One episode in particular, Elena's visit to the factory in 1967, substantiates this back-and-forth between the two. When Lila ends her marriage to Stefano in 1966, she loses her status as the young wealthy wife. She retreats to another poor suburb of Naples to live with Enzo and decides to work at a factory. Her backbreaking job at a sausage plant is made all the more alienating by the absence of unions and the sexual harassment of her supervisors and the factory owner, Bruno Soccavo (whom Lila and Elena had considered a kind, shy friend in Ischia just a few years before). Lila enters the scene undone, enveloped by the stink of cured meats, shapeless in her uniform.

> Her eyes were feverish, her cheeks more hollow than usual, and yet she seemed large, tall. She, too, wore a blue smock, but over it a kind of long coat, and on her feet she wore army boots. (snn 462)

Elegantly dressed and displaying the manners she picked up during her five years at the university, Elena triumphantly announces her graduation and the publication of her first novel. Lila's face—marred by fatigue and cracked by the cold—lights up with feeling, and she instinctively kisses Elena's hand.

But immediately afterward Lila's face narrows out of spite, and she begins telling her friend about her discovery of computer programming, a new language far more useful than the language found in novels ("[T]he dismissive tone in which she uttered the word 'novels' disturbed me"; snn 465). Elena sees the enthusiasm with which Lila talks about her new ultramodern field of research, and the potential for change linked to that interest, as a diminishment of her own achievements, which suddenly appear conventional in comparison. Once again the intensity of Lila's life, her ability to gamble away her own marvelous gifts (at the end of their encounter she burns *The Blue Fairy*, the story she wrote as a child and that Elena had brought to her to acknowledge her creative debt) in order to pull other gifts out of her hat (the new story about computers), devastate Elena, and make her feel persistently bullied: "Her life had overwhelmed me and it took days for me to restore clear outlines and depth to mine" (snn 467).

Yet Lila, too, feels unhappy about their encounter, and her unhappiness is both recorded and obscured by the narration, thanks to Elena's wary mix of uncertainty ("I don't know how strong an effect our meeting had on her") and conviction ("certainly she felt unhappy for days"):

> As soon as *The Blue Fairy* turned to ash in the bonfire of the courtyard, Lila went back to work. I don't know how strong an effect our meeting had on her—certainly she felt unhappy for days but managed not to ask herself why. She had learned that it hurt to look for reasons, and she waited for the unhappiness to become first a general discontent, then a kind of melancholy, and finally the normal labor of every day . . . (tlts 105–6)

The narrative sets these reactions one hundred pages apart (between the end of one volume and the start of another), spanning a time period of roughly twelve months, during which Elena's fate as a bourgeois artist is increasingly cemented by the growing success of her book and her subsequent speaking engagements; Pietro's new position as a university professor; and the work underway on her future marital home. One evening, at the end of this period, Lila urgently summons Elena; Lila has had a nervous breakdown after the bitter union clash that she herself instigated during her months at the factory. Lying on a cot in her humble abode, completely undone, Lila tells Elena how unhappy their meeting made her, before going on, hours later, to tell her about her courageous life as a politically active worker during what will later be called (though not in the quartet; cf. 7.2 and 7.3) the "Hot Autumn of '69."

By introducing this distance between the revelation of their states of mind and jettisoning the cause and effect of their emotions, the narrative creates an uninterrupted dynamic of ambiguity and clarity, of distortions and recognitions. Initially perceiving their meeting at the factory from Elena's point of view only, a reader may well believe that Elena was, in effect, bullied by her friend. Yet Lila's confession and brave vulnerability, emerging as they do after an account of Elena's private and public successes, alter the meaning of their encounter and of the omnipotence that Lila would seem to have manifested in Elena's eyes.

Their encounter has a third act: the perception that, to borrow Ferrante's own words at the beginning of this chapter, "one [friend] draws strength from the other . . . in the sense that they [deprive] each other of energy" (fr 233). Which is to say, both friends have carved out a new life during those twelve months, one based on a rivalry that thrives on their need to bully one another and to part ways. The narrative strategy to create distance between them is therefore a way of unveiling and placing in relation both the two friends' otherness and their symbiotic dependence on one another as they turn twenty-five. On the one hand, they are intertwined presences in the same ghostly scene. Yet on the other, they are situated in social and psychic spaces that are quite different—and asymmetric (there are similar disparities between success in the bourgeois literary world and the new epic of the worker). Elena tries to make sense of this tangle of togetherness and estrangement, comparing herself to a "knight in an ancient romance . . . wrapped in her shining armor," and Lila to a picaresque hero, a "ragged, starving herdsman, who, never leaving his pasture, subdues and controls horrible beasts with his bare hands, and with prodigious courage" (tlts 172). Lila's final heartfelt appeal—devastating in its intensity—distills the force of their bond, the way it remains suspended between an overwhelming presence and an equally overwhelming absence: "Watch me until I fall asleep. Watch me always, even when you leave Naples. That way I'll know that you see me and I'm at peace" (tlts 178). In this final exchange at the end of Lila's long story, the two friends "pass through each other as if they were air" (fr 367). Once again, symbiosis and otherness, distortion and recognition are, like the girls' fingers, interlaced.

CHAPTER THREE
Smarginatura, Frantumaglia, *Surveillance: Between Mothers and Daughters*

1. Love, the "Mad Widow," and the Queen

The word "love" first appears in the quartet in reference to Melina Cappuccio, a character who only seems minor. The backstory of this woman from the *rione* is described in the index of characters with chilling brevity. The index of the first volume, *My Brilliant Friend*, informs us that she is a "mad widow." The second volume, *The Story of a New Name,* paints a fuller picture:

> *Melina*, a relative of Nunzia Cerullo, a widow. She washes the stairs of the apartment buildings in the old neighborhood. She was the lover of Donato Sarratore, Nino's father. The Sarratores left the neighborhood precisely because of that relationship, and Melina has nearly lost her reason. (snn 8)

The stigma of madness extends to the entire Cappuccio clan. Beginning with the first volume, every family listed in the index is given a specific label. The Cerullos, for example, are "the shoemaker's family," the Grecos "the porter's family," et cetera. Following this folktale convention, the Cappucios are referred to as "the family of the mad widow."

Readers will primarily remember Melina as the author of two unforgettable deeds. First, at the beginning of the quartet, she is shown eating soap flakes straight from the bag—on the street, out in public:

> [Melina] was walking slowly from one side of the *stradone*, the wide avenue that ran through the neighborhood, to the other, carrying a paper bag in one hand from which, with the other, she was

taking something and eating it . . . holding in her palm the dark
soft soap she had just bought in Don Carlo's cellar, and with her
other hand was taking some and eating it. (mbf 40–1)

Later in the novel, ten years after the soap incident, she is
described as completely transformed by her misery. With her
daughter Ada looking on, Melina drinks the dirty water from
the bucket she uses to mop the building stairs:

> . . . bent double, she started from the top floor and, with the
> wet rag in her hands, wiped step after step . . . If someone went
> down or up, she began shouting insults, she hurled the rag at him.
> Ada had seen her mother, in the midst of a crisis because someone
> had spoiled her work by walking on it, drink the dirty water from
> the bucket, and had had to tear it away from her. (mbf 161)

In the melodramatic style characteristic of the quartet (cf.
1.2), her ingestion of this poisonous brew calls to mind her
pathological relationship and the intoxication of her soul—as
the famous Neapolitan song "La Malafemmena" has it—forcing us to visualize "the invisible wound that does not heal easily" (fr 338), i.e., her abandonment at the hands of Donato
Sarratore, the "railroad worker–poet" and Melina's former
lover. Lost love, Ferrante points out, is "the question most
crudely posed by female existence" (fr 77). Due to social and
economic inequality, for a woman the loss of a lover entails a
decline in her image, status, and place in society. Damage to
her social position makes her emotional damage more acute,
and vice versa: the day-to-day life of a jilted woman is the
"experience closest to the myth of the expulsion from earthly
paradise" (fr 86).

Melina's madness and spectacular anger reveal to Elena and
Lila the existence of new forces that can overwhelm a person's
life: the laws of passion that destabilize an individual. With
love comes extreme behavior, as yet indecipherable to the two
friends, who only know the radical but routine violence that

they have witnessed in the *rione*. When, years after leaving her, Donato gives Melina a book of poetry inscribed to her, having underlined a few pages she presumably inspired, she explodes with sensual happiness: "laughing, jumping on the bed, and pulling up her skirt, displaying her fleshless thighs and her underpants to her frightened children" (mbf 126). According to Elena, the inscribed book of poetry suddenly releases Melina from the blight of the *rione*, from her obsessive mania (until then most people believed she had made up the relationship with the railroad worker–poet), and from her role as an "ugly, lean, widowed woman" (mbf 60), elevating her to the status of romantic heroine:

> Melina wasn't mad . . . Donato really had been in love with her and still loved her. Therefore . . . we had all known not an ordinary man . . . but a poet. Therefore, right before our eyes a tragic love had been born, inspired by a person we knew very well, that is to say Melina. I was very excited, my heart was pounding. (mbf 127–28)

A few months later, when Melina's excitement has worn off and Donato's abandonment been confirmed, Lila—now a teenage shoemaker and avid reader of her friend's textbook, the *Aeneid*—is the one to interrogate Melina's passion, whereby she reconfigures the shape and scale of the neighborhood. In Lila's eyes, the *rione* becomes the quintessential mythical space of abandonment. She associates Melina's story with the story of Dido, who, on account of Aeneas' flight, not only takes her own life but, before that, discards her royal dominion over the city that she had been building "according to what is just and lawful" (fr 150).

The Queen of Carthage inhabits the streets of the neighborhood as well as the nomadic universe of *Frantumaglia*: Ferrante devotes many pages of the book to Dido and stresses the importance of the fact that Dido first appears in the *Aeneid* as a sovereign ruler in the middle of erecting a kingdom, and not as a woman in love: "When she first appears, Dido, who is very beautiful, and escorted by young suitors, is serenely active, vigilantly governing the progress of works in the city" (fr 147). But as the epic poem goes on, Dido becomes a symbol of passion in a parable about female vulnerability, a passion that drives her to betray her "polis of love." Carthage is material in perpetual transformation, the erotic birthing of an urban landscape, and, above all, a city engendered by the vigilant desire of a woman, namely Dido: "Cities are this, stone made suddenly alive by our emotions, by our desires, as we can see above all in the relationship between Carthage and Dido" (fr 149). "'When there is no love,'" confirms Lila, "'not only the life of the people becomes sterile but the life of cities'" (mbf 160).

There is a passage in *Frantumaglia* that describes at length this double "absence of sense" (fr 77) produced in the *Aeneid* by the loss of love:

> What had been started stops, the work breaks off. Like Dido, the stones wait to decide their fate . . . Aeneas abandons her. Dido, the happy woman, becomes furious, raging. The past is joined to the future, Tyre virtually reaches Carthage, every street becomes a labyrinth, a place to get lost without art, and the blood that Dido has left behind returns to stain the new city. (fr 150)

The two friends still don't know what love is, but they do know what it is to live in a city bereft of love: Elena immediately associates the image of this abandoned city with the *rione* and its "dirty streets, the dusty gardens, the countryside disfigured by new buildings, the violence in every house, every family" (mbf 160). Through these parallel loves, one amorous, one urban, Lila glimpses the transformative power of eros, which can spread from the lover's room to the civic realm, and vice versa. Elena will stake her high school and university fortunes on this insight (in fact, she writes her thesis on the fourth book of the *Aeneid*; snn 452). What connects the private and the public, passion and morals, and the individual and the city, is the relationship between individuals who seek to reimagine and transform the world, and in doing so cast love as "a political emotion" (Nussbaum) that can contribute to the development of civic consciousness, and not just to an abstract theoretical tradition. If this polymorphism of feeling endows the melodrama of the love story with utopian ideals ("solidarity, respect, a movement toward a good life for all"; fr 151) by envisioning a crack in public space (and therefore a form of *smarginatura*), the lack of love anticipates a private question in the public sphere: the decline of the *rione* lucidly described by Elena entails the deformation of women's bodies at the heart of the quartet (cf. 6).

2. *Smarginatura*

Every time Melina appears she is described from the point of view of Lila, who is secretly connected to her relative by her nickname (Melina/Lina; only Elena calls her Lila). It is young Lila who carefully studies Melina eating soap. Her gaze is so intense as to distract Elena from the widow's eccentric behavior:

> [Lila] was moving, cutting across the street, a small, dark, nervous figure, she was acting with her usual determination, she was firm. Firm in what her mother's relative was doing, firm in the pain, firm in silence as a statue is firm. A follower. One with Melina . . . " (mbf 40–41)

Lila's attachment to Melina and her gesture reveals the young girl's perilous identification with her relative. Her troubling empathy becomes still more evident ten years later, when—during the summer of 1961, a few months after Lila's marriage—Melina disappears, only to be later discovered sitting in the turbid pondwater just outside the *rione*. "She was silent: she whose attacks of madness had for ten years taken the form of shouting or singing" (snn 96). As her son Antonio and Elena escort her back to the *rione*, they cross paths with Lila.

> I saw Lila next to the gate; isolated in her house in the new neighborhood, she must have heard the news late, and hadn't taken part in the search. I knew that she felt a strong bond with Melina, but it struck me that, while everyone was showing signs of sympathy . . . she stood apart with an expression that was hard to describe. She seemed to be moved by the pitiful sight of the widow . . . But Lila also seemed to be wounded by it, and frightened, as if she felt inside the same disruption. (snn 96–97)

This "disruption" stems from Lila's awareness that she, like Melina, risks straying from reason to madness and succumbing to *smarginatura*: spilling through the established boundaries of conventional reality, as per the semantic neologism—obtained by enlarging, qualifying, or adding to meanings already present in a word (Palermo)—that Ferrante reinvents by applying the word to the psychic realm and wrenching open its common meaning. (*Smarginatura* is also a typographic term that refers to a text spilling over the margin.) Even if "she had often had the sensation of moving for a few fractions of a second into a person or a thing or a number or a syllable, violating its edges" (mbf 90–91), Lila doesn't become aware of *smarginatura* until the year before her marriage. On New Year's Eve 1958, when Lila is fourteen years old, her sensation morphs into something certain:

> . . . she had perceived for the first time unknown entities that broke down the outline of the world and demonstrated its terrifying nature . . . It was—she told me—as if, on the night of a full moon over the sea, the intense black mass of a storm advanced across the sky, swallowing every light, eroding the circumference of the moon's circle, and disfiguring the shining disk, reducing it to its true nature of rough insensate material. (mbf 91, 176)

Smarginatura is the loss of edges that give things shape, the slippage of sensory order, an inner "wave" (slc 179) of lava that comes gushing out on November 23, 1980, the day of the earthquake in Naples, terrifying Lila and prompting her to confess this sensation to her friend.

> She used that term: *dissolving boundaries* [*smarginatura*]. It was on that occasion that she resorted to it for the first time . . . She said that the outlines of things and people were delicate, that they broke like cotton thread. She whispered that for her it had always been that way, an object lost its edges and poured into another, into a solution of heterogeneous materials, a merging and mixing . . . A tactile emotion would melt into a visual one, a visual one would melt into an olfactory one . . . (slc 175–76)

Lila may christen this incredible experience, but her friend lived through it first, and only lacked the courage to name it:

> I was overcome by a kind of tactile dysfunction; sometimes I had the impression that, while every animated being around me was speeding up the rhythms of its life, solid surfaces turned soft under my fingers or swelled up, leaving empty spaces between their internal mass and the surface skin. It seemed to me that my own body, if you touched it, was distended, and this saddened me . . . It was an enduring malaise, lasting perhaps years, beyond early adolescence. (mbf 57)

It is Elena, not Lila, who narrates this experience. Having already fallen into this state of confusion in the third grade after the search for the dolls in the cellar—six years before Lila's first episode—young Elena endures a prolonged crisis of spatial perception ("lasting perhaps years, beyond early adolescence"), which morphs into a labyrinth (cf. 4.6).

The experience earns a place in Elena's first novel, written in 1967, an autobiographical tale about a girl who discovers, among other things, sex with an older man on the Maronti in Ischia. Her sexual initiation may be based on Elena's own, but the novel's main character draws on Lila's determination and the *smarginatura* that Elena experiences following the fruitless search for their dolls in the cellar. (In fact, while writing the book, Elena can only know about this sense of fragmentation from personal experience, since her friend will not name it for another fourteen years):

> I imagined a dark force crouching in the life of the protagonist, an entity that had the capacity to weld the world around her, with the colors of the flame of a blowtorch: a blue-violet dome where everything went well for her, shooting sparks, but that soon came apart, breaking up into meaningless gray fragments. (snn 433)

The motivating cause of *smarginatura* is the battle between the sexes (cf. 6.1), which, on New Year's Eve 1958, obliquely scrapes away the figure of Rino, the brother whom Lila adores (mbf 53) yet who, in his struggle to assert himself socially, has already used violence to dominate his sister (mbf 165; cf. 4.3.). Now, on the eve of the new year, during the noisy symbolic war among men to see who has the best fireworks display, Rino dissolves; his bodily form breaks up into "a disquieting patchwork of various materials" (Alfano B.) and the "disgusting brother" spills out (slc 177), "a squat animal form, thickset, the loudest, the fiercest, the greediest, the meanest" (mbf 90):

> I was afraid that the colors of the fireworks were sharp . . . that the trails of the rockets were scraping my brother Rino like files, like rasps, and broke his flesh, caused another, disgusting brother to drip out of him, whom I had to put back inside right away—inside his usual form—or he would turn against me and hurt me. (slc 176–77)

What Lila sees in Melina, what she recognizes as their shared fate, is the undoing of her person by patriarchy, her disfigurement by a painful, sorrowful, impoverished fate. Lila is also subjected to this same subsuming process, even if it takes different forms. By the time Melina is discovered in the ponds,

Lila has already been ruined—as she herself writes in her note-books—by her husband, who rapes and beats her daily. Her sensation of "imminent death" drives her to "express herself for the last time, before becoming like Melina" (snn 295). Melina is *smarginata* (dissolved) by a man's neglect, Lila by a man's presence (cf. 6.2 and 6.6). The secret bond between Melina and Lila is that between a mother and daughter. The mix of empathy, terror, and disgust that Lila feels upon seeing Melina returning from the ponds in all the unseemliness and impropriety of her madness is "matrophobia"—"the fear of becoming one's mother" (Rich, 153).

3. The Cave of the Mother

Becoming one's mother, or the relative who stands in for one's mother, means being cast into a cave as dark as the cellar into which Elena and Lila's dolls are tossed (cf. 4.5 and 4.6): both are dark places in which thousands of years of gender inequality and violence have thrown a shadow over women. In a memorable passage in *Frantumaglia*, Ferrante describes the fall: "[S]uffering casts us down among our single-celled ancestors, among the quarrelsome or terrorized muttering in the caves, among the female divinities expelled into the darkness of the earth, even as we keep ourselves anchored . . . to the computer we're writing on" (fr 107–8). What Ferrante is talking about are "ancestors," the chain of women who have been humiliated or oppressed: the interminable links that continue to compromise the silenced, shadowy non-history of the female sex. They are ancestral mothers, whom every mother, and therefore every daughter insofar as she is a mother, carries inside her: strong yet at the same time subordinate, like the "female divinities" of this temporal standstill.

When unbearable grief shatters the outer shell of her

personality, the daughter falls into a "black well" (ld 88). The metaphor, already at the center of an important debate between Alba de Céspedes and Natalia Ginzburg in 1948 (Alsop 472), now returns in new forms. Falling into the cave is relentless, and the daughter finds herself in a chthonic, pre-linguistic world inhabited by primeval matriarchs. Yet the falling woman lugs behind her—the detail is significant—a technological object: the computer on which she was writing. All of the heroines in Ferrante's novels share this type of synchronicity: they collapse into the ancient maternal cave, revise the culture (via writing), and update it (via the computer). These women narrate their experience, writing their own stories from within a destabilized state made of jagged pieces of time that do not combine to form a picture of serene and resolved emancipation. Here, the grand archetype of mothers is seen from the perspective of female difference.

Faust, too, descends to the underworld, but the ghostly female divinities he encounters there are terrible rulers of eternal re-creation (*Faust* II, I), not the humiliated, dethroned figures depicted in Ferrante. Goethe's hero may be on a perilous adventure, but it is a temporary quest for the magical "glowing tripod"; it is not due to a loss of willpower (a fall), nor does it threaten to be permanent. What makes the initial trial in *Faust* daring is his mission to rob the Mothers of a symbol of their regenerative powers. Whereas what enables daughters to rewrite their experience is a tool that they themselves supply (the computer), a tool that will become—as we will see—a way of being cyclically together, in and out of the cave.

Let's analyze how the fall into the cave of mothers is recounted in *The Story of the Lost Child*. In 1976, Elena has realized her childhood dream, entering into a relationship with Nino, for whom she has broken off her marriage to Pietro and thrust her daughters into an itinerant lifestyle. Two years later, in 1978, Lila reveals to Elena that the man she loves so much is still living with his wife (and is about to have another baby with her—something Lila doesn't have the courage to tell Elena). Pressed for an answer, Nino tells her the truth; Elena is filled with a fury that she discovers, to her surprise, has maternal roots:

> *Am I always this furious other I? I, here in Naples, in this filthy house, I, who if I could would kill this man, plunge a knife into his heart with all my strength? Should I restrain this shadow—my mother, all our female ancestors—or should I let her go?* (slc 95)

Once again, ancestors enter the picture, here even referred to as "our," meaning the ancestors of Elena and her female readers equally at risk of falling into the cave: giving vent to primal passions, unleashing the Furies, losing their social standing.

Another striking aspect is the melodramatic language that Elena employs, in clear contrast to her usual control of Italian. Elena not only sees the shadow of her mother Immacolata; her mother *speaks through her*. When, ten years earlier, Elena coolly announces that she is marrying Pietro, a member of the upper middle class who would make her "increasingly estranged from the family, indifferent to their problems of survival" (tlts 46), Immacolata angrily responds by reminding her *whose belly she came out of and of what substance she is made*:

> She attacked me in very low but shrill tones, hissing with reddened eyes: We are nothing to you, you tell us nothing until the last minute, the young lady thinks she's somebody because she has an education, because she writes books, because she's marrying a professor, but my dear, you came out of this belly and you are made of this substance, so don't act superior and don't ever forget that if you are intelligent, I who carried you in here am just as intelligent, if not more, and if I had had the chance I would have done the same as you, understand? (tlts 47)

But the mother's voice, the voice arising from the cave, is

not only the voice of persecuted and melodramatic rage ("the quarrelsome or terrorized muttering in the caves"). Her tone is primarily imbued with "a fascination with death" (fr 107): the herald of a depressed, subaltern, and vengeful fate, which the daughter counters by expressing her own "matrophobia" as her fear of and resistance to the threat of assimilation.

The line of mothers is long, and, as we have seen, mothers like Melina are no less cumbersome than natural mothers like Immacolata. Another primeval figure is the *poverella* in *The Days of Abandonment*: the ghost of a Neapolitan woman who kills herself after her marriage ends when the novel's main character, Olga, is just a child. Olga, too, is aggrieved after her husband leaves her, but unlike Melina and the *poverella*, her loss "changes her without annihilating her" (fr 187). In Olga's adulthood, the Neapolitan woman returns with the same dark and fairy-tale-like features Olga remembers from childhood, a figure transformed by grief into an animal ("a gray-blue fish," "a silver anchovy"), her identity dissolved:

> The *poverella* was crying, the *poverella* was screaming, the *poverella* was suffering, torn to pieces by the absence of the sweaty red-haired man . . . She rubbed a damp handkerchief between her hands, she told everyone that her husband had abandoned her, had cancelled her out from memory and feeling, and she twisted the handkerchief with whitened knuckles . . . A grief so gaudy began to repel me . . . Now she came down the stairs stiffly, her body withered . . . Once my mother exclaimed: *poverella*, she's as dry now as a salted anchovy. From then on I watched her every day . . . wanted to discover her new nature, of a gray-blue fish, grains of salt sparkling on her arms and legs . . . I heard people say that our neighbor . . . had drowned herself near Capo Miseno . . . . I stayed in a dark corner of the house dreaming the story of the *poverella*'s waterlogged, lifeless body, a silver anchovy to be preserved in salt. (doa 16, 52)

During the "four months of tension and grief" (doa 118)

following her abandonment, Olga dwells on the threshold of infanticide and madness, constantly besieged by her memories of the *poverella*:

> [The children's] look was such that I thought that, like certain characters in tales of fantasy, they might see more than it was in reality possible to see. Maybe I had beside me, stiff as a sepulchral statue, the abandoned woman of my childhood memories, the *poverella*. She had come . . . to grab me by the hem of my skirt, before I flew down from the fifth floor. (doa 43–44)

Olga's mother initiates a game of side-eyes, a female tradition of dismissing one another that distorts both the *poverella* and Olga herself:

> And my mother laughed bitterly at the bitterness of that story and of others she knew, all the same. Women without love lose the light in their eyes, women without love die while they are still alive . . . Sometimes she gave me the feeling that she didn't like me, as if she recognized in me something of herself that she hated, a secret evil of her own. (doa 44, 52)

The mother/*poverella* imposes her own negative legacy, dragging the daughter into the vortex of an ancient world where she risks repeating the same suicidal act carried out by countless unknown women. Abandoned by her husband, at odds with her own motherhood and her children, whom she views as the cause of her abandonment, the "stink of motherhood" (doa 92) having repelled her man and precipitated her desperation and death, the *poverella* is a symbol of the inextricably difficult coexistence of two opposing states: motherhood and womanhood.

The same tension afflicts many of the mothers in Elena Ferrante's oeuvre: Amalia, the seductive mother in *Troubling Love* (1992); Olga, the Medea-like mother in *The Days of Abandonment* (2002); Leda, the mother in *The Lost Daughter* (2006) who runs away, just as Elena will, in her own way, at various stages of the quartet; and finally Lila, the abortive mother (in the first two years of her marriage to Stefano). Moreover, mothers gain power from these forms of detachment and indifference, which often trigger in the daughter an obsessive attachment and idealization (Giorgio 148), as is the case with Delia in *Troubling Love*. There is a profound link between impurity and the reemergence of the ancient mother. The daughter also experiences motherhood as "abjection" (Kristeva), that bottomless origin, that clash of opposites that appears to be unarticulated, unpremeditated, impervious to historical transformations: "In this way the opening of the mother, the opening to the mother, appear as threats of contagion, contamination, falling into sickness, madness, death" (Irigaray 15).

4. Matricide

The daughter falls into the cave with the same "savagery" (Wood) with which Ferrante's protagonists explode the myth of motherhood, flaunting its abject side with deeply disturbing images, displaying its opposing undercurrents of disgust and primary envy (cf. 2.4). In this sense the writer positions herself as the heir to a rich tradition of Italian women writers—including Fabrizia Ramondino—who placed motherhood and the conflicts motherhood generates for daughters at the center of their creative endeavors (Benedetti[2] 102–106, Giorgio). In *The Lost Daughter* Leda describes her pregnancy as "a bloody liquid; suspended in it was a mushy sediment inside which grew a violent polyp" (ld 123) and "an insect's poison injected into a vein" (ld 37), while the pregnant belly of Rosaria is a "protruding navel like an eye" (ld 29). In *The Days of Abandonment* Olga calls her breastfeeding body "a cud made of living material" (doa 91) and sees in her daughter traces of death and her own self ("I imagined her old, her features deformed, near death or already dead, and yet a piece of me, the apparition of the child I had been, that I would have been"; doa 89).

In *The Story of a New Name* Lila describes her pregnant body as "a box of flesh with a living doll inside" (snn 112), while Elena echoes her when talking about her own condition as an "expanding nodule that at a certain point would come out of her sex" (snn 372). Finally, in *Those Who Leave and Those Who Stay*, she gives a chilling appraisal of motherhood:

> The two children seemed to have confirmed that I was no longer young, that the signs of my labors—washing them, dressing them, the stroller, the shopping, cooking, one in my arms and one by the hand, both in my arms, wiping the nose of one, cleaning the mouth of the other—testified to my maturity as a woman, that to become like the mammas of the neighborhood wasn't a threat but the order of things. It's fine this way, I told myself. (tlts 276)

This particular fury at her ability to reproduce is in truth a form of "matricide" (Klein[2]): an attack on the mother as well as an attempt by the daughter to come to terms with her, bringing to light the deep-seated reason why one simultaneously clings to and seeks to get free of the other (Elwell 237). This hostility toward mothers in fact feeds the "subversive power" (Wehling-Giorgi[1]) of a new feminine consciousness, now finally in a position to name and revise the current of violence running through the mother-daughter relationship.

Matricide as performed by the daughter—Ferrante remarks in her review of Alice Sebold's novel *The Almost Moon* (fer[1])—is one of the great omissions in our collective imagination. No myth (Electra acts "on the mandate of her ancestors" and "cribs her reasons from her male sibling Orestes") and, to this day, nearly no novel has portrayed the murder of the mother, the concrete fulfillment of her fantasy, even when that desire—as Melanie Klein's psychoanalytic studies show—is clearly apparent in the daughter's psyche. Why is this act so unspeakable, so impossible to depict in literature? Because, the writer speculates in her review, "a daughter's fury moves like a wild animal . . . the knowledge about ourselves that it unearths repels us and automatically derails the pleasant models that have long comforted us."

In *Troubling Love*, during Delia's childhood, the lust for murder is repeatedly depicted as a form of obsessive and jealous love for the elusive, seductive mother (Wehling-Giorgi[2] 223):

> When I was a child, I would spend the time of her absences waiting for her in the kitchen, at the window. I longed for her to appear at the end of the street like a figure in a crystal ball. I breathed on the glass, fogging it, in order not to see the street without her. If she was late, the anxiety became uncontainable, overflowing into tremors throughout my body . . . "When you get back I'll kill you," I thought, as if it were she who had left me shut up in there. (tl 12–13)

The mother's physical wounds become objects of adoration and sexual arousal. Incapable of feeling closely connected to her mother's body (access to which Amalia denies her), the daughter turns to oral contact (licking, sucking) as a form of incorporation, and considers committing the same violence against her own body. For according to a principle of symmetrical displacement, hurting oneself means hurting one's mother (Wehling-Giorgi[2] 223):

> My mother's wounded finger, pierced by the needle before she was ten, was more familiar to me than my own fingers precisely because of that detail. It was purple, and the nail appeared to sink into the crescent. For a long time I'd wanted to lick it and suck it, more than her nipples . . . I intended to make a hole in my finger, too, to make her see that it was risky to deny me what I didn't have. (tl 63–64)

In the end the young protagonist believes that she has actually murdered her mother by making false accusations about her, telling her father, a madly jealous man and the source of Delia's own morbid jealousy, that she saw her mother having sex with her suitor Caserta. Once relayed, the lie exposes her mother to the husband's brutal violence:

> "I wished only to confess aloud that, then and later, I had hated not [Caserta], perhaps not even his father: only Amalia. It was she I wanted to hurt" (tl 133).

As with Elena in the quartet, in Delia's story matricide is a necessary step to access guilt and make "reparations" (another of Melanie Klein's key words) in relation to one's mother. In other words, only by becoming aware of your violent intentions can you begin to symbolize loss and emptiness, the basis of any possible equilibrium. Thanks to Melanie Klein, says Elena Ferrante, "Today the body of the mother is a source of good and, more importantly, wicked feelings of the human animal" (fer[1]). These images of matricide, this violent repertoire of daughter versus mother—and versus herself, insofar as she is a mother—are liberating, because they call into question maternity and its false transparency, permitting women to inhabit this universe authentically: that is, to live in it as problematic subjects rather than as objects of a fictitious patriarchal idyll (Wehling-Giorgi[2] 226).

5. Repressive Surveillance and *Smarginatura*

The name *Cronache del Mal d'Amore* (*Chronicles of Heartache*)—the title of the 2012 volume containing Ferrante's first three novels—could be applied to the author's entire body of work, which can be read as one continuous discourse about the subjective experience of women who toggle between being stricken with troubling love and being totally deprived or devoid of it. In this light, the writer's works appear connected by a remarkable number of constants. Elena and Lila are two women who spend their lives fending off a sense of loss, ushered in by their malignant mothers and by the dolls, and later resumed by gender violence and inequality, by nagging social insecurities, feelings of loneliness, the tragic disappearance of Tina, and their punishing and passionate friendship. Yet Delia, Olga, and Leda are also three Neapolitan women reckoning with loss, and thus going through a dramatic phase in their lives: the death of a mother in *Troubling Love*, the abandonment of a husband in *The Days of Abandonment*, and the separation from grown daughters in *The Lost Daughter*.

Ferrante's stories speak from the margins. At the center of the plot there is always a boundary, a transition from repressive surveillance to *smarginatura*, from emancipation to social derailment. Indeed, one constant among her heroines is an initial tension of self-control. In *Troubling Love* Delia describes herself as "strong, lean, quick, and decisive; not only that, I liked being confident of being so" (tl 37). In *The Days of Abandonment* Olga recalls her composure: "I had, finally, taught myself to wait patiently until every emotion imploded and could come out in a tone of calm" (doa 12). In *The Lost Daughter* Leda thinks back on her practice of keeping her "pregnancy under control": "I managed to vanquish even the long and violent labor pains . . . leaving of myself . . . a proud memory" (ld 122–23). In *The Story of a New Name* Elena burnishes her practice of self-discipline during her years at the Normale in Pisa: "I learned to subdue my voice and gestures. I assimilated rules of behavior, written and unwritten. I kept my Neapolitan accent as much under control as possible" (snn 332). Finally, in *The Story of the Lost Child*, Lila tells Elena that she has dedicated her entire life to keeping *smarginatura* in check: "She muttered that she mustn't ever be distracted: if she became distracted real things . . . would gain the upper hand over the unreal ones, which, with their physical and moral solidity, pacified her" (slc 176).

But each of these stories acquires meaning only when the

process of deconstruction, fueled by loss, shatters the heroine's protective shell—the flimsy armor of the "I." In *Troubling Love* the transition triggers a few physiological symptoms, namely fluids, which plague Delia right after her mother's funeral: not only vomit, menstrual blood, and tears, but other external and internal liquids as well (rain, vaginal lubrication, sperm). In *The Days of Abandonment*, after her husband leaves her, Olga becomes estranged from social life, flouting the rules of personal hygiene and decorum ("I looked at my ankles, my armpits, when had I last waxed them, when had I shaved? I who until four months ago had been only ambrosia and nectar?"; doa 97), a pathological use of vulgar words ("[My husband] ought to feel a terrible pain in his prick; doa 78), and unbridled aggression ("I struck him like a battering ram with all my weight, I shoved him against the glass, he hit it with his face"; doa 70). These signs of progressive *smarginatura* come to a head on the crucial day of her crisis, at the start of which Olga covers her face with a "mask" (doa 105) of makeup. Clearly the gesture is symbolic, since it is shorn of any purpose and indeed conflicts with Olga's irrational behavior.

The Lost Daughter also hinges on a climactic narrative structure. Leda's transformation, already underway for months (once her daughters have gone, she regains the slender body of her youth; ld 11), overlaps with a series of disturbing details at the start of her vacation that undermine the apparent idyll of her holiday: rotten fruit, a dead cicada, and a potentially burst abdomen (ld 14). In the quartet, Lila constantly incarnates this crisis, not only in the form of the *smarginatura* she perceives externally, but above all in that which she sees in the metamorphic narrative of her own life, made of failures and triumphs, social invisibility and radicalism (just think of her working-class existence after her comfortable marriage to the grocer, itself abruptly traded in for the union battles during the "hot autumn" of 1969 and then for the visionary project at Basic

Sight), until her definitive breakdown precipitated by the loss of her daughter.

For a large part of her life, the stable and outwardly restrained Elena is haunted by the threat of a transformation she fears is lying in wait for her: her mother's limp. For Elena, this physical defect is the matrophobic sign that Immacolata is embedded in her body. The trait is so associated with Immacolata, and, along with her "wandering eye," so significantly connected to her social inferiority as a "disposable living being" (mbf 208), that as a child Elena tries to exorcise it by following the resolute stride of Lila, the "terrible, dazzling girl" (mbf 47). Yet during her first two pregnancies, from 1969 to 1973—an unhappy period in her motherhood, when she is a lonely housewife—she begins to suffer from a painful cramp in her hip, which causes her to limp. Falling into the cave, brought back down to the inferior, subordinate level of her mother and "ancestors," Elena quickly turns to physical therapy to ward off the threat of regression.

6. *Frantumaglia*

To define this structurally unstable dimension of womanhood, Ferrante uses a term her own mother invented. Like Elena Greco—not insignificantly, her (nom de plume's) namesake—and all of the female protagonists of her novels, when discussing herself the writer first considers what she has inherited from her mother: *frantumaglia*, her mother's "word for grief". Ferrante's mother refashioned the dialect word ("*frantummàglia*") to refer to "how she felt when she was racked by contradictory sensations" (fr 99). The discussion of *frantumaglia* is divided into two parts. In the first, Ferrante defines this "vertiginous foundation" (Setti[2]) of the "I" from the point of view of her mother, seeing as she—a woman of the people—manifested concrete signs of it. In the second, Ferrante decodes the word using a visual language that draws on her own personal and intellectual experience.

These two stages attest, in her essay, to the oblique genealogy that is created between mother and daughter the moment the latter manages to overcome her matrophobia: a recognition, unstable but significant, born of alterity *and* great affinity. In the first stage, Ferrante lists the everyday symptoms that her mother ascribed to *frantumaglia*: waking up in the middle of the night, talking to yourself and then being ashamed of your soliloquies, plaintively and distractedly singing under your breath, suddenly going out of the house having left the stove on, crying "tears of *frantumaglia*" for no reason. What emerges is the portrait of a woman trapped inside the domestic walls and disoriented by "a miscellaneous crowd of things in her head, debris in a muddy water of the brain" (fr 99). Ferrante's essay is thus plotted along a matrilineal line, with its most significant poetic nuclei activated by the construction of a "family lexicon" (fr 100).

The crucial passages of the chapter on *frantumaglia*, from which the work gets its name, are structured around this extremely concrete story. For example: "Vortexes" (the paragraph on *Madame Bovary*), "The Beast in the Storeroom" (on moral themes), "The Image of the Mother" (on the debate around psychoanalysis and womanhood), and "Cities" (on urban topographies and their importance to one's formation). The vortexes provide the form as well as the content and title of the text. Indeed, the collection of essays develops by oscillating between the writer's actual identity and her pseudonym, by an autobiographical contract that wants to be both conclusive and kept in suspense. "A Writer's Journey" thereby displays an inherent contradiction—the real life of a literary ghost—hovering between "the imagined and the real."

Something similar emerges when Ferrante tells the story of

her diary in adolescence ("the diary itself began to turn into a fiction"; (fer[2]), or, for example, when she points out that all writing entails some form of fiction-making (fer[3]). In the second part of Ferrante's discussion, *frantumaglia*, that "disquiet not otherwise definable"—it is "impossible now to ask [her] mother what she really meant by the word" (fr 99–100)—becomes somewhat clearer through the gaze of the daughter. The opacity of her mother's symptoms is associated with "a catalogue of images" (fr 100). The daughter is keen to point out that these visual representations of distress (representations that are therefore prone to drift away from rational speech) "have more to do with my problems than hers." In this way she carves out a space for herself within motherhood, a nesting doll in the discourse.

These "problems" must be understood as belonging not only to the character/Ferrante in the essay, but also to her heroines. Driven by grief and a loss of self-control, all of them encounter *frantumaglia*. In fact, the first image that characterizes the writer's fragmentation—"an unstable landscape, an infinite aerial or aquatic mass of debris that appears to the I, brutally, as its true and unique inner self" (fr 100)—shores up the psychic and narrative stability of her two protagonists:

> [They are] women who hold on to their I, strengthen it, become hardened, and then discover that cutting your hair is enough to cause a collapse and lose solidity, to feel yourself a chaotic flow of debris that is still useful and of no use, polluted or reclaimed. (fr 103)

Ferrante-as-daughter describes the dissolution of repressive surveillance and its false sense of security, which sets in motion the first three novels and is one of the recurring devices of the quartet, as "an effect of the sense of loss, when we're sure that everything that seems to us stable, lasting, an anchor for our life, will soon join that landscape of debris that we seem to see" (fr 100). The depths to which Olga sinks on the last day of her crisis are explicitly associated with the writer's own symptoms, "a hum growing louder and a vortex-like fracturing of material living and dead: a swarm of bees approaching above the motionless treetops." The *smarginatura* that Lila experiences in Naples on New Year's Eve, when she is beset by violent sounds and colors, calls to mind the "bright-colored explosion of sounds, thousands and thousands of butterflies with sonorous wings." What the writer describes as the "excruciating" perception of "the heterogeneous crowd from which we, the living, raise our voice, and the heterogeneous crowd into which it is fated to vanish" (fr 100) is Delia's matrophobia: the terror of not managing to draw a boundary for her own body, of dissolving, of being invaded by the forms of her mother. Distinguishing herself requires radically refusing the seductions of her mother Amalia and committing a form of matricide (Klein[2]) by erasing every trace of her origins ("All of it remade, so that I could become me and detach myself from her"; tl 64). Yet paradoxically, this way she remains trapped inside the uterus of the ghost mother, the eternally dependent "wizened child" (tl 11).

For Ferrante, another blurred line, another "anguish of death" is "the fear that the capacity to express [herself] would get stuck—as if the organs of speech had been paralyzed" (fr 100). Something similar happens to Olga both at the outset of the day of her breakdown ("I realized that my grammatical tenses weren't correct; doa 89) as well as when, two days earlier, she runs into her ex-husband on the street, accompanied by his twentysomething girlfriend (thus discovering the deceit that had gone on behind her back for five years). She flies into a rage, assaulting them and then addressing the curious onlookers incoherently, with "fragments of sentences like captions" (doa 72). *Frantumaglia* as dehumanization—the risk of one's body becoming increasingly reduced to "a thing, a leather sack leaking air and liquids" (fr 100)—is once again transcribed in the bestialization of Olga, who, like her dog, urinates and defecates in the public park: "Suddenly I was afraid I would dissolve into liquid, a fear that gripped my stomach . . . Smiling scornfully—with scorn for myself—I pulled up my nightgown, I peed and shit behind a trunk" (doa 97–8). An analogous anguish appears in *The Lost Daughter* when Leda shakes the doll that she has stolen and to her disgust imagines "stomach filth" immediately associated with the "swampy life" into which, at any moment, she might sink (ld 85–88).

As you can see, these portraits of *frantumaglia* present an "I" eclipsed by things, challenging Cartesian dualism and the subject-object hierarchy from a perspective that combines feminist critiques of male rationality with the "posthuman" (Ferrara 132). The chronology that corresponds to *frantumaglia*, a "storehouse of time without the orderliness of a history, a story" (fr 100), undermines not only a coherent picture of the writer's life but the forms of her narratives. Chronological "vortexes"—as the paragraph in *Frantumaglia* under discussion here is called—disrupt the lives of Delia, Olga, Leda, Elena, and Lila: "crowding around them, simultaneously, in a sort of achrony, is the past of their ancestors and the future of what they seek to be, the shades, the ghosts" (fr 108). Losing control of these aesthetically conformist, socially evolved, and surveilled bodies produces, "like it or not, . . . a stunning resurrection of the dead" (fr 366). For the daughters who sink into the cave, the linear progress of female recognition coincides with the eternal return of destiny, in which the lives of ancestors, mothers, daughters, and even classical heroines interconnect. If Melina is Dido, Olga is Medea, and Delia is Ariadne keeping a firm grip on the thread of Naples's labyrinth, as well as Persephone searching for Demeter (cf. 4.7 and 6.5), then historic time is imbued with mythic time: "[T]oday it's my turn, in a moment my daughter's, it had happened to my mother, to all my forebears, maybe it was even happening to them and me simultaneously, it will happen" (doa 89). The present teems with "secondary figures, elusive antagonists, ghosts resurfacing from the past to goad the protagonists into making a sort of pact with their 'unbearableness of the feminine'" (Manetti[2]).

In addition to four visions, there are sixteen flashbacks in *Troubling Love*. The constant shuttling between the past and present overwhelms Delia, compelling her to "link voice to voice, thing to thing, fact to fact" (tl 29) and thus dredging up her memory of being abused. In *The Days of Abandonment*, the apparitions of the *poverella* are a calamity, ensnaring the present and superimposing Olga's childhood memories of underclass Naples onto bourgeois Turin, where she lives as an adult: "That's where I was, accents of the south cried in my head, cities that were far apart became a single vice [sic], the blue surface of the sea and the white of the Alps" (doa 47). In *The Lost Daughter* Leda's envy of Nina (the happy young mother at the beach resort near the little town where Elena spends a vacation studying and preparing for her first year of university) continually summons snippets of time in a negative epiphany, which shackles her to her family tree, to fragments of her childhood, her love life, her sex life, and her own imperfect motherhood: "I seemed to be falling backward toward my mother, my grandmother, the chain of mute or angry women I came from" (ld 71).

Given the complexity of its narrative canvas, in the quartet this "confusion of time" (fr 107) takes an even more complicated form. On a first, more conspicuous level, the regressive force of chronology exerts pressure on the lives of Elena and Lila to the point of dissolving their boundaries. For the two friends, the threatening metamorphosis of time stems not only from the perpetual risk of falling into the mother's cave but also from the symbolic container of the entire sociohistorical tableau: Naples, the liminal city that comprises and blurs the hypermodern with the archaic, and technological and commercial transformation

(Basic Sight) with abject violence (cf. 4 and 7.5, 7.6). On a second level, the process of decomposition seeps into the form of the story itself and, because of that, is an even more powerful, if less visible, energy in the work. The *frantumaglia* of time problematizes the linear progression of the story through the tension created by the contemporaneous forces of the hyper-genre (cf. 1.1). The apparent linearity of the biological, existential, and historical cycles is sabotaged by the anticipation of the finale in the story's opening ("Eliminating All the Traces," the prologue of *My Brilliant Friend*) and by the greatest symbol of dispersed ("*smarginata*") cycles—the dolls—in the epilogue of Volume Four (cf. 1.2). Polyphony operates in a comparable manner (cf. 1.5 and 2.6). It can be read as a continuous revision of the present of one character via the past of the other (and vice versa). In the end the novel's focus on the development of the artist gradually wanes. Elena's growth as an author is in fact constantly interrupted by her own metanarrative (cf. 1.6), which compares her texts—her laborious conquest of the present—to Lila's writing: the model of a mythic time, no longer verifiable, that dates back to childhood (*The Blue Fairy*) and youth (the eight notebooks that Lila gives Elena in 1966).

7. Expressive Surveillance

Frantumaglia can be defined as a liminal process (Turner 50), a rite of passage, when a person enters an extraordinary state of metamorphosis and painful creativity. As in initiation rites (such as *frantumaglia*), this disorderly and transitional phase is followed by a post-liminal phase during which the transition to a new stage in life is consolidated. Similarly, in Ferrante's writing, pain settles into awareness, what was decomposed is recomposed, and repressive self-surveillance gives way to "expressive" surveillance (Alsop 472). The established history of male dominance—which, even in the most developed parts of the world, has resulted in a system of pressures, restrictions, and biases—makes this process of fragmentation and fusion cyclical for women, who, says Ferrante, are "increasingly constrained in our actions to subject ourselves to punishing trials involving the reorganization of our private life and admission to public life" (fr 89). For Ferrante, "[the] female 'I' in particular, with its long history of oppression and repression, tends to shatter as it's tossed around, and to reappear and shatter again, always in an unpredictable way" (fr 322).

Certain features of contemporary female identity can be detected in the stories of Delia, Olga, Leda, Elena, and Lila; in the stories of Ferrante's own childhood in *Frantumaglia*; and in the fable of Celina, the doll-heroine of *The Beach at Night*. As characters, they are capable of repurposing their shattered state and turning it into a paradigm of experience, affected yet not consumed by tragedy and obsoletion. When, at the height of her fury, Olga exclaims "*La femme rompue, ah, rompue*, the destroyed woman, destroyed, shit" (doa 57), her extreme vulnerability after being abandoned does not result in suicide—as it did for the heroines of romantic sagas (another book about female desperation that she recalls is *Anna Karenina*) and the many *poverelle* in all too recent history—nor an existential failure of the kind Simone de Beauvoir described in her 1967 short story "La femme rompue". Instead, she will sidestep the "model of broken women" and survive (fr 107). Suffering may modify "the image of time" and the chronological vortex swirl "the debris of different epochs" (fr 107–8), but it is equally true that the one habitable landscape is made up of the wreckage in the storm's aftermath.

In Ferrante's stories there is always a profound reason for the disorder of time: disorder presents us with an inclusive chronology that does not pass over mothers, but redeems them "as a storehouse of sufferings, of rejected ways of being" (fr

107). "Survival" (Didi-Huberman) moves in two directions, enabling one to accommodate the past in the present, though the two may collide or take the form of a "disturbing image." The plurality of timelines prevents women from being subjected to self-colonization or to the logic of complying with the progress of history imposed by repressive surveillance. On the contrary, survival is predicated on intermittently coming into contact with one's maternal genealogy. In short, on heredity (Irigaray 30). Ferrante underscores the shaky yet substantial benefits of those existential and narrative arcs that—unlike the first phase of repressive surveillance—no longer follow Platonic models of perfection but rather the messy truth of "new equilibriums," within which the chronologies of mother and daughter, the inheritance of grief, and creative and vital claims can coexist:

> Old ghosts arrive . . . the same ones with whom the women of the past had to reckon. The difference is that these women don't submit to them passively. Instead, they fight, and they cope. (fr 203)

Frantumaglia is therefore not just an entropic process, but a ritual, wherein women enact a "transformative performance" (Turner 69) with significant dramatic and cinematographic contents (de Rogatis[1] 72). During the metamorphosis caused by *frantumaglia*, the protagonists of Ferrante's novels lose their grip on reality and cross the "threshold of repugnance" (Milkova[2] 92). This perception suggests the lapse of boundaries protecting the "I." The texts are structured around an "aesthetics of disgust" (Milkova[2] 94): in the course of the narrative Delia, Olga, Leda, Elena, and Lila live "on the edge of chaos" (fr 377), constantly nauseated and decentered because of the dissolving boundaries between their body, intellect, behavior, and language. Disgust looms over them, forcing them across the threshold of tolerance and normality, placing them in a "flexible, slippery position" (Milkova² 97–98) in and out of the social, cultural, and psychic status quo.

Ferrante underscores the cognitive and creative import of this disgust: "Better to make a mistake with the incandescent lava we have inside, better to provoke disgust with that, than to assure ourselves success by resorting to murky, cold finds" (fr 123). This ritual process blends with and reemerges from a "physical primitivism" (fr 78), a capacity "to push ourselves along, in contact with the living material, to where language becomes reticent and leaves a space, enclosed between obscenity and scientific terminology, where everything can happen" (fr 222). Then the content settles into a carefully constructed form on two different levels, between the magma of the deep nucleus and the frozen light of the word, between "seals that are broken" (fr 373) and the case history of their rupture (cf. 1.3).

Not for nothing, in *The Beach at Night*, words are Celina's most precious possession. Words allow her to staunchly resist the violence of the Mean Beach Attendant and his hook, "hanging on a disgusting thread of saliva," (ban 18) that seeks to rip them from her chest. Once again, the focus is on the link between *frantumaglia* and surveillance, but surveillance here is no longer the "ugly word" associated with our protagonists' initial self-policing, with the functions of a sentinel, jailer, or spy (fr 104). Expressive surveillance is "an emotional tendency of the whole body, an expansion and an inflorescence on and around it" (fr 104); it is also a stylistic, growing defense of the self *not in retrospect, but while* one spirals downward and violently perforates the hidden depths: "We have to watch ourselves, attend to our very individual expansion into the internal lands that are ours, and drill [there]" (fr 123). The metaphor of a *"rampicante"* life, a life that grows and flourishes on rugged, sloping terrain, distinguishes Ferrante's protagonists as vigilant women who surveil themselves and others, as "heroines of our time" (fr 105).

8. Heredity and Clothes

In Ferrante's writing, one of the crucial ways to experience these continuous transitions from *frantumaglia* to new equilibriums is in the daughter's relationship with the mother, which follows a cyclical trajectory, from furious rage to "reparation" (Klein[2]), from collapse to resurrection. Read as the formation of a vision and a poetics, *La frantumaglia*, which is set in motion by a mother's word, travels the same path. To understand the meaning of this trajectory it may be useful to reconstruct the stages of two mother-daughter relations: that of Immacolata and Elena in *The Neapolitan Novels* and that of Amalia and Delia in *Troubling Love*.

Following her third pregnancy in 1981, eleven and eight years after her first two unhappy pregnancies, Elena cultivates a completely different attitude toward the affliction that brings her closer to her own mother and makes her feel *smarginata*: She no longer corrects her limp. In fact she nurtures it "like a bequest preserved in [her] body" (slc 222). Lila points out the irony of her friend's decision, saying, "You invented that limp in order not to let your mother die completely, and now you really do limp" (slc 369). This observation inspires Elena's contribution to "a magazine that was devoting an entire issue to the female body" (slc 367), suggesting to the reader that the mother has finally been accepted not only in the body but in the mind and intellectual world of her daughter. Between Elena's first two pregnancies and her third, a decisive event takes place: the physical decline and death of Immacolata. Returning to Naples in 1979, after an extended period in Tuscany and Milan, Elena grows close to her mother again. While her mother grows increasingly ill, Elena carries and breastfeeds her third daughter, Imma, the result—according to her mother—of Elena's degrading, adulterous affair with Nino. Shattering her usual veneer of omnipotence, Immacolata's illness makes her vulnerable, and she is finally able to open up to her daughter: "It was this frailty that slowly opened the way to an intimacy we had never shared" (slc 150). During the slow arc that will culminate in Immacolata's death, Elena sees her matrophobia in a new light ("I had considered her an insensible and vulgar woman"; slc 221), detecting traces of love in an otherwise hostile relationship:

> I was moved by her clinging to me in order not to get lost, the way I, a small child, had clung to her hand. The frailer and more frightened she became, the prouder I was of keeping her alive. [. . .] She revealed that the only good thing in her life was the moment I came out of her belly, I, her first child. [. . .] She revealed finally, without circumlocutions, that her only true child was me. [. . .] [I]t was in those slow hours that I truly felt I was her favorite child. When she embraced me before I left, it was as if she meant to slip inside me and stay there, as once I had been inside her. That contact with her body, which had irritated me when she was healthy, I now liked. (slc 149, 151, 208)

This revision forces the reader to go back and find something positive in Immacolata's behavior during the archaeology of her rapport with Elena: small gestures registered as anomalies in her daughter's narrative because, until transformed by illness, they were incompatible with her matrophobic distortion.

Among these gestures, the most significant is Immacolata's intervention when Elena is about to give up taking her junior high makeup exams because the family is unable to pay for private lessons. With a sudden outburst that surprises the child, who is accustomed to hearing only words of delegitimization and scorn for having the gall to want to set herself apart from her mother ("'I've always known that you thought you were better than me and everybody else'"; snn 328), for wanting to redress her illiteracy and ignorance, Immacolata makes the following crucial remark: "'Nowhere is it written that you can't do it'" (mbf 105). This remark, and above all the air of trust and recognition that it implies, is so unusual and shocking for Elena that she looks her mother over carefully as if she were afraid she might not recognize her: "She was the same: luster-less hair, wandering eye, large nose, heavy body." While still discerning the usual distortions in her mother, this one note of encouragement and emotional availability mobilizes Elena. "Starting the next day," she says, "I began to study."

To return for a moment to the farewell between mother and daughter-cum-mother, the synchronicity of life and death—underscored by the fact that the granddaughter bears her grandmother's name—is no longer experienced as another link in the chain that yokes together subordinate women, but as a vital lineage:

> What was the body of a woman: I had nourished my daughter in the womb, now that she was out she was nourished by my breast. I thought, there was a moment when I, too, had been in my mother's womb, had sucked at her breast. A breast as big as mine, or maybe even bigger. (ld 202)

When Immacolata dies, Elena—now distinguished by her social standing (as a member of the middle class), cultural status (as a feminist writer; her second book is an essay about the invention of woman by men) and existential freedom (for love, she has broken off her marriage to Pietro)—is able to recognize and transcend her matrophobia.

Maternal inheritance is thus divided into two different and complementary bequests. The first is the chance to feel finally one with the mother, to give in to her need for the protective union that Elena has constantly refused (and offloaded onto her friend Lila; cf. 2.3 and 2.5). This unprecedented feeling of closeness to her mother leads Elena to describe Immacolata's grit with a loving metaphor:

> Right after her funeral I felt the way you feel when it suddenly

starts raining hard, and you look around and find no place to take shelter. For weeks I saw and heard her everywhere, night and day. She was a vapor that in my imagination continued to burn without a wick. (slc 221)

The second bequest is, instead, connected to the part of Elena that has always felt threatened by the mother's cave, which is to say, by her creative and intellectual mandate. Withdrawing from the competition with her daughter during the last year of her life, Immacolata is finally able to recognize herself in Elena, thus providing the bedrock for her daughter's sense of self:

> She died convinced that because of how I was made, because of the resources I had accumulated, I would not be overwhelmed by anything. That idea worked inside me and in the end helped me. (slc 222)

This newfound confidence permits Elena to enter into contact with "the symbolic order of the mother" (Muraro) and calmly confront a crucial trial in her writing career. For two years her publishing house has been awaiting her second novel, which she—caught up in her private affairs (the move to Naples, the failure of her relationship with Nino)—has not even managed to begin. On the wave of determination propelled by her mother, Elena has an idea: she digs up the manuscript of a novel that had been rejected eight years earlier and resubmits it (slc 255–5). It will turn out to be a smash.

"Amalia had been. I was Amalia" (tl 139). The last words of *Troubling Love* acknowledge the magical presence of the mother. With this heartbreaking climax, Ferrante modifies the scope of the family novel, placing at its epicenter a story about mothers that turns mysterious and disquieting. No longer the mother as sentimental recollection, domestic affair or nurturing rite, but as a means to investigate perversion: Delia's two days "without respite" (tl 109) in Naples center on the naked corpse of her mother and her obscene, mysterious death. *Troubling Love* is a detective story, because the truth about the mother and the meaning of her life can only be reconstructed by investigating Amalia: by retracing her steps, by filling in a space that had seemed empty, by finding her true shape amid the "bodies of fabric" (fr 154) of her clothes (a key metaphor in the novel) like a plaster mask, by reformulating the verdict of her abandonment, by correcting the distortions of envy and rivalry. This investigation revolves around the mother's concealment, around the metaphorical murder of the "unloved beloved" (fer[1]) in the mother-daughter novel, and challenges the way our culture places a higher value on the Oedipal bond with the father and with vicarious figures of male power and authority, reducing to a domestic drama of rivals the pre-Oedipal bond with the mother: "the single great tremendous original love, the matrix of all loves, which cannot be abolished" (fr 123).

In fact, Ferrante points out that the title of her novel, *Amore molesto*, refers to Freud's essay "Female Sexuality" (1931), in which he remarks that during the first phase of a little girl's life her father is "only a *troublesome* rival." (In the Italian translation, "*un rivale* molesto.") In the empty cellar of the Coloniali-Pasticceria—the cave of *Troubling Love*—Delia recovers the femininity that her mother, distorted by the patriarchy, had so powerfully embodied, and which the daughter rejected; she relives the true origin of that rejection, connected to her childhood envy of Amalia's supposed adultery; finally, underneath the lies, she uncovers the truth about a sexually abused child. In order to reveal the mystery surrounding her mother, she needs to surveil herself creatively while at the same time abandoning herself to the metamorphosis of *frantumaglia*. When she first appears, the daughter is extremely rational and repressed—donning "a carapace" (fr 161), shouldering Amalia's coffin with the men in her family (tl 16)—but very soon she turns that detached condition on its head, becoming hyperfeminine and hypersexual, exposing herself to the lusty looks of men on the crowded streets of Naples: both detective and femme fatale in this noir tale (Small 307). The naked body of Amalia—a figure of anguish dead *or* alive—is contrasted with the semi-clad body of the daughter, made unforgettable in a few sequences in the 1995 film adaptation by Mario Martone. "That body in red," Ferrante says, "devoured by an obscure and troubling passion [. . .] is, I believe, an important moment for the iconography of the female body today" (fr 56).

A series of chance events in the course of her investigation will in fact require Delia to put on two tight-fitting and slinky dresses, the first red and the second blue, thus setting in motion a slow process of delving into her suppressed memories. Her recollection of the violence she endured is associated with her bond with her mother, who had intended to give her those seductive clothes as a birthday gift. The source of those clothes, the writer reminds us, is "murky" (fr 161): once again recalling that tangle of truth and lies that Amalia's seductive energy had produced in her daughter. This performance of seduction may be considered an initiation into femininity, a rite of passage for one to accept her maternal inheritance (de Rogatis[2]) during which the clothes become "a means of communicating" and key to gaining an awareness of the other that otherwise would have been precluded (Sambuco 200).

Delia ultimately reconnects with her mother and her buried memory when, combing through the run-down rooms of the Coloniali-Pasticceria, she finds her mother's blue suit (the last outfit Amalia ever wore) and puts it on. Putting herself in her dead mother's "shoes" (Conti 112), and thereby reckoning with her own conflicted feelings of matrophobia and primary envy (cf. 2.4), becomes even more demanding when the mother in question turns out to have been, like Amalia, a seamstress who for decades made, remade, and mended her old outfit. The blue pants suit is more representative of her than her own, longed-for body. There are two distinct instances of Delia playing dress up. In the first she slips into two sexy outfits, attire her mother would have wanted her to wear, as if she were channeling the most transgressive and seductive side of Amalia. Next, donning the blue suit, she dresses the way her mother actually appeared in the comedy of manners (de Rogatis[3] 303). This contrast between the clothes of the seductress and the clothes of the wife/mother lays bare the fate of women, forever trapped inside the same terrible "subservient dress" (fr 167), which sews up a life, crushed by male domination, inside the subordinate role of one who can only express her own desires through the desires of another. In short, if the nun and her habit are one, she risks finding nothing in the nunnery but that habit.

In the imaginary world of Stanisław Lem's sci-fi novel *Solaris* (1961), Harey, a woman risen from the dead, cannot take off her dress, because it is inseparable from her body (fr 163). Here, the story of Delia intertwines with that of Ferrante, herself the daughter of a seamstress who had just two harsh alternatives: the humiliating dress of the wife ("a bundle of rags") and the humiliating dress of high society ("the stunning appearance"). "[T]oday," says Ferrante, "I know that my mother, both in the dullness of domestic tasks and in the exhibition of her beauty, expressed an unbearable anguish" (fr 168). In *Troubling Love*, these costume changes enable Delia to recognize her mother's suffering and to insert between these two poles a third act, an alternative way—until then never considered of value—with which Amalia experienced her dress as a metaphor. The dress is also a metaphor for mending, the emblem of which is the seamstress's work and the constant modifications to the blue suit. For her mother, it is a re-creation of the "I": the "thought-out" carelessness of a woman who reconsiders "what was out of proportion, giving it the proper measure," who plays with "empty fabrics" (tl 103), who mends the tears she has sustained, who resists.

This third hypothesis is the vision of another wrinkle in time, another course of past events. In the final leg of the story Delia falls down the rabbit hole of her imagination, where the blue suit can be unstitched, returned to its original possibility as uncut fabric. But immediately after, the ghost of Amalia begins basting and sewing it; shaping her daughter's destiny, in other words (tl 125). In this case, the cut of fabric is not the creation of a body subservient to the male gaze, but the generative cut from which the daughter's life originates. Thanks to these three acts, Delia sets in motion a syntactic process that frees her from symbiosis and from matrophobia. She is no longer caught inside Amalia and the destiny of her mother, like the "wizened child" she once was. She no longer "thinks her thoughts from within her, from within her breath" (tl 74). Which is why now she can be a *different* version of her mother (the blue suit is too big for Delia). Only a part of Delia, the symbolic skin of the dress, belongs to Amalia, not her entire being. Accepting and creatively adapting her maternal inheritance ("the recognition of a closeness that needs to be accepted"; Benedetti[2] 107), the daughter works through her mourning for the parts of herself and her mother that were damaged by the patriarchal violence, and she can experience the authentically joyous, vital side of Amalia's seductiveness, her permanent laughter (Cardone 104). Surviving the trauma means reevaluating the leftovers, the excess bits, the remnants forever in search of a new shape. Delia narrates because she has absorbed the story of her mother. This polyphonic narrative anticipates that of Elena and Lila in the quartet: "I felt that that old garment was the final narrative that my mother had left me, and that now, with all the necessary adjustments, it fit me like a glove" (tl 134).

9. Another Story

In the ritual process that passes from *frantumaglia* to expressive surveillance, the daughter rewrites her relationship with the mother, deconstructing both the most striking image-fantasy of the altruistic and happy mother as well as the inhibited—therefore truer—fantasy of matrophobia. The mother-son relationship can shape male identity into an adventure that manages to unfold thanks to a break from the mother-as-absolute—and therefore is constantly threatened by rifts and regressions (Jung[2]). On the other hand, in Elena Ferrante the mother's tale takes the form of an enigma (the noir of *Troubling Love*, the reinforced door in *The Days of Abandonment*, the inexplicable dedication to a doll in *The Lost Daughter*, and the dolls lost and found in the quartet) situated in a reversible temporality. The constant return to the mother gives rise to myriad fragments in a multiple, discontinuous time frame; a rite of fusion and reparation, collapse and reemergence. *Frantumaglia* and expressive surveillance allow women to absorb abjection and pain without being overwhelmed by them. The protagonists of Ferrante's novels tell us that we need to comb through the dark spaces where our female ancestors live. To return to the author's metaphor, they reiterate the importance of carrying the computer into the cave and of finding the courage to write a collective story from inside the cavern.

CHAPTER FOUR
Naples, the City-Labyrinth

1. Love Shack

The ambiguous power of love emerges clearly in the late fall of 1963 during the final phase of Lila and Nino's relationship. While they live together for twenty-three days, once again love becomes—as it did for Dido (cf. 3.10)—an energy that desperately seeks to transform space. By the time Nino reappears after the summer on Ischia, physical places and the principle of reality have grown hazy for Lila: "The shelves stacked with goods had faded, the street had lost every definition, the pale facades of the new apartment buildings had dissolved; but most of all she didn't feel the risk she was running" (snn 339). Leaving her husband and the *rione* shortly after, Lila feels she has permanently exorcised the danger of *smarginatura* that had exposed her life to that "soft space, inhabited by forms without definition," and she labors under the illusion that she has finally found unity and harmony, "a structure [. . .] capable of containing her fully, all of her, without her cracking or the figures around her cracking" (snn 356). When Nino walks out on her less than a month later, he immediately shatters the illusion of stability, and the sun sets on what Elena transcribes in her narrative as "an abstract plan for a secret couple, hiding in a kind of refuge that was to be part bungalow for two hearts, part workshop of ideas on the complexity of the world, he present and active, she a shadow glued to his footsteps, cautious prompter, fervent collaborator" (snn 342). This secret dream that Lila had confided to her notebook is now re-transcribed—not without malice or ambivalence—by her friend, who describes in her own way how the "the boy" had resurrected her old friend: "The phenomenal child of elementary school, the girl who had charmed Maestra Oliviero, who had written *The Blue Fairy*, had reappeared and was stirring with new energy" (snn 341).

It's interesting to see how, in Elena's reading, this version of Lila perceives her relationship with Nino. Elena calls herself "the pale shadow" of her friend, yet here it is Lila who is "a shadow glued to [Nino's] footsteps" (snn 342). In other words, a relationship can never be one among equals; what changes is the order of the hierarchy, not its perpetuation: among women, Lila dominates; among members of the opposite sex, the same Lila automatically acts subservient. After all, a few years earlier, Elena expressed a similar desire to protect and tend to Nino, the object both women covet and vie for: "I felt the need, as I had long ago, to take care of him, to tend to him, to protect him, to sustain him in everything that he would do in the course of his life" (snn 159). After Nino abandons her, Lila scans the walls of their empty apartment on the outskirts of the city, in Campi Flegrei, and for the first time recognizes how squalid it is: "She became aware of the bad smell, of the cockroaches that came in under the stairwell door, the stains of dampness on the ceiling, and felt for the first time that childhood was clutching at her again" (snn 367). As long as the two are a couple in their love nest, swept up in their project of cultural empowerment (tensions arise after a public event with Pasolini), the squalor of the place goes unnoticed. But with Nino gone, the shabby apartment reveals itself as the permanent setting of her life, returning her to her "childhood of cruel privations, of threats and beatings" (snn 367). This transformation of space is triggered by her grief over being left and throws Lila—who is carrying a child whom she believes is Nino's, but turns out to be Stefano's—into a state of tedium and *smarginatura* unanchored to time:

> She [. . .] decided [. . .] to wait for her life and that of the baby to lose their outlines, any possible definition, and she found that there was nothing left in her mind, not even a trace of the thing that made her spiteful, that is to say the awareness of abandonment. (snn 368)

This muddle of time is a sign that Lila has fallen into the cave (cf. 3.3), a fall often manifested as a state of abjection linking the mother with a decline in social status and zip code. Olga doubles as Medea in *The Days of Abandonment* partly because her wild Mediterranean passion appears totally obscene in civilized, upper middle-class Turin; the evolved city in the North, like Corinth, stands in contrast to the barbarous Colchis/Naples (Lucamante[2] 87). Nino leaves Lila and then, tellingly, takes the step of enrolling in the university in Milan. In other words, by going north he sidesteps the risk of abjection that he had been exposed to with Lila, whereas Lila—after a brief return to living with her husband—tumbles into the cavern for good, moving to San Giovanni a Teduccio (another poor neighborhood on the outskirts of Naples) with Enzo Scanno (cf. 2.6). Lila's fall from grace deeply disturbs Elena, who receives the news while finishing up her studies at the Pisa Normale. San Giovanni a Teduccio is unknown to her, though she associates it with Bruno Soccavo's factory (where Lila will wind up working), with their summer together in Ischia, and with losing her virginity on the Maronti (cf. 6.3 and 6.4). This last episode in particular suddenly resurfaces as a degrading experience, on the wave of other humiliating incidents related to her thesis and the imminent end of university: her sense of the inequality between Pietro's future academic career and her own destiny as a high school teacher, the threat of returning to the *rione* (even if as a *professoressa*), her failure to achieve a greater breadth of freedom. Her social shame overlies her erotic shame, even here, in a tangle of time periods that marries her encounter with Donato Sarratore to her encounters with her former classmate at the Normale Franco Mari and with Pietro Airota. All of her experiences are linked by disgust:

> I'm lying to myself, I thought. Had it really been so wonderful? I knew very well that at that time, too, there had been shame. And uneasiness, and humiliation, and disgust: accept, submit, force yourself. Is it possible that even happy moments of pleasure never stand up to a rigorous examination? Possible. The blackness of the Maronti quickly extended to Franco's body and then to Pietro's. I escaped from my memories. (snn 433)

Pressed by her puzzling sense of humiliation, in twenty days or so Elena dashes off her first novel, an autobiographical story centered around her first sexual experience on the Maronti: "I found that I was calmer, as if the shame had passed from me to the notebook" (snn 433). The transitive magic is born from her need to expel abjection, although the feeling continuously returns by other avenues and in other shades, for example, in the way Elena perceives San Giovanni a Teduccio when, a few months later, she walks through the neighborhood for the first time on her way to see her friend: "To arrive at San Giovanni I had forcibly to regress, as if Lila had gone to live not in a street, or a square, but in a ripple of time past, before we went to school, a black time without rules and without respect" (snn 456). The gloomy shadows of the Maronti and those of the working-class Neapolitan neighborhood blur to one filthy shade:

> I walked along Corso San Giovanni a Teduccio with the cold wind in my face, it seemed a yellowish channel with defaced walls, black doorways, dirt. [. . .] Finally I found the street, the building. I went up the dirty stairs, following a strong odor of garlic, the voices of children. (snn 457)

Love of Nino as a form of cultural liberation, reeducation from semiliterate origins with Franco Mari, social recognition thanks to the socialist philanthropy of Pietro Airota, the pretense to reform the *rione* first with Stefano and then with Nino (who is now with Elena), the ascent into Naples's intellectual middle class: these various developments in Elena and Lila's lives are held together by a common thread, an "arduous and almost always unhappy adjustment to men and their sexuality" (fr 358), an unspoken premise that forces the two friends into vicarious positions of submission (cf. 5.7 and 6.4). Seeking protection from a male authority, disguising themselves as sexual and cultural novices, betraying their own pursuit of autonomy, Elena and Lila show that, in the Italian public sphere of the 1950s and '60s, their identity is not acknowledged in the slightest. Their one right as citizens is to the cumbersome inheritance of their origins, which comes from "a black time without rules and without respect" (snn 456), a combination of gender, class, and regional inferiority. This polyphonic sense of shame and misunderstanding determines the shape of the setting in the quartet. The setting is never mere scenery nor neutral backdrop. The plot—now concordant, now discordant—presents us with "a world learned, a world perceived, a world imagined" by the two friends: a multifocal filter that points to "impressions perceived or imagined by Lenù and, through her story, by Lila" (fr 309).

2. *Cocoricò* and *Tàmmari*

After Lila's wedding in the spring of 1961, Elena has a breakdown and considers dropping out of school—now bereft of the aura it emitted by virtue of her competition with her friend. For fifteen days she skips school and wanders up and down the city:

> I rummaged among the used books in the stalls of Port'Alba, unwillingly absorbing titles and authors' names, and continued

toward Toledo and the sea. Or I climbed the Vomero on Via Salvator Rosa, went up to San Martino, came back down by the Petraio. Or I explored the Doganella, went to the cemetery, wandered on the silent paths, read the names of the dead. (snn 28)

What appears to be an ordinary checklist of place names, the way she reports on the apparently tedious—yet unthinkable in the *rione*—routine of browsing the stalls of used books in Port'Alba, is in truth a map of places that, thanks to her studies, Elena has handily conquered. And yet, because Elena fears that from now on she will have to navigate such spaces by herself, without the ghostly presence of Lila, the city is not an engine of desire or competition. The need to inhabit space through one another, the anxiety over not being able to focus one's gaze without the gaze of one's friend, is a fundamental theme of their friendship. Three years earlier, when Elena's father shows her around the city in preparation for her first year in high school, she enjoys the Mediterranean splendor of Naples (the scene may be the one homage to Neapolitan iconography in the entire quartet), but that beauty is immediately tarnished by the thought of her missing friend. The city can only be *narrated* with Lila:

> What a pity that Lila wasn't there. [. . .] I had the impression that, although I was absorbing much of that sight, many things, too many, were scattering around me without letting me grasp them. [. . .] I, I and Lila, we two with that capacity that together—only together—we had to seize the mass of colors, sounds, things, and people, and express it and give it power. (mbf 138)

Naples regains intensity and is again intensely depicted every time a symbolic and polyphonic topography is developed: a cartography of the two friends' need for recognition and liberation, of their alternatingly convergent and divergent marginality. Consider one of the many moments in which the symbolic map of social status is grafted onto the topographic map. About a year after Lila's wedding, at the end of May 1962, Professor Galiani invites Elena to her home to attend her children's party. Learning of the situation and the anxiety it causes her reluctant friend, Lila demands she go with her, thus exacerbating Elena's feelings of inadequacy. Once inside Professor Galiani's building, the two find themselves staring at an elevator.

> We were tempted by the elevator, but then decided against it. We had never taken an elevator, not even Lila's new building had one, we were afraid of getting in trouble. (snn 153)

Even more than the interior of the house, with its library of books accumulated over generations—the inheritance of an indisputable right to a life of study and liberal professions (the name plate on the door reads "Dott. Prof. Frigerio")—this particular threshold establishes the friction between two worlds, that of the middle class and that of the *rione*, and reveals the two friends' fear of not successfully acting the part in this social milieu, of losing "in a moment of distraction the mask of self-possession" (snn 153). The matter of architectonic forms is a microphysics of social stratification, illustrating rituals founded on intangible yet clear distinctions (Hamon 4). Of the two friends, only Elena—seasoned in bourgeois conventions from her years at school—will succeed that evening in reciting the script of the middle-class activist by mimicking the styles of political speech ("fragments of phrases read in Galiani's books and newspapers stirred in my mind [. . .]. I used the elevated Italian I had practiced [. . .]. I said I didn't want to live in a world at war"; snn 160). Only Elena will play the part of the daughter of a good family, good-naturedly annoyed by her younger siblings ("I jokingly alluded to the trouble that my younger sister and brothers had always given me"; snn 155). This foray outside the *rione* makes Lila cognizant of the "humiliating difference" (mbf 192) that at the end of the evening provokes her rage, the ferocity of one who brutalizes those by whom she feels brutalized:

> [I]n their heads they don't have a thought that's their own, that they struggled to think. [. . .] If you were up there [. . .] all you'd see is parrots going *cocorico, cocorico.* [. . .] Chimpanzees that piss and shit in the toilet instead of on the ground, and that's why they give themselves a lot of airs, and they say they know what should be done in China and in Albania and in France and in Katanga. (snn 162)

If the relationships between spaces can be more significant than the spaces themselves (Moretti 71), that is because the shadow line between the two worlds is where individuals most reveal themselves. In the narrative this border zone produces a different *mode*, another perspective from which to view the faux naturalness of the world, uncovering truths otherwise buried.

I would like to point out two other significant moments in the quartet that gravitate around this border-induced turmoil. The first is a synthetic image (visual images in Ferrante are often shattered by social psychology), a kind of cameo that illuminates Stefano's social inadequacy. The second is a complex scene, Elena's account of an outing with her friends from the *rione* one Sunday evening in 1959.

Some narrative context is needed for the first image. Immediately after their marriage, Lila and Stefano depart for their honeymoon. A few hours after the ceremony, there has already been a definitive rupture between the two when Stefano betrays Lila's trust by selling the pair of shoes she designed to Marcello Solara, shoes that her future husband had acquired as a symbol of their engagement. The acquisition was in fact the down payment on a deal that Stefano would finance the manufacturing and design of the shoes and preserve the Cerullo family brand. But during the months of their engagement, he also describes the shoes as "a valuable witness to their story," the fata morgana of a protective love:

> [Stefano] saw [the shoes], had always seen in them her small, almost childish hands working alongside her brother's large ones. [. . .] He took her fingers and kissed them, one by one, saying that he would never again allow them to be spoiled. (mbf 289)

Lila marries a man she doesn't love, a man "of twenty-two [. . .] kind, decisive, courageous [. . .] of good character" (mbf 254), because his apparent courtesy and seemingly modest ways of managing his wealth give her the illusion that, as his wife, she will get out from under the arrogant Solaras and be free to compete with them (cf. 4.3). After the twist at the end of *My Brilliant Friend*, when Marcello Solara shows up at the wedding party with the symbol of that illusion (i.e., the shoes) on his feet, *The Story of a New Name* opens with Stefano striking his new bride at the end of their fight over this betrayal, revealing the dark heart of his nature: "Stefano struck her in the face with his strong hand, a violent slap that seemed to her an explosion of truth" (snn 33).

When they arrive in Amalfi, outside the confines of the *rione*, they display the clumsy unworldliness of people who have never spent a night in a hotel. In particular—we're finally getting to the first image—Lila's gaze, later set down in her notebooks and eventually conveyed by Elena's narrative, falls on her husband, in whose face and gestures she glimpses an inferiority complex thinly masked by arrogance:

> Neither had ever been to a hotel, and they were embarrassed and ill at ease. Stefano was especially intimidated by the vaguely mocking tones of the receptionist and, without meaning to, assumed a subservient attitude. When he realized it, he covered his discomfiture with brusque manners, and his ears flushed merely at the request to show his documents. Meanwhile the porter appeared, a man in his fifties with a thin mustache, but Stefano

refused his help, as if he were a thief, then, thinking better of it, disdainfully gave him a large tip, even though he didn't take advantage of his services. (snn 34–35)

This brings us to the second scene, this time set in downtown Naples. Here, too, characters trespass beyond the outer limits of the *rione*, which, based on clues from the text, ends at the central train station on the western edge of the city and is loosely inspired by Rione Luzzatti. One Sunday evening, in the middle of April 1959, Elena and Lila join Carmela, Pasquale, and Rino for a stroll along Via Toledo, in the city center. Rino and Pasquale are already familiar with the codes of social exclusion and know that it is better for everyone, given the social backwardness written all over them ("on foot, in shabby old clothes, penniless"), not to venture onto Via Chiaia and the neighboring streets "where there would be wealthy, elegant people," "dandies" (mbf 191–92). Yet the boys give in to the girls' nagging. Walking down Via Chiaia, Elena immediately senses how unfamiliar the place is ("It was like crossing a border"; 191). Her reaction is all the more surprising given that by then Elena has been leaving the *rione* every day for months to attend her classical high school. But this time she is crossing into a protected area, where the bourgeoisie exhibit all the traits of a caste:

> I looked not at the boys but at the girls, the women: they were absolutely different from us. They seemed to have breathed another air, to have eaten other food, to have dressed on some other planet, to have learned to walk on wisps of wind. I was astonished. All the more so that, while I would have paused to examine at leisure dresses, shoes, the style of glasses if they wore glasses, they passed by without seeming to see me. They didn't see any of the five of us. We were not perceptible. Or not interesting. (mbf 192)

The friends' discomfort comes to a head when they

encounter a young woman whose eccentric elegance ("The girl was all in green: green shoes, green skirt, green jacket, and on her head [. . .] she wore a bowler, like Charlie Chaplin, also green") gives way to aggressive hilarity, replete with poses ("[. . .] Pasquale stopped, he was laughing so hard, and leaned against the wall with one arm"; mbf 194). After Rino makes a vulgar remark, the girl's companion turns around and calls him a *tàmmaro*, a hick. Rino responds with his fists. In no time friends of the couple turn up ("all tall, sturdy, well dressed"; mbf 195) and a violent fight breaks out. Pasquale and Rino risk taking a beating until the Solara brothers come to their aid and react with brazen, practiced violence: "Michele [. . .] joined in, hitting with a cold ferocity that I hope never to see again in my life" (mbf 196).

The fight occurs in Piazza dei Martiri, a symbolic place that will later be the site of the shoe store financed by the Solaras, thus becoming an ambiguous maze of economic initiatives, extortion, and dirty business. The real environment is progressively absorbed by the two friends' perceptions, which turn from disbelief to terror. More than Rino's punch, it is the entire dynamic of exclusion and rage which Lila at first finds incredible, a sign of their difference hitherto hidden behind the bounds of the *rione*:

> Lila first of all hurled herself at her brother before he started kicking the young man on the ground and dragged him off, with an expression of disbelief, as if a thousand fragments of our life, from childhood to this, our fourteenth year, were composing an image that was finally clear, yet which at that moment seemed to her incredible. (mbf 194)

Elena's reaction is even more complicated. As a resident of the *rione* and a high school student with dreams of escaping her social class, she is an alien "made unhappy by [her] own alienness" (mbf 319). She doesn't fully belong to the *rione*; to the bourgeois world she belongs even less. Her feelings are therefore more ambivalent because prompted by her disgust and shame over her group's having trespassed beyond its jurisdiction, by her sensation that the chaotic magma of her neighborhood is invading Naples:

> Rino and Pasquale [. . .] seemed like strangers, they were so transformed by hatred. [. . .] I felt as if our neighborhood had expanded, swallowing all Naples, even the streets where respectable people lived. (mbf 196–97)

Three years later, at the party at Professor Galiani's house, Lila foresees that this doubleness in Elena will only grow with time. In fact, Lila includes her friend in her final invective against the *"cocoricos,"* accusing Elena of betraying her class:

> You, too, you want to be a puppet from the neighborhood who performs so you can be welcomed into the home of those people? You want to leave us alone in our own shit, cracking our skulls, while all of you go *cocorico cocorico*, hunger, war, working class, peace? (snn 163)

The two friends' filter of "a world learned, a world perceived, a world imagined" (fr 309) creates a hybrid point of view, one that bears with it an internal conflict within the *rione*, their original universe. Oscillating between friendship and rivalry, the two friends' antagonistic polyphony, insofar as it presents an interior point of view, rescues the representations of space from paternalism, false consciousness, and exoticism—the trademarks of every story that seeks to depict impoverished and squalid spaces like the outskirts of Naples.

In Neapolitan literature between the 1800s and 1900s, this model of a polarized space led to the belief that Naples was a divided city, part obsolete and part progressive, part impulsive and part enlightened, part natural and part historical (Alfano G.). On one side are the hilltop quarters of Vomero, Posillipo, and the area around Corso Vittorio Emanuele (where Professor Galiani lives and where Elena will, not insignificantly, move in 1979). On the other, the low-lying historic downtown and peripheral neighborhoods like the *rione*. The center itself is split in two: the luminous upscale universe of the *lungomare*, the Riviera di Chiaia, and Piazza dei Martiri stand in direct contrast to the notorious bleak alleys and underclass squares, which are, anthropologically speaking, contiguous to the world of the *rione*. What changes with the quartet and other contemporary narratives about Naples, such as Roberto Saviano's *Gomorrah* and Giuseppe Montesano's *In the Body of Naples* (De Caprio), is their insertion of a third element into the two cities: a bridge that makes the fault line not a mythical and fixed space but a "third space" (Bhabha 12). This strip straddles both sides, is neither the one nor the other, feels estranged yet connected to both. In the *Neapolitan Novels*, that hybrid element is the narrative voice of Elena.

3. "Plebs"

But what accounts for the diversity of the *rione*? To understand this we need to assemble details scattered throughout the quartet and described, once again, from the hybrid, multifocal perspective of Elena, whose chronicle partly exists within the mechanisms of her neighborhood and partly props up the value system of the bourgeoisie. "The plebs are quite a nasty thing," Maestra Oliviero tells Elena in 1955, as if the girl didn't belong to that economically, socially, and culturally backward universe (mbf 71). She uses the term to define those who live in the *rione*, members of an ancient Neapolitan people who inhabit a "world connected and apart from the main, a dense and crowded urban world, submerged" (Belmonte 143). The "plebs" are the legend and shame of Naples, one of the few remaining European cities whose historic center has a prominent popular character. When, in the quartet, in the 1950s and '60s, the Neapolitan bourgeoisie and petite bourgeoisie come face to face with the residents of the neighborhood, they affect a coolness toward them, at its best a form of noblesse oblige.

The teachers in particular—from elementary school to high school—promote a dissociation between the intellectual class and the common people described long ago in Vincenzo Cuoco's "Historical Essay on the Neapolitan Revolution of 1799" (1801). Maestra Oliviero refuses to read *The Blue Fairy* because Lila cannot pay for private lessons to prepare for the middle school admissions test, and she sees the painful renunciation imposed on Lila as a sign of structural inferiority ("[. . .] if one wishes to remain a plebeian, he, his children, the children of his children deserve nothing"; mbf 72). In 1960, she contemptuously dismisses Lila's marriage to Stefano: "The beauty of mind that Cerullo had from childhood didn't find an outlet [. . .] and it has all ended up in her face, in her breasts, in her thighs, in her ass, places where it soon fades and it will be as if she had never had it" (mbf 277). The same Maestra later regards Elena's mother as if she "were only a disposable living being" (mbf 208). Professor Gerace laughs when Elena mispronounces the word "oracle" by stressing the second syllable rather than the first ("It didn't occur to him that, although I knew the meaning of the word, I lived in a world where no one had ever had any reason to use it"; mbf 159). Professor Galiani asks Elena which newspapers she reads, ignoring the fact that reading the paper isn't a common activity in the *rione* ("The professor took it for granted that I normally did something that at my house, in my environment, was not at all normal"; snn 132–33). Equally uncommon is the opportunity to converse about Italian or world politics (snn 157–60). When Professor Galiani sees the engagement ring on Lila's finger and discovers the girl is only seventeen, she withdraws into an eloquent silence. A bourgeois woman with ties to the Communist Party, the teacher takes a dismissive attitude—one that has always pervaded mainstream left-wing culture in Naples—toward the plebeian populace that cannot be incorporated into the working class; (Ramondino 25). Ferrante sidesteps Southern Italian pathos by portraying discrimination as not only operating along north-south lines, as not confined to a developed North discriminating against a backward South, but as occurring within the marginalized South, within Naples, where the bourgeoisie does everything in its power to avoid mingling with the people with whom they have lived side by side for centuries.

If plebian Naples is perceived to be irreducibly other, it is important to understand which features of this untamable Caliban are most prevalent in the quartet. Little by little, Elena herself, with her binary attitude, provides us with a phenomenology that is essentially defined as *being in need* (the clauses in question are in fact almost always built on a syntax of negation). Her anthropological otherness marks her as an "intelligence without traditions" (according to the classist formula used by the Airotas to describe Nino and Elena; slc 74), prevents her from approaching life with the same resources of the bourgeoisie, and bars her from ever really becoming like them: "There was something malevolent in the inequality [. . .] It acted in the depths, it dug deeper than money" (snn 125).

A few symptoms, great and small, of this neediness: At her classical high school, Elena cannot help but sense the continuity between the world of school and that of the *rione*, where the price of acceptance is masking or censoring oneself ("With them I couldn't use any of what I learned every day, I had to suppress myself, in some way diminish myself"; mbf 319–20). Jobs in the *rione* always bear the stigma of uncleanliness. Lila's father Fernando resembles a famous actor yet is "unrefined [. . .] he had broad, stubby hands streaked with dirt in every crease and under the nails" (mbf 81). Pasquale arrives to meet Elena "out of breath and sweaty in his work clothes, spotted all over with splotches of white plaster" (mbf 127). Like Pasquale, Elena's first boyfriend Antonio shows up "in his grease-stained overalls" (mbf 279), and the first thing Elena points out are the coarse, mean features of his face ("his face was shiny and full of blackheads, his teeth here and there were bluish; he had broad hands and strong fingers"; mbf 266). When Maestra Oliviero floats the idea of attending high school, Elena looks at her surprised: "I didn't know anything about the order of schools [. . .] Words like high school, university were for me without substance, like many of the words I came across in novels" (mbf 123). At Professor Galiani's party, the seventeen-and-a-half-year-old realizes she doesn't know the proper manners with which to make "introductions" (snn 154). Earlier still, when she participates in a march for world peace—at the prompting of said professor—Elena is forced to withdraw because her brothers, whom she had to bring with her, join other kids in throwing stones and heaping insults on the demonstrators (snn 130). When the teacher with pale-blue hair who sits in on Elena's oral exam suggests that she take another entrance exam, she has never heard of the Pisa Normale nor does she quite know what a university department is (snn 324). Once she gets to the Normale she realizes that she speaks a "bookish Italian" (snn 332, cf. 5.6) and has no knowledge of the rules of etiquette ("I spoke in a loud voice, I chewed noisily"; snn 332). For a girl of semiliterate origins, she succeeds in achieving extraordinary grades at the Normale but lacks that "mental conformation that didn't reduce everything to [an] individual battle" (snn 409). In 1968, at twenty-four, she still isn't in the habit of brushing her teeth in the evening, a practice she only learns about at the Normale (tlts 81).

Finally, it comes as no surprise, given the previously mentioned glitch of matrophobia and female and social abjection (cf. 3), that for Elena, the pleb is none other than her own mother at her most violent and vulgar:

> The plebs were us. The plebs were that fight for food and wine, that quarrel over who should be served first and better, that dirty floor on which the waiters clattered back and forth, those increasingly vulgar toasts. The plebs were my mother, who had drunk wine and now was leaning against my father's shoulder, while he, serious, laughed, his mouth gaping, at the sexual allusions of the metal dealer. (mbf 329)

Anthropologically speaking, this plebian world encompasses the subproletariat and the precarious worker (Ramondino 9), yet from a social perspective it doesn't end there, as the index of characters at the start of each volume demonstrates. Setting aside the explicit references to the murky criminal world of the Camorra (the black marketeer and loan shark Don Achille Carracci, the moneylender Manuela Solara), which are always made in connection to solid jobs and investments, in other social contexts the list of occupations in the index could easily define a heterogenous world made up of the lower and upper middle classes as well as the working class: porter, shoemaker, greengrocer, baker, small businessman (represented by Silvio Solara, owner of the Solara bar-pastry shop), railway worker, cleaning lady, pharmacist, and teacher. In *Frantumaglia*, Ferrante repeatedly returns to this "plebian" city, which, according to the writer, is distinguished by a blind anxiety to pull oneself out of poverty, a certain moral ambiguity, a blend of otherness and violence, a mix of disdain and admiration for culture:

> The plebeian city I know is made up of ordinary people who don't have money and who seek it, who are of the underclass and yet violent, who do not have the intangible privilege of a good education, who mock those who think of saving themselves through education and yet still consider education valuable. (fr 370)

This could be a portrait of, say, Lila's brother Rino. Dogged by moral more than by material poverty—in part because at first his father viciously hinders his plan to design shoes, and with it, every viable attempt of Rino's to free himself (just as the father hinders Lila from continuing school because "it didn't enter into his view of the world"; mbf 70)—Rino jumps at the chance to partner with the Solaras, and gets himself mixed up in illegal activities. He ends up betraying his sister by agreeing to sell her design and the Cerullo brand to Marcello Solara, thereby humiliating Lila's efforts to gain independence, the very same efforts he had tried as a young man to protect (mbf 68–70). Even if Lila loves Rino deeply, on numerous occasions he manifests violent and contemptuous behavior toward her. Wherever he goes, he brandishes the violent ways he picked up in his neighborhood, as is confirmed during the trip to Ischia when Elena observes "the swaggering self-confidence that pushed him to violate every rule and to respond to any protests according to the habits of the neighborhood, braking suddenly, threatening, always ready to fight to assert his right to do as he pleased" (snn 219). Lacking the ability to form a plan that is not motivated by financial greed, Rino will fall into ruin and die of an overdose.

If we consider the character arc of the young well-to-do grocer Stefano (even if much of his fortune was left to him by his loan shark father), we find things aren't so different. In 1959 he can afford to buy a sports car, a vehicle that nullifies the prestige of the Solaras' 1100—a symbol of an increasingly widespread wealth—but neither before nor after his honeymoon will it lead him to venture out to another city and stay in a hotel (cf. 4.2). He goes into business with the Solaras, well aware that their wealth is even more compromised by illegal activities than his own, given their clear ties to the Camorra, and that the alliance with them will compromise his relationship with Lila, who has always stood up to them. Bewitched by

Lila, Stefano still feels intellectually inferior to her; his wife's sophistication makes him uneasy (snn 388). He is a small businessman who will become a ruined adult. Like Rino, he reveals his inability to consolidate the fortune he accumulates. A striking figure whose false good manners mask a violent and potentially homicidal male sexuality (cf. 6.1), Stefano bears all the signs of the volatile condition described by Ferrante.

4. The *Rione*

The *rione* is an "unreliable community held together by opportunistic complicities" (fr 367) so viscous as to produce the kind of gray area that Elena describes in 1986, right after the murder of the Solara brothers:

> I and countless other respectable people all over Naples had been within the world of the Solaras [. . .] the line of separation in relation to people like the Solaras had been and was, in Naples, in Italy, vague. The farther we jumped back in horror, the more certain it was that we were behind the line. (slc 375–76)

Perhaps the clearest expression of this plebeian attraction to power lies in the words of Elisa, Elena's sister, who, as soon as she begins dating Marcello Solara, realizes that she has become a person worthy of respect in the *rione*: "Before [. . .] you're nobody, and right afterward even the mice in the sewer grates know you" (tlts 323). In other cases, such complicity, though not opportunistic, originates from a shared social imaginary. For example, Lila has the courage and grit to rebuff the arrogant, lusty Solaras, yet her marriage to Stefano actually fits squarely within the Camorra logic of bravado, domination, and corruption, and is only superficially dignified by an initial respectability: "that courteous youth [. . .] seemed convinced that he could inaugurate a new era of peace and well-being for the neighborhood" (mbf 249). Lila's ostentation, "those airs [. . .] of Jacqueline Kennedy" (mbf 310), is prompted by the "race" between the two cars: the Solaras' 1100 is overtaken by the shiny red convertible that Stefano claims to have bought just for her (mbf 236) and that is, in effect, one of the bargaining chips that will launch their relationship.

Not even Elena and Lila's bond is immune to the cultural difficulty of navigating the changes to, and destructive dynamic of, social relationships in a stable and constructive way. Lila and Enzo sell Basic Sight—the product of an honest, visionary, and brave grassroots endeavor—for next to nothing. Meanwhile Elena's family ties gradually unravel over the course of the narrative: her sister Elisa disappears without ever contacting her again (slc 454) and, before that, becomes Elena's enemy by marrying Marcello (slc 209). Precisely because they spent a formative part of their lives in the *rione*, Elena's daughters strive to identify themselves as solidly middle class, in the Airota mold, or else, like Imma, as part of a cosmopolitan elite, and not subject to the same condition that Elena had fought so hard for: this is the root cause of her sense of failure at the end of the quartet. The social transformations of the *rione*, because numerous and heterogenous yet fleeting and unstable, spring from a "culture of poverty": "a culture that is simultaneously against poverty, adapted to the stresses of poverty, and mangled by poverty" (Belmonte 142). Hardly a stranger to historical and social change, ready to seize on the opportunities of the economic boom, this social sphere fritters away its creative resistance by pursuing the false models of flashiness and consumerism.

In sorting the characters by family, the opening index implies that the plot of the quartet is chiefly connected to the household nucleus and the bonds of passion, love, friendship, solidarity, competition, and hatred that take shape inside the *rione*. Ferrante's multifamily saga is a biting critique of such an institution, a rewriting of the sentimental, idealized myth that views the poor Neapolitan family as loving and mutually supportive. Every family may struggle to accept the emancipation of its loved ones, even more so in the context of Naples's underclass, which, on the one hand, strives to change, and, on the other, lacks the cultural resources to weather its traumas and treat its wounds. The quartet's depiction of domestic life shows how even the most intense—and intensely expressed—emotions, such as "cooperation, protection, friendship, and love must compromise and coexist or be defeated" (Belmonte 144) in the context of material and/or moral poverty.

If the families of the *rione* are a dramatic cross of threatening ferocity and homicidal impulses, and the ties in the neighborhood are harmful and corrupting (fr 367), that is in part due to the fact that, more than the lives of men, the lives of women are defined by a combination of subservience and violence. It is the mothers of the family whom Elena calls "angry as starving dogs." "[W]omen," she says, "who appeared to be silent, acquiescent, when they were angry flew into a rage that had no end" (mbf 38). Domestic chores may be divvied up only if the man in question is lessened by vague effeminate desires. That is the collective explanation for the behavior of Donato Sarratore (a poet no less—another sign of his lack of virility), who, after work, occasionally pushes his youngest son around in a stroller or does the shopping (mbf 39). Defending a value system based on the violent possession of their bodies, women adhere to the virile code with greater ferocity than the men: "women [. . .] knew what had to be said when the men who loved them and whom they loved beat them severely." When, on their honeymoon, Stefano begins savagely beating Lila, he earns the sympathy of the entire neighborhood: "the beatings did not cause outrage, and in fact sympathy and respect for Stefano increased—there was someone who knew how to be a man" (snn 45). Back from their honeymoon, "[n]o one, not even her mother, who was silent during the entire visit, seemed to notice her swollen, black right eye, the cut on her lower lip, the bruises on her arms" (snn 44). Even Elena adopts the stance that "a stranger must not even touch us, but [. . .] our father, our boyfriend, and our husband could hit us when they liked, out of love, to educate us, to reeducate us" (snn 52). Bringing into focus the "vital, obscene, suffering subjugation" of the "silent victims, desperately in love with males and male children" (fr 219), and pointing out that the "mother-centeredness" (Belmonte 87) in Neapolitan lower class families does not imply that the real power and autonomy of women is recognized, Ferrante topples two unfounded myths at once: first, the myth of unconditional motherly love, and second, the myth of the Mediterranean matriarchy as omnipotent and essentially different from male dominance.

5. The Ogre Don Achille and the Labyrinth

The scene in which Elena and Lila climb the stairs of Professor Galiani's building, in 1962, is an important reversal of one of the symbolic events of their friendship: the climb up to Don Achille's apartment to look for the dolls. While the exploration of the bourgeois world separates the two nearly eighteen-year-old friends, who walk—as is explicitly called attention to—without holding hands and in inverse rank (Elena first, Lila second), in the scene from their childhood, roughly nine years earlier, the ascent to the house of the "ogre" (mbf 27) profoundly unites them. Indeed, it proves to be the founding myth of their friendship:

> We climbed slowly toward the greatest of our terrors of that time, we went to expose ourselves to fear and interrogate it. At the fourth flight Lila did something unexpected. She stopped to

wait for me, and when I reached her she gave me her hand. This gesture changed everything between us forever. (mbf 29)

Clasped hands are the main symbol of their friendship (cf. 2.2) and call to mind a body that makes its way in the world by sensing and overcoming fear and its physical symptoms by joining forces with another body:

> I still feel Lila's hand grasping mine, and I like to think that she decided to take it not only because she intuited that I wouldn't have the courage to get to the top floor but also because with that gesture she herself sought the force to continue. So, one beside the other, I on the wall side and she on the banister side, sweaty palms clasped, we climbed the last flights. (mbf 65)

The expedition to the ogre's that inaugurates the story of *My Brilliant Friend* is told circularly. It encompasses two thirds of the first section, "Childhood" (in the table of contents it is subtitled, not coincidentally, "The Story of Don Achille"). After the narrative begins, the story of their adventure is interrupted the moment they join hands, and their friendship locks into place, and does not end until forty pages later, in chapter fourteen (Milkova[3]).

In between the beginning and end of the story—which dates back to when the girls are in third grade ("when we went together up the stairs that led to Don Achille's and were eight, almost nine"; mbf 34)—there is a period of childhood that precedes and extends beyond that of the circular story about Don Achille. In fact, the circular structure envelops a magmatic nucleus that actually spills over into before and after third grade. Before, with the manifestation in first grade of six-year-old Lila's genius, for example, or the time they throw each other's doll in the cellar "[n]ot too long before" their expedition to Don Achille's ("ten days, a month, who can say, we knew nothing about time, in those days"; mbf 29). And after, with the middle school admissions test (mbf 63). This centrifugal nucleus is made up of diverse, meandering, repeated stages. (Like the throwing of the dolls, Lila's head injury from the rock-throwing war with Enzo is recounted in two different chapters and from two different perspectives.) This spiraling galaxy, the overture of all the narrative threads of the quartet, casts a magic halo over the raw and violent power relations in the *rione*, predominantly characterized by childhood fights (the one form of group play), school rivalries based on class, the checkered figure of the padrone/black-marketeer/loan shark Don Achille, and by the love-mad victim Melina. This various, twisting timeline, composed of scraps, deviations, flashbacks, flash-forwards, and repetitions, is the labyrinthine timeline of childhood (Milkova[3]), a nomadism many traces of which we also find in *Frantumaglia*.

Ferrante recalls her own bewilderment at eleven years old when she and her sister were caught in a violent storm after venturing far from home without their mother's permission. The two girls give up their ice cream outing with "two boys who were scarcely older, playmates who were silently in love" (fr 141). In the rain, Naples appears to her for the first time in all its ambiguity, "alien and known at the same time, limited and boundless, dangerous and exciting" (fr 141). An urban space where the only way to find yourself is by getting lost, "an ordinary space, a known place that, with oneself, is suddenly disrupted by a strong emotion" (fr 145): "I felt [Naples] on my back and under my feet, it was running along with us, panting with its dirty breath, horns honking madly" (fr 141). Belonging gives way to estrangement ("I was aware of the city for the first time"), to feeling lost on streets that you've walked many times before but that, following the freedom and anxiety of having escaped, are now unrecognizable, repellent, threatening. The spatial model is a map that warps into a maze, that transforms into a "primary labyrinth" as soon as "the child's gaze [. . .] wanders in the mystery outside the house, far from his guardian divinities, and encounters love for the first time" (fr 144).

Young Elena loses her way on the streets of Naples just as a child by the name of Walter (Benjamin) once got lost in Berlin's Tiergarten. As an adult, Ferrante recounts this episode of her childhood by way of the German essayist's *Berlin Childhood Around 1900*. Yet in the pages of *Frantumaglia*, not only do we discover the labyrinth in which Elena and Lila get lost and find one another but the method by which this maze took shape. Speaking of Benjamin's spatial model, his "art of getting lost," Ferrante defines a type of narrative structure quite similar to the one she herself adopts to create the spiraling galaxy of "The Story of Don Achille": "the extraordinary gaze of eyeballs that are pupils in their entire spherical surface, and which therefore see not only before, not only outside, not the afterward that is in store but the ahead-behind, the inside-outside, the after in the then-now, without chronological order" (fr 143).

In the first forty pages of *My Brilliant Friend* there are various instances of synchronicity, of "the after in the then-now." One of them is the event that tears the two girls out of their anonymous childhood, the fork in the road that will forever separate them, when Maestra Oliviero offers them the chance to continue studying beyond elementary school. Within this magical loop, in the chapter before chapter fourteen—which closes the Don Achille circle—we learn of Lila's parents' opposition to the opportunity and Elena's faith in her friend's implacable determination to put up a fight: "Although she was fragile in appearance, every prohibition lost substance in her presence" (mbf 64). But the end of this first episode shatters their hopes, prospects, potential; childhood ends because time suddenly becomes quantifiable, irreversible, the real account of a girl forced to stop studying at ten years old, and her friend's continuation of the journey without her. The last eighteen pages of "The Story of Don Achille" form the falling action of their magical story. Their reading of *Little Women*—bought with the money that the ogre gives them to compensate for the irretrievable dolls—and plan to write and make money together are rites intended to rescue Lila from her fate. But already the redemptive symbol of *The Blue Fairy*, which Lila writes by herself while Elena attends private lessons to prepare for her middle school admissions test, gives off less and less light. The ogre's blood and the girl's broken arm, the murder of Don Achille and Lila's flight—"thrown like a thing" (mbf 82) out the window by her enraged father after she complains about being taken out of school—foreshadow a violent reality that will rarely regain the evanescence of child's play.

6. The Minotaur and the Two Ariadnes

In the circular story that leads Elena and Lila to confront Don Achille, there is a moment in which, shortly before making their ascent, the two girls slip into the cellar in the hopes of finding the two dolls where they must have fallen. Not finding them, Lila declares with total certainty, "'Don Achille took them, he put them in his black bag'" (mbf 56). The myth of "the shapeless mass of Don Achille," the predatory and ubiquitous thief of dolls/little girls ("running through the underground tunnels, arms dangling, large fingers grasping Nu's head in one hand, in the other Tina's"; mbf 57) triggers in Elena's mind the transformation of the entire *rione* into "an intermediary and liminal zone, an architecture without ends or borders" (Milkova[3]). Hierarchies—high and low, internal and external, horizontal and vertical—vanish, and the underground "air bubble" (mbf 57) becomes connected to Don Achille's apartment. The two poles encroach upon every other space in the neighborhood, now morphed into the vast territory of the ogre, "a spider among spiders, a rat among rats, a shape that assumed all shapes" (mbf 31). This depiction, chilling yet also charged with the magical thinking of children, gives rise to the symbolic typography of the neighborhood, its "latticework of power relations—between rich and poor, strong and weak, creditor and debtor, and, most pernicious of all, between man and woman" (Manetti[1])

> [The space] seemed to be chained between two dark poles: on one side was the underground air bubble that pressed on the roots of the houses, the threatening cavern the dolls had fallen into; on the other the upper sphere, on the fourth floor of the building where Don Achille, who had stolen them, lived. The two balls were as if screwed to the ends of an iron bar, which in my imagination obliquely crossed the apartments, the streets, the countryside, the tunnel, the railroad tracks, and compressed them. I felt squeezed in that vise . . . (mbf 57)

In the dark, dusty cellar, Lila unearths a gas mask—an object foreign to Elena—and puts it on to prank her friend. Elena is petrified: "She had put the face with the glass eyes over hers and now her face was enormous, with round, empty eye sockets and no mouth, only that protruding black chin swinging over her chest" (mbf 56). The terrifying image overlays the supernatural shape of Don Achille, "an evil being of uncertain animal-mineral physiognomy, who [. . .] sucked blood from others" (mbf 37):

> He was a being created out of some unidentifiable material, iron, glass, nettles, but alive, alive, the hot breath streaming from his nose and mouth. I thought that if I merely saw him from a distance he would drive something sharp and burning into my eyes. So if I was mad enough to approach the door of his house he would kill me. [. . .] he would suck my head the way my father did with mullets. (mbf 28)

If Don Achille is all too clearly the Beast-Minotaur, the hybrid cannibal monster inside the maze, Elena and Lila are two Ariadnes who allow themselves to be led by the thread of their desire to compete and gain knowledge, in order both to kill the monster and escape the labyrinth of patriarchal violence and to enter the labyrinth of their own passions (Milkova[3]):

> There was something unbearable in the things, in the people, in the buildings, in the streets that, only if you reinvented it all, as in a game, became acceptable. The essential [. . .] was to know how to play, and she and I, only she and I, knew how to do it. [. . .] we were both trying to understand, and understanding was something that we loved to do. (mbf 106–7, 170)

Their desire to compete and gain knowledge is improper because it subverts what their fathers think of as the natural order of things: male supremacy. In fact, after Rino intercedes on Lila's behalf so that his sister can go to school, their enraged father asks him, "[W]hy should your sister, who is a girl, go to school?" (mbf 69). Thus, the two Ariadnes are also Pasiphae, the queen whose obscene, shameful desire to couple with the animal gives birth to the monster, while the boundaries of the *rione*-labyrinth are erected in order to wall off this irrepressible desire. "[T]here is no city-labyrinth," underscores Ferrante, "without a Pasiphae who gives birth to the Beast-Minotaur, without an Ariadne and love" (fr 144). But Ariadne is also the one with a tight grip on the thread. Like Dido, who in one mythological story cunningly uses thread to extend the borders of her new city as far as possible and expropriate land from Iarbas, the King of Getulia, Ariadne is a figure of the expressive surveillance necessary to erect a city (cf. 3.7). Ferrante draws on these two mythological figures to describe the self-discipline with which, as a child, she managed to overcome her panic about being lost (Milkova[3]): "I had to stop, tug on my sister so that she wouldn't run away, grasp the thread of orientation, which is a magic thread, to tie one street to the next, making tight knots, so that the streets would calmly settle down and I could find the way home" (fr 142).

The labyrinth should therefore be read as a polymorphous metaphor. Above all it is a confusing and chaotic space, which produces "a kind of tactile dysfunction" (mbf 57) in Elena, an early form—the first in the entire quartet—of *smarginatura* (cf. 3.2). Yet the labyrinth is also a magical space that, over the course of the narrative, lapses into a place where women's most historically fraught desire, the desire for knowledge, is repressed; into a place of adventure, companionship, and female redemption from such discipline; and finally into the communal violence of the *rione*. The labyrinth represents the liminal space of violence itself, perpetuated in the neighborhood by men and women and adults and children alike, connected as they are by a "a chain of wrongs that generated wrongs" (mbf 83). It also represents a lens through which to identify the actual cause of widespread violence as stemming from a patriarchal code, from a Minotaur-like figure with expressionistically male features.

But there is something diabolical about the doubleness of the two Ariadnes: the other can sometimes revert to a looming, punishing ghost, a characteristic alluded to by the epigraph from *Faust* at the start of *My Brilliant Friend* and by the whole dynamic of Elena and Lila's bond (cf. 2). This ambivalence clearly emerges in the episode when they escape to the beach, also recounted in the first part of *My Brilliant Friend*, yet significantly outside the narrative circle we have been analyzing up till now. The joy of their adventure is established by the cheerful laughter of the two girls, who once again are holding hands. Their laughter erupts inside the pitch-black tunnel, like a form of exorcism against the disturbing recess that resembles Don Achille's cellar: "all we did was shout, together and separately: laughter and cries, cries and laughter, for the pleasure of hearing them amplified" (mbf 75). Beyond the tunnel lies uncharted territory, a measure of freedom which the girls take ownership of thanks to the "spatial practice" (de Certeau 115) of travel: "When I think of the pleasure of being free, I think of the start of that day" (mbf 75).

Before them stretches the ruined panorama of a chaotic Naples, still bearing signs of the war. Before this "landscape of ruin," Elena does not break down, because up till now she has always perceived Lila as a measure of balance, control, and composure that defies the chaos of Naples: "I felt as if she had everything in her head ordered in such a way that the world around us would never be able to create disorder" (mbf 76). At a certain point in their journey Lila seizes up, and her inability to leave the *rione* becomes apparent. But here her hesitation has another origin. There is something unspoken, something agitating her, that she cannot confess to her friend, something that drives her to dash back home in a violent storm (as in *Frantumaglia*, the rain gives rise to the labyrinth), dragging her friend along with her. That something comes to light the next day, when, upon discovering the bruises on Elena's body—her parents' punishment for running away—Lila asks her if they had given her another, far worse punishment than the beating: if they had prohibited her from continuing school. The doubts that Elena has at this point still linger fifty-six years later as she writes her story:

> Was it possible? She had taken me with her hoping that as a punishment my parents would not send me to middle school? Or had she brought me back in such a hurry so that I would avoid that punishment? Or—I wonder today—did she want at different moments both things? (mbf 79)

It's impossible to say whether or not her doubts are well-founded. What the episode makes clear is that from now on both will have to contend with another labyrinth and another beast lying in wait: the ambivalence of female friendship. In

Frantumaglia Ferrante discusses working on a story about Ariadne set in "a city of female friendship and solidarity, but free in its thoughts and in its conflicts" (fr 146), a modern rewriting of a well-known variation of the classic myth (the abandonment of the young woman in Amathus). However, the story failed to take shape because "the city was too perfect; the community of women, even in its vivacity, seemed sentimentally full of good feelings and thus inauthentic." "No," says Ferrante, "even in the case of cities dominated by women one can and must write only of city-labyrinths, the repositories of our complex and contradictory emotions, where the Beast is lying in ambush and it's dangerous to get lost without having first learned to do so" (fr 146). *The Neapolitan Novels* are also this labyrinth, in which two friends sometimes unspool the thread of life's adventure together, and sometimes let go of it; in which the Beast lying in ambush is generated both by their fear of losing one another and their desire to do so.

7. The Cellar and Heterotopia

In Ferrante's writing, the spatial model of "two Naples" (Rea) facing off in a clash of social classes and customs (cf. 4.2) blurs with its opposite, a model of the city-threshold, of the liminal city in which opposites are canceled out. The first way of representing space is dual and centripetal, the second multifocal and centrifugal; the first has a long tradition in the nineteenth and twentieth centuries, while the second starts to form after the urban transformations beginning with the last two decades of the twentieth century, in particular, "the multiplication of peripheries; the proliferation of outer loops, beltways, and circumferential highways; the spread of shopping centers, which become the quintessential emblem of these contiguities" (De Caprio).

Besides the labyrinth of the *rione*, another example of a space-threshold is the Vossi sisters' store in *Troubling Love*. Located in the upscale residential neighborhood of Vomero, the store is famous for selling high-quality, sophisticated lingerie that is too expensive for Amalia and Delia. As a young woman, Delia used to study the lingerie on display, especially a painting in the corner window (cf. 6.5). From the perspective of the city outskirts (Delia spent her entire childhood in the *rione*) and the historic downtown (where she goes to live with her mother when Amalia separates from her husband), the uphill climb to Vomero and to the shop results in a conflict between high and low, between underclass and bourgeois borders previously described in the fight in Piazza dei Martiri in *My Brilliant Friend* (cf. 4.2). Yet when Delia returns to the shop after an absence of twenty years to investigate her mother's death (her body was found in nothing but a Vossi brassiere), she finds the space totally transformed: the store no longer belongs to the three elegant sisters but to a vulgar man. At first Delia mistakes him for a bouncer, on account of his brusque, aggressive behavior, but then she recognizes him: he was her playmate back in her hard-up childhood. In and out of the changing rooms, the shop's (completely different) clientele also exhibit vulgar manners and plebeian tastes:

> [The women] talked loudly in a dialect marked by a forced cheer [. . .] displayed abundant flesh striped by stretch marks and dented by cellulite, gazed at pubis and buttocks, pushed their breasts up with cupped hands [. . .] They seemed women whose men had got rich suddenly and easily, hurling them into a provisional luxury that they were compelled to enjoy, and whose subculture was like a damp crowded basement, with semi-porn comic strips, with obscenities used as refrains. They were women forced into a city-prison, corrupted first by poverty and now by money, with no interruption. (tl 58)

The liminal city is also a labyrinth of late modernity that

erases the lines between middle- and underclass neighborhoods, brought together by their obsession with shopping, thereby generating a new variation of the "city-prison." To linger a moment over the "damp crowded basement" where these women come from: the phrase alludes to *bassi napoletani*—popular dwellings in the historic city center consisting of a single room facing the street—yet immediately calls to mind the cellar in the quartet and, with it, the nest of labyrinths in *My Brilliant Friend*. The cellar and basement are, besides a social labyrinth, a women's labyrinth closely linked to the mother's cave (cf. 3.3) and to that "fund of pleasure," "the cellar of writing" (fr 64), that long repressed attraction to weighty dramas from which the quartet emerges (cf. 1.1).

Like a new Ariadne, Delia wanders through the city and "gets lost in her childhood" (fr 144). Recovering her own story through the story of her mother (cf. 3.8), Delia will locate the thread to get out of the "labyrinth of Naples" (fr 66). The labyrinth is the form of the story itself, reconstituted as the cave, a tale with multiple timelines punctuated by regular flashbacks: that "survival" that enables mythical figures, ancestors, and daughters to inhabit the same moment (cf. 3.7). Just as in the case of Persephone (de Rogatis[3] 306), Delia is initially driven in a symbolic direction, her journey one of descending, first in the elevator and on the funicular, and later to the basement. These urban inversions of empty spaces are typical of Neapolitan geology and archaeology. A series of metaphors illustrates her adventure as an underground version of *The Adventures of Alice in Wonderland*: an "aged Alice in pursuit of the White Rabbit," falling into the "oblique well" (tl 69–70) of memory. Just as the girl is transformed in Wonderland, Delia's body undergoes a metamorphosis, shrinking and recovering the gaze and stature of her five-year-old self (tl 79). Delia also becomes a child again when, at the end of her pursuit, she enters the now empty and desolate Coloniali-Pasticceria; the counter seems for a moment to be high above her head, as it was when she was a child (tl 122). In the manner of Carroll's novel, a tiny exit is the doorway to a secret world: from the bakery a "little door" in fact leads to the basement, the place of Delia's triangular fantasies (cf. 3.8) and the setting (along with the entire establishment) of the abuse that she now, sinking into the cave, can name: "To speak is to link together lost times and spaces" (tl 133).

The cellar in the quartet and the basement in *Troubling Love* are heterotopias: utopias situated in a concrete context, "sort of places that are outside all places [. . .] in which the real emplacements [. . .] are, at the same time, represented, contested, and reverted" (Foucault 178). The allusion, in this case, is to a heterotopia of resistance, recurrent in the work of many contemporary Italian authors (like the Neapolitan writers Fabrizia Ramondino, Valeria Parella, Lalla Romano, and Goliarda Sapienza), which crosses and redeems spaces of female marginalization and suffering (Brogi[4], Guglielmi).

8. *Femminiello*, *Smarginatura*, and the City-Hermaphrodite

Stefano's younger brother Alfonso is found dead on the beach at Coroglio, between Posillipo and Bagnoli, in 1984. Beaten to death, he was tossed into the sea. It is important that the Gulf of Naples make one of its rare (merely scene setting) appearances in the quartet on the occasion of a violent death. The idyllic setting is violated three times: first because it serves as the backdrop for the body of someone who has been murdered; second because this hybrid, "male-female" (slc 164) cadaver floating out at sea is a rewriting of one of the founding myths of the city: the death of the siren Parthenope (another hybrid); third because, of all the places on the Gulf, the writer chooses the one most devastated by modernity. Though the side of Coroglio closest to Posillipo includes the beautiful island of Nisida, the other side extends all the way to the edge of the ex-Italsider in Bagnoli (clearly visible from the beach and still operating in 1984). Coroglio's identity is itself hybrid.

Alfonso's progressive metamorphosis into a transvestite "in whose habits, the feminine and the masculine continually broke boundaries" (slc 272) is crowned by Lila. She is the one who urges Alfonso to model himself on her own body. Elena describes her behavior as a reenactment of the myth of Narcissus: "She must have looked at him as at a mirror and seen herself in him and had wanted to draw out of his body a part of herself" (slc 305). This game of doubling even ensnares Michele, who, always obsessed with possessing Lila, becomes embroiled in a relationship with Alfonso based on sexual stand-ins. In Lila's drive to dominate, putting "male material inside male material" (slc 178) means gaining the upper hand by extorting the Solaras (cf. 7.6). The metamorphosis complete, Elena finds herself witness to a surprising scene:

> My old desk mate, with his hair down, in the elegant dress, was a copy of Lila. His tendency to resemble her [. . .] came abruptly into focus, and maybe at that moment he was even handsomer, more beautiful than she, a male-female [. . .] ready, male and female, to set off on the road leading to the black Madonna of Montevergine. (slc 164)

The black Madonna of Montevergine is the destination of a historic pilgrimage observed to this day by a group of Neapolitan transvestites known as the *femminielli*. Exuberant figures of diversity, both male and female (as the name implies), the *femminielli*—unlike homosexuals—have traditionally been recognized by and integrated into the fabric of the oldest Neapolitan neighborhoods through a series of specific rituals (among them the *figliata*, a simulation of child-birth), endowed with magical status, and associated with good luck, because they represent a metaphysical union of the two sexes (D'Agostino 90–98). The connection between the metropolis and the *femminiello* (first explored thirty years ago in the experimental Neapolitan theater of Roberto De Simone, Enzo Moscato, and Annibale Ruccello) returns us once again to Naples as a liminal city, a threshold city, a labyrinth of various times, codes, and genders.

However, the word *femminiello* never appears in *The Neapolitan Novels*; it is only implied with the roundabout reference to the pilgrimage to Montevergine. Ferrante was very careful not to equate the character of Alfonso with that figure of folklore, which a superficial reading of the Neapolitan term would risk evoking for wider audiences. The symbolic nature of Alfonso's transformation remains intact, translates (along with the Neapolitan dialect) nationally and internationally, and alludes to the metamorphic energy of the entire city, "a cyclical Naples where everything was marvelous and everything became gray and irrational and everything sparkled again" (slc 440). This eccentricity is based on its being a hermaphroditic city (de Rogatis[4] 290–91), the bearer of traits both masculine and feminine, ancient and contemporary. Under the pressure of violence, these codes can fuse together into an enigmatic totality. Something similar can be found in the description given in *Frantumaglia* of the aggressive gestures and mindset of peasant mothers, in a phallic word (cf. 4.4), and in the fantasy of two young girlfriends who attribute the murder of Don Achille to "a black creature [. . .] part male but mostly female" (mbf 95).

No wonder Alfonso undergoes his transformation thanks to Lila, the character who most catalyzes the dissolving of boundaries. Insofar as she is a "violator of taboo" (Van Ness 298), Lila is in fact Naples. If we try to widen our perspective on the subject, we see that the dissolving of boundaries refers to a broader metamorphic energy, triggered by Lila, by whom it is most acutely felt, yet also expressed by the whole city. From the start, Lila's legend flares up into "that terrible, dazzling girl" (mbf 47) and later into the "glow that seemed a slap in the face" (mbf 264) of the young beautiful woman likened to a goddess. Ferociously determined, hardheaded, unreasonable: over time she becomes for the *rione* "a kind of holy warrior who spread avenging light over the *stradone*" (slc 153), who emanates "something tremendous" (tlts 210). Her features are superhuman: her gaze as piercing as a "bird of prey" (mbf 105, 310), the choices she makes beyond the bounds of propriety (mbf 64). Lila has the power to animate things, to charge them with the tension of her precocious, multifaceted mind (mbf 130, 231). Her body gives off a strength that overwhelms Elena (slc 275); the intense eroticism contained in her lean, edgy, nervous body is in reality powerfully anti-erotic, or at least a departure from the traditional canon of women whom men desire. In fact, her presence elicits in men adoration and respect more than base lust (mbf 242, 252). Like Naples, Lila is the medium of a magical power woven into the tightly knit reality effect of the entire narrative cycle.

9. Naples Up Close and from a Distance

Ferrante refuses to exoticize Naples or to suppress its objective differences in the name of middle-class decorum and discipline. Bringing the *femminiello* into a national and international context is part of a larger aim to siphon the particular into the common. The writer seeks to downplay the most extreme ethnic elements, which would risk confining her story to a distinct place, one that has far too long been rendered as picturesque (de Rogatis[5] 137). An analogous strategy shapes the spaces of the *rione*, which are never restricted to a specific neighborhood, even if the neighborhood it is based upon, Rione Luzzatti, can be easily identified. Withholding its identity, the writer seeks to give shape to a universal periphery of our contemporary moment while at the same time drawing, as much as possible, on the imaginative filter that makes that periphery interesting: the point of view of the two protagonists. The quartet derives its realism from the interior world of Elena and Lila, and their perceptual categories. This bodily and ghostly space, whose molecules are a blend of urban settings and intrapsychic and social dimensions, is also deeply elliptical. The ellipsis stems from the fact that the girls' gazes ignore, by necessity, the larger map of Naples, because their subordinated perspective blocks them from seeing the entire panorama or contemplating it aesthetically. That is why large tableaus are rare in the quartet and, in general, spring from Elena's fanciful plans or hopes of escaping—for a few instants or for several months—the polyphony of the margins. That is the case, for example, of the storm surge on Via Caracciolo, which Elena contemplates while out walking with her father (cf 4.2), and the view from the house in Via Tasso where she lives from 1979 to 1981 (cf. 5.1):

> From Via Tasso the old neighborhood was a dim, distant rockpile, indistinguishable urban debris at the foot of Vesuvius. I wanted it to stay that way: I was another person now, I would make sure that it did not recapture me. (slc 116)

The ellipsis also dilates details, which are all that Elena and Lila can express of space: the *rione*, the labyrinth of stairs, cellars, apartments, the *stradone*, the tunnel, the poor countryside, the interiors of the plebian world, the signs of exclusion in middle-class domestic spaces (like the elevator and library at Professor Galiani's), the symbols of elite life (like the green outfit of the girl on Via Chiaia). Through the soundscape of dialect above all, the city "is perceived as a mode of perception on the one hand and a reflection of constrictive societal structures and acts of violence on the other" (Wehling-Giorgi[2] 225). This hyperrealism, like the lesson of Ortese, mirrors a metropolitan space that is perceived as "pressure, a dark force of the world that weighs on its subjects, the sum total of what we call the threatening reality of today, engulfing, through violence, every space of mediation and civil relationship around and within the characters" (fr 66).

In Ferrante's writing, the city is a constantly changing metaphor. On the one hand, Naples is an eccentric metropolis, a radical experience in which the familiar becomes alien and the ordinary disturbing. It's a city-labyrinth, city-underground, city-hermaphrodite, emanating from the life of Lila herself. On the other, Naples is a figurative space that anticipates the fates of Italy and Europe:

> [. . .] It's a metropolis that has anticipated and anticipates the troubles of Italy, perhaps of Europe. So we should never lose sight of it. [. . .] What we could be, on this planet, and what, instead, unfortunately, we are, can be seen more clearly in Naples than elsewhere. (fr 201, 297)

In the quartet the city is the setting of a spatial otherness that is also universalized, and therefore relevant to European history from the 1950s to today (cf. 6.7). The international success of the cycle is the success of a "glocal" narrative (Robertson 186): its ability to depict Naples, down to its most cumbersome and distinguishing features, from a global and local perspective, as "a well connoted imaginary place" (Fusillo 150). The *rione* lies outside of the city limits, isolated from them, which is why crossing the streets of upscale areas is considered a violation that must be punished (cf. 4.2). Yet on the other hand it lies within those limits, a decentralized appendage of a world historically embedded in the heart of the city. The story of the *rione* and the other poor neighborhoods at a distance from the center befits the new Neapolitan narrative's focus on peripheries, on detaching the urban topography from its historically recognized hub (De Caprio).

If that much has already been pointed out, then we should instead reflect on how this peripheral position is read by, for example, the vast English-speaking public that largely inhabits sprawling cities that generally lack an actual center and are littered with suburbs, each of which is often called a neighborhood—i.e., a *rione*. Naturally, this endless extension of "edge-cities," constellations neighboring the actual city yet at a remove from it, is familiar within an extremely diversified urban and social fabric, which runs the gamut from the gated communities of the middle and upper middle classes to subproletariat ghettos. So, on the one hand, the quartet brings the international reader into contact with an alienating experience: a chorus that constantly makes the inside communicate with the outside, the I with others, spiritual matters with passionate dramas; a porousness at profound variance with the disconnectedness of big western cities. On the other hand, the choral community of the *rione* is not an idealized artifact of the good old times but is instead perceived as a very contemporary social cluster, neither holistic nor harmoniously benevolent but lumped together in a discontinuous form of energy—blurred and violently anti-community. This desultory chorus reflects the random peripheral stretches of each geographic point lying on the edge of a major metropolis today.

Thanks to its mix of the archaic and ultramodern, Naples is a third space of contemporary European modernity, a periphery that turns into a symbolic center in the international imagination. In Elena and Lila's neighborhood we come across a series of proto-elements of such clusters: the *stradone*, the apartment blocks, the tunnels, the railway line, the skyscrapers surrounding the business district completed in the mid 1990s ("those buildings [. . .] had immediately, at high speed, lost all their luster and become dens for the desperate"; slc 335), the gray fields of the surrounding countryside (Sellitti). Along with the Neapolitan suburbs of Scampia, Ponticelli, and the Vesuvius red zone, the *rione* is part of that "laboratory of urban fragmentation" (Pfirsch) that now corrals the world's populations into metropolitan suburbs. Not for nothing, the *rione* and Scampia—another neighborhood on the outskirts of Naples—feature heavily in the media right now: the *rione* thanks to the recent TV series based on the quartet, Scampia thanks to the film and TV series *Gomorrah*. (The film and TV series are not of equal merit but that does not detract from the centrality of the neighborhood in the national and international imagination.) Like the outskirts of major metropolises, the *rione* and the bodies that inhabit it are "a fundamentally disunified series of systems, a series of disparate flows, energies, events, or entities, bringing together or drawing apart their more or less temporary alignments" (Grosz 385).

The particular, porous, and melodramatic world of Naples becomes global through the metamorphic mechanism of violence. The stories of women's emancipation, the segregated outskirts, consumerist hopes and temp workers' cravings (the latter an amorphous social class for decades considered a blemish of Naples that is turning out to be the fate of workers all over the world), the dissolution of marginalized bodies and minds: these geologies of dominion, grief, and redemption are the labyrinth of the quartet and of the world.

CHAPTER FIVE
Two Languages, Emigration, and Study

1. Emigration and Exile:
Those Who Leave *Are* Those Who Stay

I n the quartet there is an inextricable link between emigration and Elena and Lila's friendship. The dynamic of their bond is one of additions and subtractions, gains and losses (cf. 2), which creates a text that contrasts belonging with displacement: a sometimes explicit, sometimes implicit clash between Lila and Elena, between those who fall into the cave and those determined to dig themselves out of it, those who stay in Naples and those who leave Naples. Thanks to her scholastic career, continued through classical high school—and financed and sustained by Lila, who was kept from studying beyond elementary school—Elena wins a fellowship from the prestigious Scuola Normale di Pisa and departs for Tuscany in 1963. Her emigration to Central and Northern Italy is the least tragic and radical form of exile, what Edward Said calls "the unhealable rift forced between a human being and a native place, between the self and its true home" (Said 173).

It is to this rift that the title of the third volume of the quartet, *Those Who Leave and Those Who Stay*, alludes. Beginning with her formative experiences at the Normale, Elena lives her sixteen years of exile as a period of radical detachment from Naples, for during those years the social and linguistic divide between the popular *rione* and bourgeois Italy is unbridgeable. Even after four years at the university, Pisa remains a confining, alienating space for Elena: "[. . .] routes that were the same and yet alien even when the baker said hello and the newspaper seller chatted about the weather, alien in the voices that I had nevertheless forced myself to imitate from the start, alien in the color of the stone and the plants and the signs and the clouds or sky" (snn 402). At the same time, Elena's brief return to the *rione* upon finishing university feels nothing like a homecoming. This produces a sense of instability no less disturbing than that which she perceived in Pisa, now described with a weather-related metaphor: "My return to Naples was like having a defective umbrella that suddenly closes over your head in a gust of wind" (snn 436). The city is portrayed as a stepmother ready to commandeer what Elena has obtained while away from home: "upon every return to my own city I feared that some unexpected event would keep me from escaping, that the things I had gained would be taken away from me" (tlts 26). Following her first emigration to attend the university, the narrator of the quartet launches out on a relentless centrifugal movement toward emancipation from the *rione* and its dialect, and toward success as an Italian writer at home and abroad.

Elena leaves, Lila stays. Lila has always stayed. One of the first initiation rites of their childhood friendship is built on this contrast. During the girls' first adventure outside the *rione*, their flight to the beach of Naples, Lila loses herself, while Elena finally finds a reason for living (cf. 4.6). Disciplined and conformist, Elena can leave; insecure and beset by *smarginatura*, Lila can't: she needs narrow confines if she is to avoid splintering apart from an excess of self. So Lila stays and becomes increasingly entrenched in the life of the *rione*, in its escalations of violence that deform the lives of women, including that of Lila, the most intelligent, most beautiful, most ambitious woman there. At this stage the tension between form and the destruction of form becomes literal. Because if to stay means to deform oneself, to lose the distinguishing features of the "I" and body, to pursue one's own "self-destruction *in an image*" (as Lila destroys the enlarged photo of herself in the shop in Piazza dei Martiri;

snn 123; cf. 6.6.), then to leave means to define oneself in the public arena, to remake oneself, to transition into another social class. Elena pursues this feat with cold determination: graduating from the Normale, marrying a man she doesn't love because he is the son of prestigious Italian intellectuals, publishing her first book through her influential mother-in-law. If Lila is repeatedly identified, from childhood on, as spiteful, Elena is unsympathetic; she embodies the traits of "a mind of winter" that, according to Said, can become the tools necessary to survive exile (Said 186). In short, those who stay lose, those who leave win: subtraction and addition.

But when Elena returns to live in Naples, and later moves back into the *rione*, now a prominent thirty-five-year-old writer and single mother of three daughters, the self she formed in exile brands her a foreigner, a marginalized person in her own city. In fact, Lila the insider is the one to note her friend's outsider status. Lila weaves a series of mysteries around Elena, excluding her friend by openly hinting at unknowable secrets. "Facts that I didn't know and they did" (slc 164), remarks Elena. Her return to Naples is therefore an "estranging sense" of home (Bhabha 13), making her an inept and displaced character, one always late to the party and, despite her intellectual ambition, never able to spot the signs of change or danger in the city. In 1980, for example, she judges major events of the era, like the nascent drug epidemic, by using decade-old libertarian standards of the radical left: "[. . .] I stated an opinion, drawing on the days in Milan, and on Mariarosa, for whom taking drugs was a cultivated form of release" (slc 168). Noting her friend's reaction ("I perceived the irritation she felt at that word, *release*, at my way of saying it, assigning it a positive value"; slc 168), Elena realizes she has distorted reality. Ineptitude exposes her to the whims of contingency. For example, only a sudden intuition saves her from failing to meet the deadline of her book and guarantees her success when, distraught over her private life, she disregards her commitments to her publishing house and submits *in extremis* an old manuscript of a novel she had written years before and never published (cf. 3.8).

The moment Elena's journey shifts from linear to circular—that is, the moment she returns home—the dynamic between those with power and those without it is turned on its head. The one who stayed has won; the one who left has lost. Elena, the one who left, lives in the falsehood of fictional tales, the blazonry of intellectuals. Lila says to her: "the sea, from up there"—from Elena's posh home in Via Tasso—is "[a] bit of color [. . .] closer [. . .] you notice that there's filth, mud, piss, polluted water. But you who read and write books like to tell lies, not the truth" (slc 131–32). Lila, the one who stayed, reinvents herself as an entrepreneur. In the archaic *rione*, she embarks on a groundbreaking experimental project, opening Basic Sight, the first computer programming center in Italy (cf. 7.5 and 7.6). Moreover, she transforms herself into a dazzling saint, a healer of every ill; in the very same neighborhood, an alternative to the muscle of the local *camorristi*—the Solaras.

In reality, in this contrast of gain and loss, of displacement and fixity, Elena and Lila come to define one another, and their extreme fixity "develops from a condition of estrangement" (Said 176). In fact, taking a closer look, we see that the opposition of exile and belonging that the two friends embody is continuously endangered, eroded, proved wrong, and dulled when their roles are reversed. Lila transforms into Elena, and Elena into Lila. Those who leave *are* those who stay, and vice versa. Elena abandons her posh home in Via Tasso and goes back to live in the *rione*, next to Lila, because only the *rione* and Lila promise her the "mania for reality" (slc 283) she needs to write her third novel, which she finally has the courage to set in Naples.

After the earthquake of November 1980 Lila finally discloses her condition of *smarginatura*, the constant risk of being over-whelmed by the dissolution of boundaries that give things their shape and reveal reality to be "molten," fluid *frantumaglia* (cf. 3.6). Even more than Elena, Lila is composed of jagged fragments, parts that can never be made whole in her lacerating struggle for emancipation. Noting the complex cultural geology of her life, she remarks: "Between my father's shoe repair shop and this office it's only a few meters, but it's as if they were at the North Pole and the South Pole" (slc 262). As central nuclei of Elena and Lila's dual apprenticeship, Naples and the *rione* amount to dark places of the soul, which the lives of the two protagonists transform, eschew, and carry over to other points on the Italian map and to other vertiginous points of modern history. For Elena: the student movement, the feminist movement, daily politics, her writing (her second novel depicts the *rione*, with clear metanarrative echoes of *My Brilliant Friend*), her public persona as an author, presentations of her book and feminist essay, her forays into conferences and publishing houses. For Lila: her experiences as a designer, entrepreneur, interior decorator, laborer, programmer, and, again, entrepreneur, only this time in the pioneering field of computer science.

The viewpoint from Naples and the *rione* frames this issue, determining the plot of the quartet even during the many parts of the story set in other cities. For example, we have seen (cf. 4.1) how Naples manages to breach the enclaves of the Normale and worm its way into Elena's dorm room, prompting on the one hand, via the news of Lila's vicissitudes, a sense of shame and inadequacy in her new intellectual and bourgeois life, and, on the other, leading to her first form of artistic expression (her autobiographical novel). But this contamination could extend to other stations along Elena's life journey: Florence, Genoa, Milan, Turin, Paris, Montpellier, and so on. The two protagonists' breathless shuttling in and out of Naples is a way of revising and renegotiating the image of the city and, as we'll see in the next section, the city's soundscape. When Ferrante refers to this urban space as "an extension of the body" (fr 65), when she underscores the point that "accounts are never closed" (65), when she affirms that for her "the model of urban involvement is Naples pressing in [. . .] and confusing [her]" (fr 142), she means to describe a sense of belonging at one with crucifying anxiety and flight. In this sense, the writer recounts a phenomenology of exile from Naples that, in reality, affects all those who, like Lila, never move away from the city: a rooted uprootedness that many Neapolitans can relate to.

In another subversion of this contrast, exile becomes disappearance. In reality it is Lila, not Elena, who, in the general mechanism of the narrative, escapes, mysteriously disappearing without a trace (cf. 6.8). Indeed, Elena reconstructs their story in order to fill the void left by her friend: her story is a spell to raise the dead. Furthermore, Lila will never be left out of the presumed language of exile, i.e., an ability to speak Italian well. She, not Elena or Nino, is the bilingual one, for she maintains a natural, not alienated, relationship with the two universes represented by Neapolitan and Italian (cf. 5.5). This magical ability of inclusion seems to disprove the traditional distinctions between dialect and Italian, and yet the same contrast denotes the significant barrier that the two friends—and with them an entire Italian world between the 1950s and '60s—manage to surmount with difficulty. The language of the quartet is the story of that courageous endeavor.

2. A Dialectical Tide

The image of Naples is never just visual but also auditory (Alfano G. 143). In the film adaptation of *Troubling Love*, director Mario Martone makes the odd decision to place the house that Amalia moves into after separating from her husband not in an ordinary backstreet (as one would have surmised from the novel) but in a *palazzo* whose windows overlook the interior of Galleria Umberto I. Commenting on the screenplay, Ferrante writes to the director that she appreciated "the image of Delia looking out into the Galleria and hit by the echo of voices in dialect" (fr 33). In *The Days of Abandonment*, the barrage of memories of the *poverella* (cf. 3.3) is compounded by the female voices that reemerge from the past, from the childhood courtyard and the windows of the popular building, to broadcast the abandoned woman's suicide ("The news ran from one window to the next, from floor to floor"; doa 52). In *The Lost Daughter*, a group of Neapolitans in whom Leda recognizes the plebian signs of her own family ("the same jokes, the same sentimentality, the same rage"; ld 18) lopes along the beach in a *sonorous* as much as bodily jumble: "[. . .] their laughter rang out noisily. They called each other by name with drawn-out cries, hurled exclamatory or conspiratorial comments, at times quarreled" (ld 17–18). In *The Story of the Lost Child*, Elena writes and rewrites her third book, a novel about Naples, inserting and extracting dialect in different versions of the story. Writing for her is a protective shell, a diaphragm separating her from reality: "I was in the neighborhood and yet safe in that role, within that setting" (slc 273). In the final pages of the quartet, Pasquale recalls the many shapes Lila had assumed in public life ("Ah, Lila the shoemaker, Lila who imitated Kennedy's wife, Lila the artist and designer, Lila the worker, Lila the programmer"), and goes on to say she is "always in the same place and always out of place" (slc 471).

Key to identifying the continuity between these examples is this last quotation, in which Pasquale defines Elena's friend as a figure split between interior and exterior, between belonging and exile. The protagonists of Ferrante's other works have this exact thing in common: they carry everything "all inside" themselves (as Leda says; ld 87) and must therefore be external to everything, as Elena is. She returns to live in the *rione* that "does not recognize, that reduces and debases, and on occasion injures" (La Capria), and rewrites her novel there, tirelessly measuring out the doses of dialect she herself feels excluded from, thanks to the "setting" of her writing, to the onslaught of voices. Language occupies a space defined above all by the position of these protagonists' borders. Even writing at a (geographic and symbolic) distance from Naples, in a national language and space they have fought hard to conquer, these women carry inside them, along with their plebian origins, a "dialectical tide" (fr 35), an urban theater of disorderly and violent gestures, the noise of city traffic and voices shouted or slurred, which speak to them and against which they defend themselves with social redemption and the continuous intermingling of their destinies.

In *Troubling Love* the obscene Neapolitan phrase that Delia hears spoken, first by her mother over the phone, just hours before her disappearance, and later by one of Amalia's old suitors on the street, causes her to revert to dialect, makes her heart race, and triggers in her "an ugly homicidal impulse" (tl 20).

Immediately in Ferrante's work dialect is set on a lower level, in the basement of *Troubling Love*, the cellar of *The Neapolitan Novels*, and the cave of *Frantumaglia* (cf. 3.3). Like these spaces, dialect is connected to the parameters of the disgusting (Milkova[2] 98), which Delia synthesizes, juxtaposing sound with taste, when she defines the obscene phrase as "a soft river of sound that involved me, my sisters, my mother in a concoction of semen, saliva, feces, urine, in every possible orifice" (tl 19). Dialect harkens back to a psychologically and culturally oppressive universe, a prelinguistic, barbaric phase of amputated words "[. . .] ending in consonants, as if the final vowel had been thrown into an abyss and the rest of the word were whining mutely in displeasure" (tl 94). Neapolitan is signaled by an abrupt change of tone, when the mask of mannerly Italian is torn off and the language becomes explicitly violent. It is this "tone" that Delia perceives and recognizes when, in the Vossi sisters' shop (cf. 4.7), the owner who turns out to be her childhood friend expresses his impatience by switching from Italian to an aggressive Neapolitan: "Immediately afterward he would begin to push me harder and then to strike me, without regard to whether I was a man or a woman" (tl 61).

In short, the soundscape of dialect forms the basis of people's innermost fears and anxieties (Wehling-Giorgi[3] 5). The mother tongue is enfolded in the mother, an archive of socio-anthropological roots that takes possession of an individual and throws her into a state of abjection, but that refuses to be itself possessed and therefore managed. Like the long line of ancestors in the cave (cf. 3.3.), the mother tongue "is embedded in a history that is centuries-old, goes beyond the three-generational model of familiar memory." Ferrante's positing of Neapolitan as a language of disgust, violence, and phobia, is profoundly innovative given that dialect is conventionally portrayed as the idiom of affection and sentiment (Benedetti[1] 179, Lucamante[2] 86). Comparing Ferrante to other Neapolitan writers (Wanda Marasco, Giuseppe Montesano, Domenico Starnone), one notices, once again, the equivalence drawn between Naples as a landscape and a soundscape, both crowded with colliding bodies, plagued by "the voices of others" that the narrators-protagonists of a group of significant novels must fulfill a series of "moves and counter-moves to reposition." "To descend, to re-ascend, to re-cross, to escape, are all the possible moves to be made in an urban space" (De Caprio). In fact, Delia's descent into the spatial and temporal depths of the city-labyrinth serves to decode that obscene phrase. As with the invisible truth for Oedipus, only here proclaimed by the warp and weft of events, the mysterious words are Delia's own, spoken when she is a little girl: they form the linchpin of the secret separating her from her mother that she will rediscover at the end of her journey as she climbs back up out of the basement. Dialect is thus presented as a paradoxical space: while on the one hand it is an abjection to exorcise, a threat to evade, a sin to expiate, it is also a "repository for primary experiences," the one sound that can restore depth to time and truth to the mystery.

Neapolitan keeps its jewels hidden. "[M]y characters," Ferrante says, "always have the impression that Neapolitan is hostile and holds secrets that will never be able to enter completely into Italian" (fr 325–26). The cellar of time "resounds with the evil that [. . .] was done," but the voice of the past does not echo in this giant subterranean "shell" until Delia manages to reenter and recognize it as her own origin (Alfano G. 146). Retracing the steps of all her protagonists, Ferrante establishes an important link between language and *smarginatura*: "Then something breaks and these women's boundaries dissolve, and the language with which they are attempting to say something about themselves also is loosed, unbounded" (fr 336). On the basis of the cyclical movement and loss of dialect, there follows or is connected "a kind of self-governing ability" expressed in the return to a "detached language" (cf. 1.3). Hence the relationship between Italian and dialect is likened to a scuba diver's process of immersion and decompression: a strategy to keep these women characters from "falling into depression, into self-degeneration, or into dangerous feelings of revenge, aimed at themselves or at others" (336). Once again, the narrative arc travels from acoustic *frantumaglia* (not coincidentally, a neologism from Neapolitan) to expressive surveillance (cf. 3.6 and 3.7).

3. Narrating Neapolitan

From *Troubling Love* to *The Neapolitan Novels*, Ferrante adopts an apparently neutral Italian and a middle register, apparently stripping away the vividness of dialect while invoking, to varying degrees, *the tale* of dialect (fer[4]). As with the representation of space (cf. 4.9), this omission, rather than neutralizing Neapolitan, intensifies it, so that readers perceive Neapolitan as a pervasive, ghostly presence. All literary imitations of dialect must first reckon with the psychic and social image of this spoken language. Neapolitan has a long literary and theatrical tradition, but today its explicit use is fitted either to the pathetic register of the love song, the comic register of the euphoric mask, and the pulp register of crime fiction, or else to a creative and experimental pursuit of an ironic, meta-reflexive, twice-removed Neapolitan. The explicit uses of Neapolitan that lead to mannerism and stereotypes are clearly incompatible with Ferrante's ambitions, yet the writer also finds unviable those ironic and experimental approaches now prevalent in a wide variety of theatrical, literary, and musical pursuits in Naples. Though the results vary, qualitatively and ethically speaking, all four immediately mimetic expressive forms fall short of the focus of Ferrante's aim: the need for a woman to narrate the violence fueled by dialect—a woman whose bilingual and socially hybrid voice can, as it shuttles back and forth between, in, and out of Naples and other Italian places, simultaneously register and exorcise the mixture of rage, fear, anxiety, and shame of female and Neapolitan subalternity.

Filtering out dialect, making it implicit, Elena's narration immediately acquires a squint-eyed, fluctuating perspective: viscerally linked to the *rione* and its "language of violence" (tlts 174) by a kind of positivism of family heritage, but also distant, alien; as animated by her inextricable roots as by her phobic need to flee. What Leda says in *The Lost Daughter* extends to all the author's protagonists: "Languages [. . .] have a secret venom that every so often foams up and for which there is no antidote" (ld 20). But we can understand these women's relationships to dialect by applying the violent metaphor that Leda uses to describe her own flight from Naples. "I had run away," she says, "like a burn victim who, screaming, tears off the burned skin, believing that she is tearing off the burning itself" (ld 88). Here, the language/city is both the membrane that houses the "I" and the painful white-hot mark that brands her.

In order to make this borderline position and open-ended reckoning emerge, one of Ferrante's most frequent and widely developed techniques is to signal, through direct or indirect speech, that the bilingual character on whom the narrative voice is focusing at that moment is speaking in dialect or in Italian, reaffirming or breaking with her own habits of speech in that specific context. The writing is studded with these "metalinguistic insertions" (Librandi)—produced by labeling verbs associated with communication as "in dialect" or "in Italian"—that serve to shape the quality and position of these hybrid, bilingual voices:

> I regained my balance and pulled myself free, shouting, to my own amazement, insults in dialect. (tl 67)

> I pronounced an ugly obscenity in my dialect, and with such an angry snap in my voice that I was afraid the children had heard me. (doa 38)

> [. . .] to herself [Nina] cried in dialect I have to go, and to me in Italian: I don't want to see you anymore, I don't want anything from you [. . .]. (ld 139)

> Finally [Nino] said, in school Italian: "When we grow up I want to marry you." (mbf 58)

I went so far as to say [to Stefano] pompously, in Italian, that I would do everything possible to help them to be happy. (snn 86)

[. . .] [Lila] answered unwillingly, in dialect or in an ugly Italian that imitated dialect patterns. (tlts 191)

[Lila] looked me straight in the eye and revealed, in curt phrases, in Italian, that Nino had never left his wife. (slc 93)

But metalinguistic insertions often recur—in the quartet especially—to signal the emotional tone with which someone who only speaks dialect communicates their thoughts in Neapolitan:

Gigliola said to me rancorously, in dialect, "Now your friend is acting like a princess. But does Stefano know that when Marcello went to her house she gave him a blow job every night?" (mbf 271)

The whole time, even when he spoke of his own brutality, [Stefano] used a dialect full of feeling, defenseless, like the language of certain songs. (snn 86)

The guard was yelling at the oldest boy, the fat one, shouting at him in dialect: You cross that line, cross it, shit, then you're entering private property without permission and I'll shoot. (tlts 131–32)

I recognized in the background Marcello's thick voice, loaded with dialect [. . .]. (slc 202)

In the second example given above, Ferrante repudiates the stereotypical melodiousness of *napoletanità* through her use of a metalinguistic discourse. This is in fact the one instance of the language's sonorousness, and this "dialect full of feeling, defenseless, like the language of certain songs" is employed by Stefano to convince Elena that he loves Lila. The language is shown to be sneaky, a masquerade of vulnerable sincerity, here used by a male figure who is in fact violent to his core. The narrative not only refers to what the characters say but also to how they say it, thereby highlighting social and gender inequalities and the stress they cause.

"Narrating" Neapolitan, instead of directly transcribing it, forces readers to think through dialect, rather than experience it firsthand. These metalinguistic interruptions invite readers to interpret not only the content of what is being said, but the way in which it is filtered through the Italian language. The first part of the quartet in particular (from *My Brilliant Friend* to *The Story of a New Name*) is a "portrait of the consequences of the Italian language's having gained a toehold in the dialect-speaking communities and of how its presence has accelerated our process of Italianization" (Villarini 197). The *rione* represents the typical state of the language during the 1950s and '60s, when the large majority of dialect speakers were not necessarily familiar with the Italian language or else seldom came across it (perhaps during their early education, or while watching television). That is why, during those two decades, bilingual people, like Elena, Lila, Nino, and Donato Sarratore, are an exception in Italy. Just as there is a geographic divide between bourgeois Naples and the outskirts (cf. 4.2), there are sharp distinctions between the two languages in the quartet, because every "middle way" automatically excludes one or another community, producing "a false dialect that [is] a sort of trivialized Italian" (fr 365). Elena often associates this mixed plebian language with frustration and shame:

> Pasquale even tried to answer in Italian but he gave up. (mbf 171)

> [My brothers] tried to speak to me in Italian and often corrected their own mistakes, ashamed. (snn 377)

> [My father] forgot his labored Italian and began to tell in dialect witty stories about his fellow employees. (tlts 92)

[H]e was making an effort to speak in Italian and the difficult language was coming to him with a foreign accent. (slc 250)

During this period in history, Italian inevitably becomes a symbol of social privilege (Cavanaugh 51). On the one hand, it signals a rhetorical advantage. On the other, it estranges those few people who can speak it. In the quartet the family dynamic is the measuring rod of this process, which creates hierarchies and rifts, gratifying Elena's matrophobia, for one (cf. 3.2 and 3.3). When she returns to her family in 1967, freshly graduated from the prestigious Scuola Normale di Pisa, she realizes that her fluency with the language is a check against her mother's usual intrusiveness:

> She tried to contain her disapproval, maybe she didn't even feel capable of communicating it to me. Language itself, in fact, had become a mark of alienation. I expressed myself in a way that was too complex for her, although I made an effort to speak in dialect, and when I realized that and simplified the sentences, the simplification made them unnatural and therefore confusing. (snn 437)

Then again, four years earlier, when Elena tells her family *in Italian* that she is going to take the exam for the Normale, "as if it were not a subject that could be reduced to dialect," their inevitable discomfort makes her feel like "a stranger who [has] come to visit at an inconvenient time" (snn 325). The few bilingual speakers in the *rione* can use this mechanism of exclusion (Villarini 195) to pull rank (though not always successfully). An example of this can be seen once again in the mother-daughter relationship. After Lila's wedding, Immacolata hits Elena for going off with Antonio, because the boy's poverty could compromise Elena's social ascent. It is interesting to note the link between the linguistic context and the psychic: the mother puts her daughter in a double bind, in "the contradictions of inheritance"(Bourdieu[1]) typical of the popular world, where gaining independence and speaking Italian is seen as a betrayal of one's origins, yet not emancipating oneself disappoints the mother's expectations that her daughter will better her lot (Maksimowicz 220). Elena reacts to being hit by straining to use perfect—if shouted—Italian "with bitter joy." Elena's manner of speaking makes the content of her speech more powerful, as she blames her mother for having destroyed the one thing she needs to study—her glasses. Immacolata suddenly stays her hand:

> My glasses flew to the floor and immediately I shouted with bitter joy, and not a hint of dialect, "See what you've done? You've broken my glasses and now because of you I can't study, I'm not going to school anymore."
> My mother froze, even the hand she had struck me with remained still in the air, like the blade of an axe. (snn 28)

How language functions to exclude others is especially well illustrated by a three-way conversation during Elena's adolescence, in the course of which she switches from dialect to Italian in order to impress Lila and make her understand that she is not like Carmela (Villarini 196). From that moment on, the two friends dip in and out of Italian, engaging and then excluding the third person from the conversation, whom they reduce to a "pure and simple listener." The friends' polyphony makes room for a linguistic space, one they can finally inhabit, "well-crafted words" that, beginning with the photo romance, illuminated her "heart and mind" as never before in school:

> "Why do you say no?" Lila asked me in dialect.
> I answered unexpectedly in proper Italian, to make an impression, to let her understand that, even if I spent my time talking about boyfriends, I wasn't to be treated like Carmela.
> "Because I'm not sure of my feelings."
> It was a phrase I had learned from reading *Sogno* and Lila seemed struck by it. As if it were one of those contests in elementary school, we began to speak in the language of comics and books, which reduced Carmela to pure and simple listener. Those moments lighted my heart and my head: she and I and all

those well-crafted words. In middle school nothing like that ever happened, not with classmates or with teachers; it was wonderful. [. . .] And so, returning suddenly to dialect, [Lila] advised me to become Gino's girlfriend but on the condition that all summer he agree to buy ice cream for me, her, and Carmela. (mbf 103)

There is however a significant and frequent exception to the rule. Where power (economic and symbolic) and sex are concerned, the method of exclusion breaks down. Two years later, when Elena responds in Italian to the arrogant courtship of the Solara brothers, Marcello, sitting in his 1100—a symbol of wealth in the late 1950s—reads her code-switching as a sign of flirtation and therefore of her availability (the episode will be returned to, with significant twists, at the close of the quartet, right after and right before the death of the two Solara brothers; slc 365–66 and 375):

I shouldn't have but I did. Instead of going straight ahead [. . .] I turned and, out of a need to feel attractive and lucky and on the verge of going to the rich people's school, where I would likely find boys with cars much nicer than the Solaras', said, in Italian:
"Thank you, but we can't."
Marcello reached out a hand. I saw that it was broad and short, although he was a tall, well-made young man. The five fingers passed through the window and grabbed me by the wrist [. . .]. Marcello's fingers around my wrist made my skin turn cold, and I pulled my arm away in disgust. (mbf 134–35)

4. A Latent *Napoletanità*

As we have seen, Ferrante breaks up the Italian language with metalinguistic interruptions and a dialect that is "silent and at the same time cumbersome" (Librandi). Particularly in the quartet, the neutral and seamless language of the family saga and generational novel has a dysphonic quality, an alternating voice, in addition to the previously analyzed metalinguistic tesserae and healthy dose of Neapolitan. Certain dialect words—almost exclusively vulgar—flare up "as if [to threaten]" the Italian (fr 234):

> As we left I heard Lila saying indignantly to Enzo, in the thickest dialect, "He touched me, did you see: me, that shit [*chillu stronz*]. Luckily Rino wasn't there. If he does it again, he's dead." (mbf 152)

> Nino didn't like [Pasolini], he twisted his mouth, said, "He's a fairy [*ricchione*], all he does is make a lot of noise" [. . .]. (snn 358)

> My brothers—[my mother] cried—had had to beat up the butcher's sons, who had called me a whore [*zoccola*] [. . .]. (tlts 89)

> On the list [Alfonso] put his brother Stefano (he laughed; *he fucks my wife only to demonstrate that we're not all fags* [ricchioni] *in the family*) [. . .]. (slc 213)

Ferrante always performs a careful balancing act. On the one hand she avoids filling the page with too much Neapolitan, and on the other never completely muffles the sound of dialect. It buzzes just beneath the surface, as if it were a serious threat poised to emerge and transform, where appropriate, the background noise into a voice both aggressive and coarse.

Let's examine two cases in which the tone of this voice surfaces. When, in 1959, the group of friends from the *rione* find themselves on Via Chiaia and realize that they have trespassed beyond the borders of their ghetto and onto the gated grounds of the bourgeoisie, Elena transcribes a derogatory joke in dialect about the shoes of a sophisticated girl ("*Perché, song' scarp' chelle?*" [What, those are shoes?"] mbf 193). Very rarely is an entire Neapolitan phrase brought over, for reasons linked to the narrative strategy of the quartet. This "long" quotation in dialect signals that the mood among the group of friends is growing increasingly tense and prepares the reader for the brawl to come (cf. 4.2).

Even when we encounter "a crescendo of obscenities in dialect" and sexual abuse in direct speech, Neapolitan is filtered out. The following scene takes place during Lila's days working at the factory. In the midst of union negotiations with Soccavo—the factory owner—Michele Solara emerges as the company's real owner and engages Lila in a highly tense one-on-one. At one point, the young *camorrista* loses his cool:

> [Michele] turned toward Lila with a jolt of impatience and said emphatically, in a crescendo of obscenities in dialect: "But with her it's difficult, it's not so easy to kiss her off. And yet you see what she looks like, she has small eyes, small tits, a small ass, she's just a broomstick. With someone like that what can you do, you can't even get it up. But an instant is enough, a single instant: you look at her and you want to fuck her. (tlts 169)

In another example, the transcribed obscenity intrudes on the interior monologue of a bilingual character. In 1976 Elena, now Nino's lover, fantasizes about confronting his wife Eleonora. Here Elena's inner voice becomes "a turmoil," mixing "Italian and words from childhood," because, as Elena herself recognizes, thanks to her jealousy, "[another] me wanted to rise up from the depths, where she had been buried under a crust of meekness":

> I don't know how long I stayed beside the phone. I was filled with hatred, my head was spinning with phrases like: Yes, come, come right now, bitch, it's just what I'd expect, where the fuck are you from, Via Tasso, Via Filangieri, Via Crispi, the Santarella, and you're angry with me, you piece of garbage ['*sta cessa*], you stinking nonentity ['*sta loffa*], you don't know who you're dealing with, you are nothing [*mappìna*]. (tlts 407)

Another interesting form of latent *napoletanità* is the para-dialectical nature of certain expressions, arrived at through concealed Neapolitan insertions (the original expressions appear in brackets in the following examples from *Those Who Leave and Those Who Stay*):

> How many [. . .] had disappeared from the face of the earth because of illness, because their nervous systems [*la nervatura*] had been unable to endure the sandpaper of torments [. . .]. (tlts 24)

> Lila burst out laughing, she returned to dialect: "The last time I went to a doctor he sent me to the beach and it brought me a lot of grief [*ho passato un sacco di guai*]. (tlts 192–93)

> [Lila] continued almost without a pause, in a low voice so as not to wake the baby: [. . .] my mind's no help to me [*ho la testa che non mi aiuta*] [. . .]. (tlts 104)

> I ventured:
> "Maybe the two of you have to impose some order: Lina shouldn't get overtired [*non può esagerare con la fatica*]." (tlts 300)

In the context of this repertoire of latent *napoletanità*, the use of the popular term *"cesso"* (for toilet, i.e., bathroom) is particularly significant:

> I went to the bathroom[*cesso*] to see what was wrong and discovered that my underpants were stained with blood (mbf 93)

> Then [Lila] called, turning to the door of the bathroom [*cesso*]: "Come, Nino, you can come out, it's Lenuccia." (snn 330)

> [. . .] [My mother] hid in the bathroom, and when they urged her tactfully [. . .] she responded: he answered inevitably: [. . .] what do you want, why don't you leave me in peace in the bathroom [*cesso*], at least. (slc 150)

> [Nino] woke up—at a certain point the words emerged in dialect—he found Silvana in the bathroom [*cesso*], and even before peeing he pulled up her skirt and stuck it in. (slc 330)

*

In various circumstances *cesso* is chosen over the neutral *bagno* (the more commonly used term for bathroom throughout the quartet, it is deployed along with *cesso* in the third example above), whether in relation to a bilingual speaker, such as Lila (in the second example) or Elena (in the first and fourth examples), or in relation to someone who only speaks dialect, such as Elena's mother (in the third example). The use of *cesso* by bilingual speakers like the narrator signals the emergence of the popular world and its resistance to the neutral bourgeois language telling the story. When it is used by those who only speak dialect, it signals an attention to the spoken word of the underclass (as in the third example, spoken by Immacolata). The second example is particularly significant because *cesso* here is galling—as is the later appearance of the hotly fought over Nino—with respect to the affectionate scene that precedes it. Indeed, Lila has just heard of Elena's acceptance to the Normale and welcomes the news with a display of deep feeling ("She embraced me warmly, she kissed me on both cheeks, her eyes filled with tears, she repeated, 'I'm really happy'"; snn 330).

In certain cases, dialect emerges from a magmatic nucleus that tends to dissolve the Italian through the translation of Neapolitan intonation. Though they appear rather infrequently, these inchoate forms acquire meaning in the soundscape that Ferrante creates because they capture best the tone of melodrama. Melodrama is not an extemporaneous feature of the quartet but an intrinsic part of a conscious and meta-reflexive recycling of underclass repertoire, by which the Neapolitan backdrop is included while its boundaries are dissolved (cf. 1.1. and 1.2). To this realm of linguistic *smarginatura*, conveyed by a very interesting weave of indirect, free indirect, and direct speech, we can ascribe the two following examples, two angry outbursts rendered, as Nicola

Lagioia says, "magisterially" (Lagioia 374). The first is Antonio's jealous dust-up with Elena, right after the lunch at Lila's wedding:

> He threw away the cigarette, grabbed me by the wrist with a barely controlled force and cried—a cry locked in his throat—that he was there for me, only for me, that it was I who had told him to stay near me in the church and at the celebration, yes, I, and you made me swear, he gasped, swear, you said, that you won't ever leave me alone, and so I had a suit made, and I'm deep in debt [. . .], and to please you, to do as you asked, I didn't spend even a minute with my mother or my sisters and brothers: and what is my reward, my reward is that you treat me like shit, you talk the whole time to the poet's son and humiliate me in front of my friends, you make me look ridiculous, because to you I'm no one, because you're so educated and I'm not, because I don't understand the things you say, and it's true, it's very true that I don't understand you, but God damn it, Lenù, look at me, look me in the face: you think you can order me around, you think I'm not capable of saying That's enough, and yet you're wrong, you know everything, but you don't know that if you go out of that door with me now, if now I tell you O.K. and we go out, but then I discover that you see that jerk Nino Sarratore at school, and who knows where else, I'll kill you, Lenù, so think about it, leave me here this minute, he said in despair, leave me, because it's better for you, and meanwhile he looked at me, his eyes red and very large, and uttered the words with his mouth wide open, shouting at me without shouting, his nostrils flaring, black, and in his face such suffering that I thought maybe he's hurting himself inside, because the words, shouted in his throat like that, in his chest, but without exploding in the air, are like bits of sharp iron piercing his lungs and his pharynx. (snn 22–23)

In the second example, we observe instead the linguistic *smarginatura* of maternal rage during one of Immacolata's outbursts. In the troubled young couple's bourgeois apartment in Florence and with Pietro present, Immacolata tries in vain to stop Elena from throwing away her marriage:

She slapped me violently, shouting nonstop: Shut up, you whore, shut up, shut up. And she tried to grab me by the hair, she cried that she couldn't stand it any longer, that it wasn't possible that I, *I*, should want to ruin my life, running after Sarratore's son, who was worse, much worse, than that man of shit who was his father. Once, she cried, I thought it was your friend Lina leading you on this evil course, but I was wrong, you, *you*, are the shameless one; without you, she's become a fine person. Damn me that I didn't break your legs when you were a child. You have a husband of gold who makes you a lady in this beautiful city, who loves you, who has given you two daughters, and you repay him like this, bitch? Come here, I gave birth to you and I'll kill you [. . .] Her voice choked, angry and at the same time truly grieved, eyes staring, she gasped: You're not my child anymore, he's my child, him, not even your father wants you anymore, not even your siblings; Sarratore's son is bound to stick you with the clap and syphilis, what did I do wrong to come to a day like this, oh God, oh God, God, I want to die this minute, I want to die now. (slc 63–5)

Another deluge of Neapolitan volatility largely narrated in Italian occurs during the clash between Lila and Stefano, right after their wedding, when, enraged and desperate, Lila remonstrates him for having betrayed her by giving Marcello Solara the shoes she designed (cf. 4.2):

Stefano let her go on, but when she tried again to open the door and escape he said to her coldly, Calm down. Lila turned suddenly: [. . .] calm down when all three had treated her like an old rag, a rag for wiping up the floor. I don't want to calm down, she shouted, you piece of shit, take me home right now, repeat what you just said in front of those two other shit men. And only when she uttered that expression in dialect, shit men, *uommen'e mmerd*, did she notice that she had broken the barrier of her husband's measured tones. A second afterward Stefano struck her in the face with his strong hand, a violent slap that seemed to her an explosion of truth. (snn 33)

In the first and third examples, we see how the *smarginatura* of melodrama operates on a linguistic level: a spontaneous and impulsive outpouring is immediately countered by a meta-discursive aside that reveals Lila and Elena's doubleness. On the one hand, both are swept up in the emotion of the scene, while on the other they mentally decode the impact their language has on their interlocutors. In the last example Lila senses that she has crossed a line by calling Stefano and his kind a particular "expression in dialect" (*"uommen' e mmerd"*). Unusually, the insult recurs twice in quick succession: first in Italian and then in Neapolitan (here set off, unusually, by italics) "to underscore that it is separate from the neutral language of the narration" (Librandi). In the previous example, Elena instead registers that Antonio loses control not only because he is jealous but because Elena has been putting on airs by employing Italian, a vocabulary and syntax impenetrable to him: "He heard scarcely any dialect in my voice, he noted the long sentence, the subjunctives, and he lost his temper" (snn 22).

5. A Foreign Language

Elena's first year of middle school concludes with her narrow promotion to the next grade and a meeting between her teacher and mother regarding the uncertainty of her future. During their conversation, which Elena witnesses, the girl feels a "double humiliation":

> [. . .] I was ashamed because I hadn't done as well as I had in elementary school, and I was ashamed of the difference between the harmonious, modestly dressed figure of the teacher, between her Italian that slightly resembled that of the *Iliad*, and the misshapen figure of my mother, her old shoes, her dull hair, the dialect bent into an ungrammatical Italian. (mbf 93)

The Italian that "slightly resembled that of the *Iliad*" is—we can reasonably infer—a refined and sophisticated language with poetic overtones, like that of Vincenzo Monti's 1825 neo-classical translation into hendecasyllables of the Greek poem (to which, in all likelihood, Elena is alluding). The contrast between teacher and mother is made chillingly stark by the presence of Italian, which enters into the scene as both a living language and an archaic foreign language (or a classic one; from the perspective of an adolescent during the 1950s, the two are interchangeable). This national language stands in stark contrast to the mother's dialect "bent into an ungrammatical Italian." Their polar opposite languages mirror their physical attributes: the "harmonious" figure versus the "misshapen"; the teacher's respectable dress versus "old shoes, [. . .] dull hair."

Once again, the quartet turns out to be an inquiry into the sociolinguistic history of Italy (cf. 5.3). In the 1950s, the teacher's bookish Italian is not an eccentric or isolated detail but a typical feature of a certain type of standard education (Villarini 199). Due to the relatively recent formation of a national language in Italy and the concurrent "static" of dialects, during this time period the spoken Italian cultivated by the middle class still had no firm models and historical precedents to refer to (De Mauro). That is why the language of the middle class developed not out of concrete social customs but from an abstract process; unlike the immediate forms of dialogue and daily exchange, this spoken language drew from a literary tradition that was necessarily obsolete (from the nineteenth century translation of a major classic, for example). While this bookish register is only somewhat extraneous to the lived experience of a middle-class teacher, it is absolutely unrelated to those who speak dialect, even to the few bilinguals such as Elena. There, standard Italian becomes more than ever useless during moments of heightened tension. In fact, since standard Italian is perceived as a foreign language, it exposes the speaker to the risk of losing control, a risk that is unacceptable in a situation in which one should always practice self-discipline. This happens when Lila, looking radiant, having gained a new status as a young bride, enters the crowded Bar Solara shortly after her honeymoon and dazzles Marcello, who has had to stop pursuing her:

> The verbal exchanges that followed were all in dialect, as if tension prevented any engagement with the laborious filters of Italian pronunciation, vocabulary, syntax.
> "What would you like?"
> "A dozen pastries."
> Michele shouted at Gigliola, this time with a slight hint of sarcasm:
> "Twelve pastries for Signora Carracci." (snn 73–74)

It makes total sense that, for Elena, the Italian she learns at school is "a mask of self-possession" (snn 153) "worn so well that it was *almost* a face" (402). It is a "disguise" that she dons, erecting a barrier that goes beyond inchoate origins: a carefully and artificially crafted barrier built with parroted literary passages and the highfalutin style of scholarly translations and cultured speakers. Rote imitation is the prominent feature of Elena's learning:

> [. . .] I went over my lessons again, in panic, frantically pasting strange languages into my head, tones different from those used in the neighborhood. (mbf 157)

> [. . .] I would articulate, in good Italian, statements I had memorized from Professor Galiani's books and newspapers. (snn 133)

The physical bearing of this language is inspired by dramatic recitation, the pretense of engagement:

> I would mention, let's say, "the atrocious reality of the Nazi extermination camps," or "what men were able to do and what they can do today as well," or "the atomic threat and the obligation to peace [. . .]." (snn 133)

> I adopted a friendly demeanor that I had never considered

myself capable of, I immediately engaged in casual conversation, I came out with a fine, cultured Italian that didn't feel artificial, like the language I used at school. (snn 156)

In a couple of hours I wrote an essay on the role of Nature in the poetry of Giacomo Leopardi, putting in [. . .] finely written reworkings from the textbook of Italian literary history. (snn 323)

The sentences came easily, I uttered them with an inspired cadence. (snn 324)

Those who gain emancipation by introjecting Italian's superiority over dialect perpetuate a cycle of violence, taking revenge on those even more dominated than themselves: people who only speak dialect. Such is the case when Elena intervenes in the decision about Lila's wedding dress. Using polished Italian studded with "premises in the confident voice of someone who knows clearly where he wishes to end up" ("a technique I had learned in school"), she convinces Pinuccia and her mother (her friend's future sister and mother-in-law) to abandon their first choice. Immediately after, Lila pulls Elena aside and, having sensed the manipulative quality of her habits of speech, says fiercely: "You learn this in school? [. . .] To use words to con people" (mbf 294). The fine, "vigilant Italian" (snn 195) with which Elena loves to converse with Nino is generated by stifling her origins, the plebian dialect that is, yes, the abjection required to guard against the national language.

Even before she moves to Pisa and senses that the South is cut off from the rest of Italy, the contrast between school and the *rione* forces Elena to come to terms with a series of binary oppositions. The clash between the civilized world of Italian and the primitive world of dialect is the proving ground for conflicts between nationalism and localism, progress and regression, North and South: conflicts broadly applicable to various situations in the West that helped inspire the idealization of progress in the years after World War II (Love 71).

Elena finds herself torn between these two poles and, because she is a hybrid, she experiences "deterritorialization" (Deleuze and Guattari 19), a double nomadism: she is a foreign speaker of a national language that is itself alien to the majority of the country that still speaks dialect. As is clearly demonstrated by the speech habits of Alfonso, who outside of school only speaks Neapolitan, dialect precludes not only arguing but thinking about more complex concepts:

> [W]hile in school [Alfonso] used a good Italian; when it was just the two of us he never abandoned dialect, and in dialect it was hard to discuss the corruption of earthly justice, as it could be seen during the lunch at the house of Don Rodrigo, or the relations between God, the Holy Spirit, and Jesus, who, although they were a single person, when they were divided in three, I thought, necessarily had to have a hierarchy, and then who came first, who last? (mbf 260)

Just as when the group of friends from the *rione* enter the upscale environs of Naples (cf. 4.2), dialect here signals an insurmountable divide and gives rise to a "humiliating difference" (mbf 192).

But exclusion is progressive: the more one pursues an education, the more one must reckon with the structural limitations of her dialect origins and her extremely rhetorical spoken Italian. When Elena attends the Normale in the early 1960s, she is repeatedly forced to confront an elite national student body selected on the basis of a very challenging entrance exam—not only in the classroom but in her day-to-day life at the college. In this regionally diverse environment unified by excellent spoken Italian, Elena's artificial language interwoven with bits of dialect has a touch of the absurd: "I immediately realized I spoke a bookish Italian that at times was almost absurd, especially when, right in the middle of a much too carefully composed sentence, I needed a word and transformed a dialect word into Italian to fill the gap" (snn 332). We can measure the cost of this language, born of self-repression, if we compare it with that of Lila. One of the many signs of her brilliance—or at least the ghostly representation of it provided by Elena—is in fact her language: "[. . .] she spoke in dialect like the rest of us but, when necessary, came out with a bookish Italian, using words like 'accustomed,' 'luxuriant,' 'willingly'" (mbf 48). Vivid, vibrant, inflected with the versatility of Neapolitan but cleansed of any dialectical seepage, Lila's Italian is the seat of her soul. Her language isn't animated by shame about her origins ("Lila was from the proletariat but rejected any deliverance"; slc 403) and, because she is pulled out of school, will remain unaffected by the discipline of a bourgeois education.

6. Gains and Losses

The striking contrast between the descriptions of the middle school teacher and Immacolata (cf. 5.5.) puts the professor in a pantheon of cultural gatekeepers whom Elena elevates to the status of ideal mothers, women invested with the job of rescuing her from her real mother's authority and cave (cf. 3.3). First among this category is Maestra Oliviero—whom Immacolata calls, not without reason, an "imbecile [who] always thought she was more of a mother than I am" (snn 454). The pantheon also includes Elena's distinguished Italian teacher, Professor Galiani, as well as, finally, Pietro Airota's mother Adele. Before their marriage, during the period when the publication of Elena's novel coincides with her engagement to Pietro, Adele emerges as a protective figure, capable of promoting the book's release and, right after its publication, the public debates and events to further promote it. Elena constantly points out and imitates Adele's elegance "without pretension" (snn 408) ("I put on makeup, I fixed my hair, I

dressed according to the taste I had developed from Adele";
tlts 219). She calls her mother-in-law "a mother as mine had
never been" (tlts 26). But this adoption isn't born of affection.
At work here is more of an adoption of social customs, the itch
to be launched into a higher class. The qualities Elena admires
in Adele are in fact always connected to the latter's "social capital" (Bourdieu[2]), the privilege of the bourgeoisie to gain influ-
ence, achieve recognition and trust, and mobilize consensus
around their own pursuits:

> If she needed something, she [. . .] put together the chain
> that led to her goal. She knew how to ask in such a way that saying
> no was impossible. And she crossed ideological borders confi-
> dently, she respected no hierarchies [. . .], and she addressed all
> with cordial detachment, as if the favor she was about to ask she
> was in fact already doing for them. (tlts 182)

Yet this adoptive affiliation doesn't last long. Very soon
Elena clashes with the benevolent paternalism of her mother-
in-law, and of the entire Airota family, husband included,
which Elena herself first solicited:

> I also felt, just then, that in no way did my mother-in-law's cul-
> tivated conversation arise from a true need to exchange ideas with
> me [. . .] she liked saving me more than listening to me. (tlts 245)

On the other hand, even the relationship that Adele initiates with Elena is somehow opportunistic, since it is aimed at
controlling the young couple ("We lived now like that, amid
constant battles: he quarreled with his mother, he ended up
saying something that made me angry, I attacked him"; tlts
247). This triangular relationship is the last variant of rivalry that
Elena endures, and seeks out, with all the female figures who
introduce her to the world of culture. If for Maestra Oliviero she
fails to match up against Lila's brilliance, for Professor Galiani,
too, the brilliance of the autodidact is striking and sets in

motion a similar rivalry between the two friends. Significantly, the one professor who really recognizes Elena, the professor at the end of her high school graduation exam who suggests that she sit for the selection exam for the Normale, goes unnamed ("I never met her again, I don't even know her name, and yet I owe her a great deal"; snn 324) and is enshrined by a fairy-tale aura. The elderly teacher, who—the detail is emphasized—has "an accent [Elena doesn't] recognize, but anyway far from Neapolitan" and "freshly coiffed, pale-blue hair" (snn 323), seems like a mysterious vision of the blue fairy thought up by Lila years earlier (cf. 2.2 and 2.6).

Although the quartet devotes a lot of room to teachers—included for good reason in the index of characters under the section "Teachers"—and the two protagonists' rapport with educational institutions (just consider the depiction of elementary school in the first pages of *My Brilliant Friend* and later of Elena's life from middle school to the Normale), this narrative focus has a double significance. In the quartet, culture is in fact only partially represented as a repository of democratically shared consciousness, as an "ideology of education" (fr 371) and social mobility that was, in some ways, effectively achieved in the West up until the last few decades of the past century. The stress lies not only on what Elena gains by her social ascent, but on what she loses: losses that revolve around her constant sense of alienation, frustration and precariousness. These educators/Pygmalions may have transformed her life, yet clearly the primary object of Elena's desire—their recognition—remains largely out of reach.

In the narrative this unattainability not only depends on her ambivalence toward these ferry-women, but on the class limitations intrinsic to the cultural and educational institutions they are identified with (cf. 4.3). All these formative worlds perpetuate a form of "symbolic violence" (Bourdieu[3]) because they contribute, in indirect and oblique ways, to the persistence of one indelible mark: Elena's disadvantaged upbringing. As Ferrante points out, "[. . .] class origins cannot be erased, regardless of whether we climb up or down the sociocultural ladder. Even when our circumstances improve, it's like the color that inevitably rises to one's cheeks after a strong emotion" (fr 356). In Pisa, Elena tries to alter her "bookish" Italian (cf. 5.5.), submitting to a strict regimen that, however, has to do not with the language itself so much as a series of "practices" and "dispositions" (Bourdieu[4]) connected to the body and its conduct (Love 76):

> I learned to subdue my voice and gestures. [. . .] I kept my Neapolitan accent as much under control as possible. [. . .] When one of the girls appeared hostile, I would focus my attention on her, I was friendly yet restrained, obliging but tactful, and my attitude didn't change even when she softened and was the one who sought me out. [. . .] I approached the most aloof, the most severe, with serene smiles and an air of devotion. (snn 332–3)

Her physical reeducation does not involve learning vocabulary words or the rules of syntax but instead a series of implicit categories, invisible architectures of knowledge borrowed from the upper classes and their "habitus": a combination of recurring external practices, a "matrix of perceptions, appreciations, and actions" (Bourdieu[4] 72). Elena can do nothing but ape the manners of this bourgeois world, now and then choosing "the best disguise": "[. . .] the pleasure of reeducating my voice, my gestures, my way of dressing and walking, as if I were competing for the prize of best disguise" (snn 402). Symbolic violence presupposes that those subjected to it are somehow complicit, even when that violence takes the form of value judgments or standards that profoundly delegitimize and humiliate the subject. That happens to Elena who, when teased by another student at the Normale for her Neapolitan cadence, makes the servile choice to parody herself: "I felt wounded, but

I laughed, too, and gaily emphasized the dialectal accent as if I were the one making fun of myself" (snn 332).

Playing a part is a far cry from real assimilation. The habitus in fact presupposes an interiorization cemented in those public and family rituals that gradually mold individuals and mark them as belonging to this or that social class. Long before he has concluded his studies at the university, Pietro Airota already knows that his thesis will become a book, and he can explain to Elena that what one studies counts less than the method with which one studies (snn 406). Pietro is guided by a combination of practices he inherited from his family: his is, involuntarily, a habitus of the master. For her part, when Elena realizes that, despite being an excellent student, she doesn't have that "instinctive orientation," that overarching vision that would allow her to see "the map of prestige" (snn 403)—meaning the hierarchy of knowledge and intellectual superiority ("the names of the people who counted, the people to be admired and those to be despised"; snn 403)—she reckons with the fact that she did not assimilate middle class practices but rather those of the underclass world to which she belongs. This classist framework of knowledge troubles the false assumption of meritocracy by revealing that there is an inextricable link between one's achievements at school and one's family resources or lack thereof (read: social class).

Moreover, the practices of one's plebian origins can be disguised only to a certain extent. For example, when Elena is unjustly accused of stealing by a classmate, she reacts by violently slapping her accuser and unleashing a volley of insults in dialect. This sudden abandonment of propriety, and Italian, frightens the other students looking on: "I was classified as a person who always made the best of things, and my reaction disoriented them" (snn 333). Not having learned and cultivated Italian in an imitative and self-repressive manner within an educational institution (her competence is, from an early age, that of a creative autodidact, shorn of any feeling of inferiority; cf. 5.5.), Lila alone remains significantly estranged from the dialectal regression produced by surges of emotion, which inevitably befalls Elena, Nino, and Lila's own son, Rinuccio. Despite the many troubles of her married life and, later, of her life as a laborer, Lila manages to teach her son Rinuccio excellent Italian. (The efforts that this cultural outcast will constantly invest in the education of both her children are titanic.) Fluency essentially transforms Rinuccio's voice and manners. However, as soon as he begins speaking Neapolitan, he reappropriates the codes of the *rione*. In the following excerpt Elena poignantly describes this daily fluctuation between the mask and profound truth:

> Meanwhile Rinuccio asked politely, "May I go play, aunt?" He waited for me to say yes, he ran into the hall with the other child, and immediately I heard him yelling a nasty insult in dialect. [. . .] When the quarrel in the hall didn't stop, we ran out. The two boys were hitting each other, throwing things and yelling fiercely. (snn 460)

Elena's own metamorphosis is partial. Insufficient to rescue her from the role of cultural parvenue, as the *"normalisti"* see her, her reeducation generates a change in her manners and voice that the inhabitants of the *rione* pick up on immediately, prompting them to give her an unfortunate nickname:

> On the street, in the stores, on the landing of our building, people treated me with a mixture of respect and mockery. Behind my back they began to call me the Pisan. (snn 437).

Elena cannot mask her change by speaking Neapolitan, since her new bearing, copied from the bourgeois world, makes her weak and strange in this situation. Inspiring aggression in the dialectical world, the "Pisan" becomes "secure prey":

> Good manners, cultured voice and appearance, the crush in

my head and on my tongue of what I had learned in books were all immediate signs of weakness that made me a secure prey, one of those who don't struggle. (snn 456)

7. The Language of the Colonized

In the quartet the question of language is also a question of gender. Elena is trained at the university to constantly imitate male words and attitudes. The most symbolic space at the Normale for those students and professors who "excelled because they knew, without apparent effort, the present and future use of the labor of studying" (snn 403) is in fact made up exclusively of men. Besides not being Elena's mother tongue, the Italian language does not represent the perspective of women and their historical marginalization. The young woman's usurpation is, like the symbolic violence she unconsciously adopts, twofold. As a plebian she is forced to disguise herself as a member of the middle class, and as a woman she must manage "to be male in intelligence" (slc 56), to dominate word and thought as if she were a man: "[N]o one knew better than I did what it meant to make your own head masculine so that it would be accepted by the culture of men; I had done it, I was doing it" (tlts 281). Elena's language is therefore doubly foreign. Among the Normale elite, women are subjugated by the same male vanguard touting Marxist sympathy for the oppressed. Following certain professors' advice and lectures, Elena tries, for example, to form a habit of "[getting] excited whenever I came upon passages in which the effects of social inequality were well described" (snn 335). The male elite functions as "a nobility" (Bourdieu[3] 73), a radiant aristocracy whose aura lends prestige to their inferiors. When Elena begins dating Franco Mari, a classmate at the Normale known and admired by all for his communist militancy, sociability, and upper-middle-class confidence, she becomes visible by extension: "[his] aura [. . .] automatically extended to me, as his fiancée or girlfriend or companion, as if the pure and simple fact that he loved me were the public sanctioning of my talents" (snn 404). The gender inequality practiced by this fore-ordained elite fulfills an already widespread custom in the education system. In fact, in 1962, during Professor Galiani's party (cf. 4.2), Elena notices that the oldest male students find it improper to argue with their teacher and exclude her from their mental jousting, considering her instead a "bestower of the palm of victory" (snn 158).

This intellectual variant of male dominance is not confined to the academic realm, nor to educational institutions in general. As is clearly shown by Elena's description of the nascent forms of the student movements beginning in 1968, the cross-class, cross-sectional habitus of domination has a major impact on political gatherings, which presume to be revolutionary compared with the conservative university system. Her female peers routinely emulate the heroes of this revolution, just as they did at school. Once again, the gender dynamic that Elena observes in the political arena is governed by the need to "adapt their thoughts to your brain" (tlts 63).

The Neapolitan Novels portray a young woman's coming of age during the 1960s and '70s as the systematic training of an inferior being whose feelings waver between "resentment and inferiority" (tlts 243). This colonization of mental and linguistic space inspires Elena's second book, an essay on "the invention of woman by men" (tlts 353; cf. 7.4). Through a daring rereading of the stories of the Bible, the essay investigates those writing strategies that, in the story of Genesis, guarantee Adam's linguistic supremacy over Eve, so much so that the essay has the first man say of her "[s]he is therefore a pure suffix applied to my verbal root, she can express herself *only* within *my* word" (364). Elena's inquiry into the symbolic violence of male domination comes from a lifetime of appropriating their language, during which she had felt "invented by men, colonized by their imagination" (slc 56). Frantz Fanon's reflections on the alienation of colonized subjects, who appropriate the power of colonists by replicating their gestures and incorporating their world and ritual practices, can help us understand the essence of Elena's language education. Colonized people are in fact chameleons, pressured by the educational practices of colonial governors and missionaries to think of themselves as camouflaged, disguised subjects disoriented by a natural sense of confusion (Fanon).

Analyzing such forms of symbolic violence from the perspective of gender, another postcolonial studies scholar, Gayatri Spivak, asks the same question that emerges from this passage of the quartet: can the subaltern speak? "If in the context of colonial production, the subaltern has no history and cannot speak," writes Spivak, "the subaltern as female is even more deeply in shadow" (Spivak 257). Here, "speaking" refers to an assertive and creative capacity capable of deconstructing the dual symbolic (or, according to the scholar, "epistemic") violence that Elena experiences. A contradiction creeps into this already complex dynamic: women are encouraged, on the one hand, to adopt masculine words and manners, while on the other hand they are forced by male domination to assume a passive role, one of accepting and confirming. If her female companions in the movement must imitate the vision and practices of their charismatic leaders, they must also enter into relation with their leaders through a code that hovers between the erotic and maternal: "[. . .] in war films where there were only men, it was hard to feel part of it; you could only love [the young revolutionary heroes], [. . .] feel pity for their fate" (tlts 63). Men's obsession with verbal supremacy is described in this scene, as a group discussion about politics quickly turns into a humorous reflection on animal behavior: "The result was that we found ourselves, we three women, in the situation of drowsy heifers waiting for the two bulls to complete the testing of their powers" (tlts 75).

Elena's self-discipline serves to hide the "woman in her most alarming manifestation," yet her desire to assimilate confirms her own inferior nature as a "crude organism that cracked the fragile surface of discourse and appeared in a pre-logical way" (tlts 404). The female interlocutor is removed and removes herself from the conversation even when the matter under discussion concerns women's rights and was raised by women themselves. Here is one of many such scenes:

> [Franco] and Pietro ended up having a learned discussion on the couple, the family, the care of children, and even Plato, forgetting about Mariarosa and me. My husband left [. . .] pleased to have found someone with whom he could have an intelligent and civilized conversation. (slc 105–6)

In and out of university Elena diligently awaits what others think; her posture is that of the receptive listener. Her education in keeping quiet starts with Nino and is perfected as early as her high school years:

> [Nino] seemed content with my presence only if I was silently listening, which I quickly resigned myself to doing. Besides, he said things that I could never have thought, or at least said, with the same assurance, and he said them in a strong, engaging Italian. (mbf 217)

Because the power dynamic between Elena and Lila, though complex, is never predetermined, their verbal interactions are always extremely animated and pliant ("we tore the words from each other's mouth, creating an excitement that seemed like a storm of electrical charges"; snn 195). With Nino, the relationship follows a fixed code of subordination and encouragement, which Elena constantly capitalizes on:

[I] listened to him spellbound, saying only, "How clever you are." And as soon as the moment seemed apt, I volubly if somewhat inanely praised his article. (snn 179)

Searching for something to say that would please him, I ventured [. . .] (snn 194)

He gave me an admiring look, and said, "That's exactly what I think." (snn 194)

I felt that I had to pay attention to say what he wanted me to say, hiding from him both my ignorance and the few things that I knew and he didn't. I did this, and felt proud that he was trusting me with his convictions. (snn 195–96)

Demonstrating the pervasiveness of masculine rule across social classes, Elena performs the role of passive interlocutor with Pietro too, in whom she detects a profound need for reassurance:

In order not to upset him I also learned not to say what I thought. He didn't seem to care, anyway [. . .] he preferred me to be only an approving listener. [. . .] the attention had to be affectionate; he didn't want opinions, especially if they caused doubts. It was as if he were thinking out loud, explaining to himself. (tlts 277–78)

As their relationship wanes, the idea emerges that Pietro chose Elena for her lower social status, for the chance to exert his authority and bolster his masculinity:

[M]y husband never praised me but, rather, reduced me to the mother of his children; even though I had had an education he did not want me to be capable of independent thought, he demeaned me by demeaning what I read, what interested me, what I said, and he appeared willing to love me only provided that I continually demonstrate my nothingness. (tlts 298)

8. The Confessions of an Italian

The omission of dialect leaves room to *imagine* the ghost of dialect (Librandi), so every reader can project part of themselves onto that psychic and social aura, albeit along carefully drawn lines. The issue bears on translations of the quartet, which rarely speak to realities where dialect thrives to the extent it does in Italy. In the case of the English translation, for example, Ann Goldstein resorts to slang. Yet far from diminishing the translated text, her decision enlarges it, because the desired effect is achieved: anglophone readers are forced to use their imaginations to guess what the dialect is, where it appears in the Italian text (a question often posed to Goldstein during her public events for the quartet) and above all what it represents, what meanings are attached to it. One of the striking aspects of the translator's public events is that many of the questions about language from her American audiences are posed by Italian Americans trying to reappropriate their beloved Italy from a distance.

Out of Elena and Lila's bond, with its escalation of loss and gain, its contrast between displacement and belonging, emerges the important subject of how Italy has been shaped by internal emigration, a subject suppressed by our national consciousness. With few exceptions—the minor characters in Elsa Morante's *History* come to mind—our literature has overlooked the subject. In today's globalized world, which has produced dramatic diasporas, the topic of emigration has become international, and *The Neapolitan Novels'* ability to broach the subject by portraying not only an alienated and polyphonic friendship but an estranging hybrid language, a cross between dialect and Italian, is one reason for the quartet's universal success. The language of the quartet is both neutral and para-dialectal, born on the very margin of two linguistic worlds, a third space full of "plastic possibilities" (Lucamante[2] 91) that imbues the present with the temporal progress of the *rione* and articulates cultural differences by bypassing the easy game of opposites. In its creation of a hybrid language, the novels resemble *The House by the Medlar Tree*, Giovanni Verga's groundbreaking novel that wove regional otherness into the fabric of the national language. With its mix of inside and outside, the Italian of the quartet suggests that there is no clear difference between those who leave and those who stay, because those who leave *are* those who stay, and vice versa. Those who remain in Naples live in self-exile while those who leave remain inextricably linked to the city and understand that link to be "a matrix of perception, the term of comparison of every experience" (fr 65).

Once "dialect, kept below the surface, affects the plot and characters" (De Caprio), it turns into a structuring plank of the text. By its absence, Neapolitan fully transforms into a speaker, a central protagonist of the endless web of storylines spun by Elena and Lila. Given its ability to show the uneven dynamics within which the storylines are produced, the quartet can be defined as a "very pointed treatise on the existing relation between the Italian language and dialect from the postwar years to today" (Villarini 193). More generally, in all her writing Ferrante meditates on the extraordinary history of a nation that has managed to build a unified linguistic consciousness in a relatively short time span (little more than a century and a half) and along the way inflicted losses and casualties. In one of her recent editorials in *The Guardian*, Ferrante states that she is Italian because she writes in Italian, while also specifying that she can only take pride in her national language provided that she practice it as "[. . .] a point of departure for dialogue, an effort to cross over the limit, to look beyond the border—beyond all borders, especially those of gender" (fer[5]). There is no more appropriate formula for the language of this quartet, which might be renamed the *Confessions of an Italian*, to borrow the title of Ippolito Nievo's novel (Manetti[2]). The quartet is the story of a rift, a disconnect, a fault line between the dominant male language and new female (or feminist) expressivity, between national pride and regional rootedness.

Yet the quartet also bridges the gap between nation and city, Europe and Italy, the language of men and the new words of women. To Elena, Naples is a "third space" (Bhabha 56), an intermediary element that demolishes the rigid binary dividing the primitive South from the modern North, a space that reveals the synchronicity of time, how the archaic and ultramodern coincide (cf. 7.5 and 7.6). In the quartet, Naples embodies disenchantment with progress. It is "the great European metropolis where faith in technology, in science, in economic development, in the kindness of nature, in history that leads of necessity to improvement, in democracy, was revealed, most clearly and far in advance, to be completely without foundation" (slc 337). This heartrending overlap of times—the same we find ourselves living in now, in today's globalized reality—dismantles the moral dualisms that have pitted and continue to pit Northern Italy against Southern, bourgeois civilization against premodern naturalism; stereotypes later revisited and incorporated by those outside Italy's national borders, which have often served to cast all of Italy as the Mediterranean, and to some degree African, threshold of the European continent. During the nineteenth century, as modern nation-states and colonial capitalism hardened, Northern Europe fashioned itself as the image of modernity by, in part, consigning Italy to the picturesque. Such a narrative has introduced clear hierarchies in the formation of European identity (Moe 194). Questioning this symbolic geography and its false ideology of progress, unmasking it via Elena and Lila's education in the dialect of emancipation and symbolic violence, the quartet—and with it Italian history from the 1950s until today—finds itself a site of imaginary experimentation for those peripheries in the global world that are gaining a new centrality.

1. The Labyrinth of Violence

T he quartet is the story of two friends who join forces to "step beyond" borders (fr 327), to break through the real and symbolic spaces of oppression to which they have been confined for ages. Breaking barriers is a narrative mechanism checked by violence, by abuses great and small that Elena and Lila endure every time they try to cross the frontier. No matter the social class, male authorities react by creating this corrective system to defend those prerogatives thrown into question by the historical emergence of second-class citizens and their subjectivity, by their refusal to play a secondary and supporting role. "Loss of power," writes Hannah Arendt, "becomes a temptation to substitute violence for power" (Arendt 23).

In Ferrante's writing, violence is connected to the labyrinth (cf. 4.5 and 4.6). In fact, abuse is depicted as the culmination of a process, short or long, of waywardness on the part of the victim, a sense of disorientation that, from childhood on, leads the two protagonists astray. The same sense of disorientation resurfaces for two other children: Dede (the daughter of Elena and Pietro) and Mirko (the son of Nino and Silvia, a young university student and political activist). The children are described, for example, as "a chain of shadows who had always been on the stage with the same burden of love, hatred, desire, and violence" (tlts 291). This cycle of abuse connects Silvia's rape at the hands of a fascist in 1973, the slap that Pietro—an educated middle-class man—gives Elena in Dede's presence around the same time, and Lila's rape twelve years earlier. The atmosphere of violence transforms the way the two children behave:

> They were pretending to be a mother and father with their baby, but it wasn't peaceful: they were pretending to have a fight. I stopped. Dede instructed Mirko: *You have to hit me, understand?* [. . .] I observed Dede carefully; she seemed to resemble Pietro. Mirko, on the other hand, was just like Nino. (tlts 291)

This intimate scene of child's play unmasks the deep truth about a private and domestic sphere where patriarchal manners and hierarchies are passed down and sanctioned, even when the public sphere has, in part, grown out of them. The imaginative imbalance is the crux of the issue—unresolved to this day—when we talk about femicide and stalking. It is no coincidence that the two children, though from different social classes, resemble men who are apparently evolved and progressive. The doubled physiognomies hint at the transference of violence that is not restricted to those of lower social extraction, and at the recurring fate of the backward *rione* (indeed, only Nino comes from the *rione*). The scene speaks to a particular mix of male oppression that can surface through a complex web of physical and symbolic violence, which, in uneven and measurable doses of strength and manipulation, is expressed by the bourgeoisie no less than by the plebeians. As Ferrante points out, the other face of "pure, crude, bloody violence" is the "good-natured irony of educated men who belittle or demean [women's] achievements" (fr 326–27). *The Neapolitan Novels* are a phenomenological study of the physical and verbal ways that directly and indirectly lead men to perpetrate various forms of violence against women.

The labyrinth is a structure of perception generated by displacement. The two protagonists respond by gradually repositioning themselves, placing themselves at the center of the action, decoding the ambiguous symbols that surround them and ridding those symbols of their illusory indeterminacy. They enter the labyrinth of violence because the cultural standards of their world hide a truth that ends up assaulting them, like the Minotaur, revealing itself in all its horrific nature: the evidence of a virility conceived of as systemic oppression, where fathers oppress daughters, husbands wives, boys girls, brothers sisters, and—as a vicarious form of patriarchal authority—mothers daughters. As the writer points out, the primary vehicle of physical violence is normalization, the inability of families to call it out. Says Ferrante: "I grew up in a world where it seemed normal that men (fathers, brothers, boyfriends) had the right to hit you in order to correct you, to teach you how to be a woman, ultimately for your own good" (fr 349). In the code of the *rione*, abuse is regarded as a form of protection and love practiced by a father, brother, or husband on his daughter, sister, or wife (cf. 4.4).

The labyrinth of violence also entails losing your physical form, being deformed by progressive *smarginatura*. It is in fact the male body that displays the first symptoms of dissolving boundaries (cf. 3.2): Lila's brother and new husband undergo horrible metamorphoses that, from within them, from a cleft in their souls, give vent to a barbaric violence aimed at women.

> The loss of those boundaries in her brother, whom she loved more than anyone in her family, had frightened her, and the disintegration of Stefano in the passage from fiancé to husband terrified her. I learned only from her notebooks how much her wedding night had scarred her and how she feared the potential distortion of her husband's body, his disfigurement by the internal impulses of desire and rage or, on the contrary, of subtle plans, base acts. Especially at night she was afraid of waking up and finding him formless in the bed, transformed into excrescences that burst out because of too much fluid, the flesh melted and dripping, and with it everything around, the furniture, the entire apartment and she herself, his wife, broken, sucked into that stream polluted by living matter. (snn 355–56)

In an endless cycle of deformation, male domination in the *rione* is depicted as a form of cannibalism:

> [The mothers of the *rione*] had been consumed [*mangiate*], literally eaten] by the bodies of husbands, fathers, brothers, whom they ultimately came to resemble, because of their labors or the arrival of old age, of illness. (snn 102)

Yet despite the many scenes of plebian physical violence in the quartet, Ferrante has stated that she is actually more interested in the "covert" acts of violence in her story:

> [. . .] the world in which the girls grow up has some obviously violent features and others that are covertly violent. It's the latter that interest me most, even though there are plenty of the first. (fr 233–34)

Whereas the popular universe is inhabited by the likes of Amalia in *Troubling Love* and Lila in the quartet, "uncontrollable girls and women who in vain are repressed by their men" (fr 276), Elena's life among the middle-class reveals that, due to its indirect and oblique manifestations, bourgeois violence colonizes the mind and can produce a sense of disorientation that one never completely recovers from. Female creativity is an energy that resists these forms of incorporation, this loss of forms, and creates *other* forms (Wehling-Giorgi[3] 11). The modes of male oppression and female creation of new forms to compensate for *smarginatura* operate on two distinct yet connected levels. In the following paragraphs, I shall describe these two levels and what connects them. With regards to the first, the modes of male oppression, I will linger in particular over the recurring link between sex and violence in the quartet: sexual practices in fact emerge as a transversal form of control over female identity. I will discuss Stefano's rape of Lila (the first of many) and then the bourgeois suppression of violence in connection to sex and talk of sex.

As for the second level, the female creation of new forms that compensate for the *smarginatura* that women are physically and psychologically subjected to, I will focus on a series of images created by the female protagonists of Ferrante's novels in order to visualize and exorcise the pressure of male domination. These images are powerfully evocative symbols and, at the same time, turning points in the plot: two of them are closely connected to visual images (a painting and an enlarged photo panel), while the third is a scene at the end of the quartet that fulfills the same function as a painting. I am referring to the death of Gigliola, a scene that brings to an end the violence that she endures over the entire course of the narrative (Wehling-Giorgi[4] 208). Finally, in the last section of this chapter I shall talk about another effect of violence, which becomes, at the same time, a form of dramatization: the disappearance of two women—Lila in the quartet and Amalia in *Troubling Love*—as a sign of male oppression and, despite everything, of female resistance to that oppression.

2. Lila's Rape

Around the end of March 1961, when after her honeymoon Lila sees Elena again, she bitterly confesses to her friend that she has been wrong about everything ever since the day the two girls climbed the stairs to Don Achille's apartment looking for their dolls (snn 46). From that moment on she had gotten her hopes up (hopes that would be crushed two years later when she was taken out of school) about the prospect of new adventures: a sequence of dreams that led from the dolls to *Little Women* to *The Blue Fairy* to her shoes and, finally, to Stefano, who, for sheer love, would have founded a shoe factory for her, transformed the life of the *rione*, and enriched them both. This trail of illusions guides Lila into the labyrinth, leading her astray in the confusion instilled in her by the imagination of the *rione*. According to the cultural code of the neighborhood, it is normal for a young girl to stop going to school after the fifth grade, just as it is normal that she be driven to transform that violence into a fairy tale about love and wealth not for herself alone, or not only for herself, but for her family too.

Violence weaves other webs of oppression in Lila as the collective imagination forces her to suppress her suffering and even hold it up as a form of love and devotion: to her father, who didn't want her to study; to her mother, who didn't know how to protect her; and to her brother, who proves increasingly violent and hungry for revenge. Lila gets engaged to Stefano for her family. She realizes too late that she is lost in the labyrinth; she has already stumbled upon the Minotaur. On their wedding night, Stefano's father takes possession of his son's body. Stefano dissolves and out comes Don Achille, the fairy tale ogre, the monster of the maze (cf. 4.6).

> He was never Stefano, she seemed to discover suddenly, he was always the oldest son of Don Achille. And that thought, immediately, brought to the young face of her husband, like a revival, features that until that moment had remained prudently hidden in his blood but that had always been there, waiting for their moment. (snn 41)

The clearest indication is his "voice of an ogre, like his father's," which alters the meek and sententious speech that Stefano has used since childhood to feign wisdom and mask his spitefulness: "[. . .] his father terrorized him by his mere presence and he, in reaction, had trained himself to that half smile, to slow, tranquil gestures, to a controlled distance from the world around him, to keep at bay both fear and the desire to tear open his chest with his bare hands and, pulling it apart, rip out the heart" (snn 352–53).

Upon their return from their honeymoon, Elena is also

disturbed by echoes of the past, by the bark of Stefano hurling "odious curses" at Lila. The "voice of an ogre, like his father's" (snn 80) exposes the frightening truth lurking underneath the "recital of women," the jokes about male defects that the two friends exchange in an attempt to normalize, if only for a few minutes, Lila's marriage. But the ominous signs of the Minotaur are already present hours prior to her wedding night, before and after they reach Amalfi, their destination. Lila is incredulous when Stefano smacks her full in the face on their car ride to the coast because, up until that moment, despite the shocking epilogue to their wedding party (with Marcello Solara wearing her shoes, the symbol of Stefano and Lila's engagement; cf. 4.2), she is lost in the labyrinth. She still believes in Stefano's calm veneer, in his desire to change, in the purity of their fairy tale—even if it is constantly manifested as a status symbol, a sports car (cf. 4.4)—and in the bargaining of her childhood dreams for luxury items:

> Stefano seemed to seek in her the most palpable symbol of the future of wealth and power that he intended; and she seemed to use the seal that he was placing on her to make herself, her brother, her parents, her other relatives safe from all that she had confusedly confronted and challenged since she was a child. (mbf 265)

This labyrinth of consumer goods is suddenly shown for what it is, a "glittering zero" (snn 36), like the wedding ring that Lila now finds on her finger, which dispels all her illusions, which traps her in the maze of the monster. Her husband's body begins to break up, because "something in and around him broke" (snn 37): his legs become "short and fat" (snn 35), he flashes "white jaws, a red tongue in the dark hole of his mouth" (snn 37). In a handful of hours, Lila is beset by a feeling of estrangement, of "a world that [has] lost its contours" (snn 38):

The screws holding together her new condition of wife, the restaurant, Amalfi, seemed to her so loose that at the end of dinner Stefano's voice no longer reached her, in her ears there was only a clamor of objects, living beings, and thoughts, without definition. (snn 37)

Lila's speech dissolves to the point that she must reach for a rhetorical language to find the words with which to describe another sign of animality that she perceives in Stefano: "[the gold ring] shone amid the black hairs, hairy fingers, as the books said" (snn 36).

The couple's inability to speak about sex is related to this disintegration of the contours of language. Stefano is bewildered by Lila's refusal ("'I don't want you'"; snn 39), "as if the three [sic] words were in a foreign language," and reacts by making an illogical and ill-matched comparison. "I love you more than my mother and my sister," he says (snn 40). The association of the scene's palpable menace with filial and fraternal love is perplexing, and it evokes a code of virility governed by dependence on the female body and by the desire to take revenge on it: on the body of the mother, out of which the helpless newborn issues, and on which his whole psychic life depends; and on that of the wife, whom this adult male wants to enter as master (Melandri 98–101). At the center of this dynamic lies the link between sex and power, the conception of sexual intercourse as a ritual of female submission and conditioning. The following words cross Stefano's mind, words fueled by what he has inherited from his family and neighborhood, commands that feed his own commands:

> "Now you're really pissing me off, Lina."
> He repeated that remark two or three times, each time louder, as if to assimilate fully an order that was coming to him from very far away, perhaps even from before he was born. The order was: be a man, Ste'; either you subdue her now or you'll never subdue

her; your wife has to learn right away that she is the female and you're the male and therefore she has to obey. (snn 40–41)

More than once in the middle of the rape, the focus shifts to Stefano, to his thought processes and to his body. The decision is novel even for today's collective imagination, which tends to depict rape from the point of view of the offended and violated body of the woman (think of the many advertisements addressing domestic violence) and therefore appeals to our compassion for the violated victim rather than to our moral judgment of the aggressor. Entering Stefano's thoughts and aroused body, Ferrante guides our attention toward a figure often left in the shadows of rape scenes, and therefore, to some extent—even if involuntarily—protected: toward the rapist and the poverty of many forms of male sexual identity.

All of Stefano's thoughts and dialogue gravitate toward legitimizing his violent act. If he slaps Lila, it's because she provoked him. "See what you've made me do," he asks, "See how you go too far?" (snn 33). If he can have her despite her refusal, it's because he was turned on: "[He] pointed to his wine-colored pajama pants, and mumbled with a crooked smile: See what happens to me just when I look at you" (snn 40). (According to Joanna Bourke in *Rape: Sex, Violence, History*, this is one of the most common "rape myths.") If he imposes his desire on her, it's because her refusal is only a female whim masking her willingness and lust. "How difficult it is to keep up with this girl," he thinks, "she says yes and means no, she says no and means yes" (snn 40). The "no" means "yes" argument is still repeatedly used to defend rape in court (Bourke 50–88). But the most significant passage is when, pinning down the arms of his wife, who has already been brutalized, Stefano exposes his phallus and presents it to Lila triumphantly, as if it were the most seductive aesthetic symbol that he had yet to give her, as if it were a new dress, jewels, standard of living:

> He now had his hands free and leaning over her he slapped her lightly with the tips of his fingers and kept telling her, pressing her: see how big it is, eh, say yes, say yes, say yes, until he took out of his pajamas his stubby sex [. . .] Now I'll make you feel it, Lina, look how nice it is, nobody's got one like this. (snn 42)

Close-up, his erect, exposed phallus (Lila's face is very close to her husband's sex) is offered up as a promise of happiness in which pleasure and submission amount to the same thing for a woman:

> [. . .] you don't realize how much I love you, but you will know, and tomorrow it will be you asking me to love you as I am now, and more, in fact you will go down on your knees and beg me, and I will say yes but only if you are obedient, and you will be obedient. (snn 42)

"I love you" is a phrase that from this moment on will recur with great frequency, crowning the brutal physical violence that Stefano inflicts on Lila's body, confirming the recurring link between oppression and the labyrinth, where words are empty and abuse disguised as a facet of love.

The following scene takes place two and a half years after their wedding, when Lila tells her husband that she wants to leave him:

> It was at the end of that speech that she received a blow that knocked her off her chair. She got up while Stefano moved to grab her, she ran to the sink, seized the knife that she had put under the dishtowel [. . .]. Stefano stopped [. . .]. He turned his back on her and, still muttering resentfully [. . .] went to the table and ate another pastry.
>
> Then he left the kitchen, retreated to the bedroom, and from there he cried suddenly, "You can't even imagine how much I love you" (snn 352).

To return to their wedding night, the rape scene is made by constantly alternating viewpoints: his gaze alternates with hers, and the juxtaposition becomes extremely revealing just as Stefano gratifies himself by placing his sex in the middle of both their gazes. This phallus that a sentence before was the idol of all male prowess now becomes, from Lila's perspective, a monstrous puppet grafted onto the body of another body:

> [. . .] his stubby sex [. . .], extended over her, seemed like a puppet without arms or legs, congested by mute stirrings, in a frenzy to uproot itself from that other, bigger puppet [. . .]. (snn 42)

The penetration, performed with "passionate brutality," happens in Lila's absence; after all her writhing and resistance, Lila sinks into a semiconscious state (disassociation is a recurring phenomenon in trauma victims). However, deep down, she is still aware that her body is being violated. Lila finally knows what name to give things, knows who the Minotaur is, knows that she has lost her way in the labyrinth, knows she will have to find a way out:

> When, after some awkward attempts, he tore her flesh with passionate brutality, Lila was absent. The night, the room, the bed, his kisses, his hands on her body, every sensation was absorbed by a single feeling: she hated Stefano Carracci, she hated his strength, she hated his weight on her, she hated his name and his surname. (snn 42)

3. Made Badly at Sex

In the *rione* male violence is naturalized by a code of honor that states, "I'll beat you to death for your own good." Elena reflects on the mechanisms of this normalization the moment she sees it dismantled and repudiated by Lila, who, after her rape, displays "acquiescence without respect" (snn 53) toward her husband. Unlike Lila, other women in the *rione* essentially take pride in the abuse they endure because it proves that their men are virile:

> Our mothers, after they were slapped by their husbands, [. . .] despaired, they wept, they confronted their man sullenly, they criticized him behind his back, and yet, more and less, they continued to respect him. (snn 53)

For cultural and historical reasons related to modern rationalism and the systematic conditioning of people's consciousness, bourgeois violence significantly ratchets up emotional abuse, which is to say abuse aimed at colonizing women's minds (cf. 5.7). As a result, its form of domination is subtler, forking in various and apparently unconnected directions that are almost always undetected by both the dominator and the dominated. Because the instruments of imaginative consciousness and creation become complicated and specialized in the bourgeois world, the dominated party increasingly tends to incorporate and naturalize her relationship to domination (Bourdieu[3]). This form of violence has a symbolic depth so sophisticated as to cause a nearly continuous sense of confusion in the victim as well as a profound, though elusive, identification with the logic of the aggressor.

Let's look at how middle-class violence functions with respect to sex and the dominating practices connected to sex—a key element of the Italian imagination in the 1960s. As we saw in Chapter 5, Elena's verbal exchanges with educated men are humiliating (cf. 5.7). Her sexual encounters are even more so. With unflappable indifference, young middle-class men in the 1960s—often socialists, communists, and aspiring revolutionaries—ignore the physiology of female pleasure and a woman's right to orgasm. Franco Mari (cf. 5.7) concedes, with a pinch of annoyance, his knee or stomach so that Elena, rubbing against him, can get a bit of pleasure too (tlts 175). From Elena's point of view, the idea of sexual liberation advocated by young revolutionaries from the Normale is fraught with an even more underhanded form of female submission than the one experienced in the *rione*. Women go from having to seem chastened and obedient to having to appear free and open-minded—a far more ambiguous form of submission:

> It's complicated to explain what it cost me to adapt to the idea of sexual freedom that Franco ardently supported; I myself hid the difficulty to seem free and open-minded to him. (snn 405)

If Franco represents the revolutionary side of middle-class culture, Pietro embodies its tame progressiveness, yet Elena's experience with him is no less humiliating. Once married, Pietro practices such prolonged and pained lovemaking sessions that Elena begins to regard solitude as "a consolation prize" (tlts 253). In no time, marriage seems to her "an institution that, contrary to what one might think, stripped coitus of all humanity" (tlts 309). In the popular universe of the *rione*, routine humiliation is, for the two friends, more extreme but also easier to identify. Not for nothing, Lila sums it up with a merciless phrase: *the bother of fucking*, "the great excitement, the lack of satisfaction, the sense of disgust" (tlts 176). If "afterward" consists of humiliation, "before" is, for young women, forced abstinence. "Is it possible," Elena asks, questioning her friend's marriage and the sexual mores of the *rione*, "that *the disgust, the humiliation* begin *afterward*, when a man subdues you and violates you at his pleasure solely because now you belong to him [. . .] ?" (snn 53). Antonio rejects Elena's sexual requests and his own pressing desire because he wants to "do it the way it's done with a wife, not like this" (snn 27). Yet the man of the *rione* and the student from the

Normale share the same reluctance to have premarital relations:

> [Pietro and I] walked for a long time. We kissed, we embraced on the Lungarno, I asked him, half serious, half joking, if he wanted to sneak into my room. He shook his head, he went back to kissing me passionately. There were entire libraries separating him and Antonio, but they were similar. (snn 436)

Abstinence and premarital virginity are in fact requirements of good sexual behavior for a woman, even among the bourgeoisie, the difference being that the latter punish transgressions via a relentless web of innuendo and exclusion created by the male and female students of the country's cultural elite. Elena herself winds up accused of being an "easy girl" (snn 405) because she visited Franco Mari's room one night and traveled alone with him to Paris and Versilia. In fact, when she first meets Pietro, he expresses regret for not having defended her "good name" (snn 406).

Elena launches her writing career with an autobiographical novel (cf. 4.1) about this nucleus of sexual consciousness, which she had systematically suppressed until the birth of the feminist movement the following decade. The plot is centered on the rewriting of a real-life event: losing her virginity to Donato Sarratore on the beach of the Maronti during the summer of 1962. What compels Elena to narrate her experience in 1967, in her room at the Normale, is a sense of shame: "At this distance I understood that that first experience of penetration, in the dark, on the cold sand, with that banal man who was the father of the person I loved had been degrading" (snn 431). Her first sexual experience casts a shadow of disgust over her later experiences with Franco and Pietro and drives her to write (cf. 4.1). Yet what emerges from her memory and is later described in the novel—as far as we can reconstruct it each time the plot of her debut novel overlaps with that of the quartet—only partially coincides with her account of the actual experience in *The Story of a New Name*. Furthermore, Elena's first work is that of an unreliable writer, as readers of *The Neapolitan Novels* are well aware (cf. 1.6).

But what, in this case, are the reasons for that unreliability? In order to understand them, we must go back to the passage in the quartet about the night at the Maronti and how Elena comes to term with it:

> The entire time, I didn't once regret having accepted what was happening. I had no second thoughts and I was proud of myself, I wanted it to be like that, I imposed it on myself. (snn 291)

Her encounter with Donato Sarratore is a moment of, at times, intense and enigmatic physical pleasure that remains unprecedented in her life: "I was overwhelmed by a need for pleasure so demanding and so egocentric that it canceled out not only the entire world of sensation but also his body, in my eyes old, and the labels by which he could be classified—*father of Nino, railway worker-poet-journalist, Donato Sarratore*" (snn 292). This encounter is preceded, two years earlier, during another summer in Ischia, by the night Sarratore furtively molests Elena's then-barely-fifteen-year-old body. As Elena recalls it, "I said, did nothing, I was terrified by that behavior, by the horror it created, by the pleasure that I nevertheless felt" (mbf 232).

Throughout the story of the quartet, Nino is, instead, the equivalent of the female ghost that haunts men's erotic fantasies, an elusive seraph who mirrors the triangle of desire of countless women who vie for him. But in the few passages when he steps out of this role of fleeting apparition and speaks, he appears no less normative than the other men Elena dates. When the two meet up in Milan in 1968, on the occasion of a book event for Elena's novel, Nino privately tells Elena, just after the event, that "[Lila's] really made badly: in her mind and in everything, even when it comes to sex" (tlts 36). It is significant that a man obsessed with serial erotic encounters has the gall to judge standards of intimacy. It is especially significant that Elena absorbs his words without immediately questioning their soundness. On the contrary, she makes him the arbiter of moral judgment (even after having met another young woman, Silvia, whom, like Lila, Nino impregnates and abandons):

> [Nino], I said to myself, is experienced. He has known many women, he knows what good female sexual behavior is and so he recognizes when it's bad. (tlts 176)

As an object of cultural idolatry, Nino is for Elena the person who automatically establishes the standards of Eros. What Nino has in common with Donato Sarratore is his clumsiness with words, his ridiculous "poeticizing," his voracious sexual appetite.

While sex with Nino, in 1976 (fourteen years after her experience on the Maronti), is described, in the style of ideal love, as a fusion of two people ("So pleasure was this: breaking, mixing, no longer knowing what was mine and what was his"; tlts 388), with Nino's father Elena makes a stinging discovery about herself:

> I had a hidden me—I realized—that fingers, mouth, teeth, tongue were able to discover. Layer after layer, that me lost every hiding place, was shamelessly exposed, and Sarratore showed that he knew how to keep it from fleeing, from being ashamed, he knew how to hold it as if it were the absolute reason for his affectionate motility, for his sometimes gentle, sometimes fevered pressures. (snn 291)

Elena can abandon herself to pleasure on the beach of the Maronti because she is disentangled from the sexual morality that both the underclass and working- and middle-class worlds have in common: the confinement of female Eros to marriage and moral subordination. On the one hand, Sarratore's sexual prowess places Elena in the erotic role of the passive virgin, arouser of intense physical passion: "[. . .] unlike Antonio, he claimed no intervention from me, he never took my hand to touch him, but confined himself to convincing me that he liked everything about me, and he applied himself to my body with the care, the devotion, the pride of the man absorbed in demonstrating how thoroughly he knows women" (tlts 291–92). On the other, her abandonment to male pleasure does not force her to relinquish her intellectual or moral identity, which is and will be the condition of all her other sexual experiences. Unlike Antonio, Franco, Pietro, and Nino, Donato is the object of Elena's liberating disdain. Disentangling her from male tutelage, Elena's disdain opens her up to the exciting realm of sexual initiation. Right after the two have sex, Elena's one concern is to find the right "tonality of threat" (snn 292) capable of dissuading him from pursuing her again. In the course of their exchange in Italian, Elena is stunned by her capacity to be authentic, which originates—she guesses—from the fact that she can finally translate into Italian the threat that, in general, can only adequately be expressed in dialect:

> All the way back I continued to threaten him, partly because he had returned to his sugary-sweet little phrases and I wanted him to understand clearly my feelings, partly because I was amazed at how the tonality of threat, which since I was a child I had used only in dialect, came easily to me also in the Italian language. (snn 292–93)

Yet something else is lying underneath the bilingualism (cf. 5.3) of the two interlocutors in this scene. Elena's relationship with Nino, another bilingual speaker, is, contrariwise, a linguistic performance aimed at demonstrating to one another that they have the credentials to enter the Italian middle class. This fiction is not unmasked until 1981, when Elena catches him in a quickie with the waitress in the bathroom of their home, and the son is finally revealed to be worse than the father. Her exchange with Donato, on the other hand, gives rise to a central truth: Elena's aggressive sexual needs enter the scene boldly and void of simulations and dissimulations.

4. The Power of the False

Elena's humiliation the night on the Maronti stems from having to hold together her pursuit of pleasure and vengeance (as if to make up for the love between Lila and Nino) and her sense of self-corruption, of being filthy, as she remembers it eighteen years later: "I found it equally inconceivable that, as had happened to me, [Elena's daughter Dede] could lie under the heavy body of a grown man, at night, on the Maronti, smeared with dark sand, damp air, and bodily fluids, just for revenge" (slc 138). But more humiliating are her later sexual experiences with men her own age. Whether produced by the obscene game with the father of the boy she loves and idealizes or guaranteed by a no-man's-land outside moralizing sexual practices, Elena's improper enjoyment on the Maronti chafes against the image of herself that she aspires to—as evolved, cultured, and middle class. In turn, her pursuit of emancipation is proven false by the sexual practices of the bourgeoisie: at the Normale, in her wedding bed, in apparently liberated or traditional guises, sex for Elena amounts to patient and frigid submission. For Elena, to live and to experiment means finding herself in a space where the truth is spoken only through a filter of partial falsehood or, vice versa, finding herself in a false dimension that can only be communicated via the truth. The introjection of symbolic bourgeois violence is manifested in this loss of direct contact with experience. If the traces of the path that led her to certain desires and needs have been lost, she will reconstruct them in her memory, recount them in her novel, and publicly discuss them by knitting together truth and lies.

A colonized member of the bourgeois world, Elena is oppressed by "the power of the false" (Deleuze 131), even in her most intimate moments (cf. 5.7). At the same time, the story she can tell is precisely that profound and emblematic truth about the sexual education of women during those years. No wonder the novel is a hit, the immediate focus of journalists' heated polemics about the habits of young people. Given this weave of truth and lies, not only the novel itself but her public appearances and many private exchanges about the work gravitate around something unspoken, a suppressed topic that eludes Elena herself. Subjected to the derision or brazen curiosity of the residents of the *rione* ("Then suddenly [Carmen] asked, slyly, how long does it take to get to the dirty pages?"; tlts 61); criticized by university professors who throng her public events ("[. . .] an older man with thick eyeglasses [. . .] cited the slightly risqué pages, in an openly hostile tone"; snn 471); dismissed by revolutionaries like Franco Mari ("'Behind the petty love affairs and the desire for social ascent you hide precisely what it would be valuable to tell'"; tlts 80), Elena can never address the subject of sex authentically.

On the night in San Giovanni a Teduccio (cf. 2.6), Lila, in the throes of *smarginatura*, confesses her own disappointment with sex "in the crude vocabulary of the neighborhood": "fucking had never given her the pleasure she had expected as a girl" (tlts 174). Hearing her friend's admission, Elena realizes that she herself doesn't possess a language adequate to say something similar. Neither dialect nor, strangely, the Italian in which she wrote her novel, helps: "the dialect disgusted me, and although I passed for an author of racy pages, the Italian I had acquired seemed to me too precious for the sticky material of sexual experiences" (tlts 174). Here, too, there is something underneath the limitations of bilingualism. Whereas Lila manifests an authenticity "more basely, more viscerally—involved" (fr 276), her lucidity finds no perch in Elena's bourgeois life. In fact, Elena digs in her heels: "For me it's not like that" (tlts 174), she says defensively. Lila rightly, if harshly, points out the contradiction between what Elena has said and the "dirty stuff" written in her novel:

> "In the book you wrote something else. [. . .] Dirty stuff ended up in there [. . .] stuff that men don't want to hear and women know but are afraid to say. But now what—are you hiding?" (tlts 175)

The fact that the popular world sometimes grants emancipated women glimmers of freedom still inconceivable in the bourgeois world finds confirmation in 1969, when the two friends discover the Pill. Only Lila will have the determination to use it (with Enzo; it is significant that theirs is the only truly equal and experimental relationship in the quartet). Elena on the other hand yields to Pietro, that "educated youth who wanted only a civil marriage":

> I told him that I intended to take the Pill in order not to have children, that it seemed to me urgent to try first of all to write another book. I was sure that he would immediately agree. Instead, surprisingly, he was opposed. First he made it a problem of legality, the Pill was not yet officially for sale; then he said there were rumors that it ruined one's health; then he made a complicated speech about sex, love, and reproduction; finally he stammered that someone who really has to write will write anyway, even if she is expecting a baby. I was unhappy, I was angry [. . .]. We quarreled. Our wedding day arrived and we were not reconciled: he was mute, I cold. (tlts 228)

Typical of symbolic violence is this tendency to conceive of the relationship as a space for corrective and manipulative practices, so-called gaslighting (Calef and Weinshel 44), by which the man perceives and is perceived as the guarantor of socially acceptable positions and practical schemes, which are, in turn, indelibly inscribed on the body of the dominated party (Bourdieu[3]). Though she protests against Pietro's arguments, in her actions Elena immediately accepts them: she does not take the Pill and becomes pregnant on her wedding night (tlts 231). That Elena is lost in a labyrinth unlike the one Lila finds herself in becomes clear when, during the night in San Giovanni a Teduccio, speculating about some impossible-to-utter truth, she initially manages to articulate only a silent lie, to recite an interior monologue defending her bourgeois experience of sex:

> I would have had to admit that being penetrated had disappointed me, too [. . .]. But I would have had to add that Franco [. . .] before entering me and afterward let me rub against one of his legs, against his stomach, and that this was nice and sometimes made the penetration nice, too. (tlts 175)

In light of the supposed beauty of the rubbing that the man concedes, another unconfessed thought about that night appears far more truthful. Elena finally recognizes in herself and in her friend the same cruel disapproving behavior of Nino: *being made badly at sex* means seeking, despite everything, to live:

> *To be made badly when it comes to sex* means, evidently, not to be able to feel pleasure in the male's thrusting; it means twisting with desire and rubbing yourself to quiet that desire, it means grabbing his hands and placing them against your sex as I sometimes did with Franco, ignoring his annoyance, the boredom of the one who has already had his orgasm and now would like to go to sleep. (tlts 176)

5. Images: The Painting in *Troubling Love*

That brings us to the images that convey a "narrative of resistance" (Wehling-Giorgi[3] 10) to the *smarginatura* of men's abuse. *Smarginatura* is also an affirmative or creative process that releases intense willpower from the female body, "a break from the need for hatred, the urgency for revenge or justice" (snn 103). This surge of resistance generates a ramified, transversal phenomenology. It is what inspires the painting that Delia recalls and later contemplates in *Troubling Love* and the collage made of the enlarged photo of Lila in the store in Piazza dei Martiri.

The painting in *Troubling Love* makes its first appearance as a memory and later as a real object that helps reveal the mystery of why—as Delia puzzles things out—it was given by her mother's ex-husband to her suitor (tl 118–19). This back-and-forth between the artwork remembered and the true account of it, between the fuzzy memory and the actual painting, defines other works and reproductions in the novel, such as the painting of the Gypsy and the identity cards of Delia and Amalia. In *Troubling Love*, perhaps the most visual of Ferrante's works (Milkova[4] 2), the blurry quality of the images is very closely connected to the theme of violence. Seesawing between memory and reality facilitates a constant focalization of scenes that by association evoke the originating scene of her suppressed, and therefore indemonstrable, trauma. The recollection-image (Deleuze 106) is an objective correlative of the abuses endured, and, most especially, of the way in which those abuses exist in a latent state, between suppression and sudden epiphanies. The double role of the object, part memory and part record, is developed in the story of the painting. When Delia is a child, the painting is the object of young Delia and her father's admiration displayed in the window of the Vossi sisters' shop (cf. 4.7). Her father even claims the painting is his.

Besides being linked by blood, father and daughter share an artistic vocation: the former is a mediocre painter, the latter a comic-strip artist. This supposed right to the painting and the recollection of the demeaning ways her father drew her mother's naked body in the other painting (the series of the Gypsy, sold for decades at county fairs) converge to define a potent visual nucleus of suppression.

When Delia stops before the window of the Vossi sisters' shop, at the beginning of her two-day investigation into her mother's death, she discovers that the painting is no longer there, but she puts off recalling the image itself:

> Two women, so close and so identical in movement that their profiles were almost superimposed, were running openmouthed, from the right side of the canvas to the left. You couldn't tell if they were following or being followed. The image seemed to have been cut away from a much larger scene, and so only the left legs of the women were visible and their extended arms were severed at the wrists. (tl 55)

At the end of her investigation, Delia will rediscover the painting in her father's house. Though having only caught a glimpse of it out of the corner of her eye, Delia describes it again:

> The two shouting women whose profiles almost coincided— hurled from right to left in a mutilated movement of hands, feet, part of the head, as if the table had been unable to contain them or had been bluntly sawed off—had ended up there [. . .]. (tl 118)

As shown by the discrepancy between the two descriptions, the moment Delia meets her father, the central figure of male oppression and the old trauma she endured, the image is presented in a slightly different way: in the second description, the two women are seized by a terrifying violence. Their mouths are no longer generically "open" but screaming. Their bodies are "mutilated," as if they were being punished for their irrepressible movement. There is no question about whether they are running or being chased; the picture brings to mind two fugitives on the run. The two women in the painting symbolically recall Delia and Amalia, mother and daughter, and—as in the myth of Demeter and Persephone (de Rogatis³ 286)—tragically separated twins: the two almost overlapping figures look like fragments of an unfinished whole, nesting dolls without the whole set to contain them. If on the one hand both are fleeing male violence (Lombardi 290), on the other they are both moving forever in pursuit of a desire. The open mouth, which Delia lingers over in her first recollection of the painting, may either refer to the terrified cry or to the vital passion of mother and daughter: two crucial elements in the novel's plot. Through this blur of memory and reality, through this metamorphic story of the object, Delia frees the two women's bodies by placing them outside the frame of the lingerie store—a place attached to male erotic codes—and the realm of her father's troubling love (Milkova⁴ 2). The body, no longer an object but a subject, is released from the male gaze and recreated from Delia's female point of view, which thus challenges her father's genealogical and artistic domination (Milkova⁵ 172).

6. Images: The Photograph of Lila

In the quartet, Lila is compelled to alter the photo of herself as a young bride awaiting her nuptials in a similar process of reappropriation. Her creative act conveys her resistance to Stefano's abuse, which began on their wedding night. Aside from reframing the image, as in *Troubling Love*, the female point of view intervenes materially to irreversibly and poignantly transform the object.

Immediately after her wedding Lila gives her dressmaker a

photo of herself in her bride's gown. For several days the beautiful image is displayed in the shop window on the Rettifilo, and—according to the dressmaker, whose stories soon become legendary in the *rione*—it rouses the interests of men from high society (an Egyptian prince and a journalist) and show business (Renato Carosone and Vittorio De Sica) (snn 87). The window display also gets the attention of the Solara brothers, who swiftly urge Stefano to enlarge the photo and make a big decorative panel for the shop in Piazza dei Martiri; in the photo, Lila is in fact showing off one of her shoes. After lengthy negotiations, her husband agrees. In this way, the enormous photo panel turns out to be a kind of gigantic visual synthesis of male domination: it celebrates the nuptials by which Lila "had lost her shape and had dissolved inside the outlines of Stefano, becoming a subsidiary emanation of him" (snn 124). It highlights a detail—the bridal shoe shown off by Lila—that recalls how Lila had been betrayed by Stefano, her father, and her brother during the transaction involving the shoes and the shop in Piazza dei Martiri (which will bear the name Solara and not, as had initially been stipulated, Cerullo). Finally, like Lila herself, the image becomes "merchandise to barter" (snn 112) in her husband's negotiations with the Solaras—to whom she is forbidden to speak.

Despite this chain of events that comes to define her and is crystalized in the photo—itself an act of expropriation of her lived life—Lila manages to impose her will by altering the image, because Michele Solara, obsessed with her intelligence no less than her beauty, senses the creative value of her collage and supports her. In September 1961 she wrangles a few days to work on the large panel just before the inauguration of the shop and involves Elena in her experiment. Their alliance, doubling the female gaze and empowering both women, enlarges the creative act:

> I joined in with the devotion that I had felt ever since we were
> children. Those moments were thrilling, it was a pleasure to be

beside her, slipping inside her intentions, to the point of anticipating her. [. . .] They were magnificent hours of play, of invention, of freedom, such as we hadn't experienced together perhaps since childhood. Lila drew me into her frenzy. We bought paste, paint, brushes. [. . .] Lila had always been good with lines and colors, but here she did something more, though I wouldn't have been able to say what it was; hour after hour it engulfed me. [. . .] We suspended time, we isolated space, there remained only the play of glue, scissors, paper, paint: the play of shared creation. (snn 118, 121–22)

The "play of shared creation" magically suspends their violent reality (cf. 2.2):

[. . .] I still think that much of the pleasure of those days was derived from the resetting of the conditions of her, or our, life, from the capacity we had to lift ourselves above ourselves, to isolate ourselves in the pure and simple fulfillment of that sort of visual synthesis. (snn 122)

Lila creates by destroying: cutting, stripping, erasing whole parts of herself. Creation takes the form of self-mutilation and, occasionally, self-erasure (Wehling-Giorgi[3] 11). "The self-mutilated photo," writes Wehling-Giorgi, "stands as one of the novels' central visual metaphors of resistance against the colonization of the female body" (Wehling-Giorgi[4] 208):

Lila was happy, and she was drawing me deeper and deeper into her fierce happiness, because she had suddenly found, perhaps without even realizing it, an opportunity that allowed her to *portray* the fury she directed against herself, the insurgence, perhaps for the first time in her life, of the need [. . .] to erase herself. [. . .] With the black paper, with the green and purple circles that Lila drew around certain parts of her body, with the blood-red lines with which she sliced and said she was slicing it, she completed her own self-destruction *in an image*. (snn 122–23)

There are specific reasons for her rage at her own body. On

the one hand, Lila ravages that part of herself ("her belly") that represents a new, unwanted life: she will soon miscarry, on the day of the opening, confirming the self-abortive evil, the witch-craft that her husband accuses her of (snn 85; Wehling-Giorgi[1]). On the other hand, Lila ravages her own face till it becomes an effigy, producing a monstrous, "one-eyed" image of a female cyclops looming over her clients with her one spangled eye:

> The body of the bride Lila appeared cruelly shredded. Much of the head had disappeared, as had the stomach. There remained an eye, the hand on which the chin rested, the brilliant stain of the mouth, the diagonal stripe of the bust, the line of the crossed legs, the shoes. [. . .] I couldn't take my eyes off it. Lila was no longer recognizable. What remained was a seductive, tremendous form, the image of a one-eyed goddess who thrust her beautifully shod feet into the center of the room. (snn 119, 126)

Lila tears down the fiction of the traditional story about her-self, crystalized in the original image of the happy wife, and replaces it with a powerful, desperate artistic truth. Indeed, this new image speaks of a body that has survived male violations by violating itself, rebelled against mutilations by mutilating itself, denied its own erasure by erasing itself. Lila produces a hideous distortion of her frail womanly body, out of which rises a mytho-logical goddess-cyclops. Gigantic, threatening, ready to avenge the death of her human form by engendering just violence, the "one-eyed goddess" is captured in the act of hypnotizing or crushing the clients/slaves gathered at her feet.

7. Images: Gigliola's Corpse

According to a very ancient tradition, "horror has a woman's face" (Caverero[3] 23). The terrifying visage of the Gorgon, torn from her body, hence from her harmonious entirety, is an image of an offense that recurs even in contemporary horror films.

Femininity and horror mingle in another key scene in the quartet. In 2005, Elena and Lila discover Gigliola's corpse lying on one side in the filth of the neighborhood gardens (Wehling-Giorgi[4] 207). Their childhood friend's body still has the long hair she wore in her youth, but aside from that, the spoil of senility has ruined her. Age, the key ingredient of horror, has thinned her once full head of hair, the former dark color has been dyed an unnatural, fiery red. Twice Elena's gaze lingers over this detail:

> Her hair, once brown, was now fiery red, and long, the way she'd had it as a girl, but thin, and spread out on the loose dirt. [. . .] I thought of that face in profile on the dirt, of how thin the long hair was, of the whitish patches of skull. (tlts 24)

The detail encapsulates the whole: the corpulent body in a shabby old coat, ravaged beyond recognition:

> [. . .] she was extraordinarily fat, and was wearing an unfashionable dark-green raincoat. Lila recognized her immediately, but I did not [. . .] Her beautiful face was ruined, and her ankles had become enormous. One foot was shod in a worn, low-heeled shoe; the other was encased in a gray wool stocking, with a hole at the big toe, and the shoe was a few feet beyond, as if she had lost it kicking against some pain or fear. (tlts 24)

The scene at the heart of the first chapter of *Those Who Leave and Those Who Stay* is a kind of prologue positioned at the beginning of "Middle Time," a season that covers ages twenty-four to thirty-two: a formative, particularly rich and adventurous stage of the two friends' lives. Confirming the *smarginatura* of the biological and existential cycles set in motion by the first and final sections of the quartet (cf. 1.4), here too youthful formation is put into perspective by the deformation of the prologue. In the span of a few pages, Gigliola's corpse becomes a frame for several forms of violence and its boundary-dissolving effects. At the outset Elena emphasizes how this "enormous" body has been transformed and its powers of seduction have faded: "How she must have suffered from that transformation, she who had been beautiful and had caught the handsome Michele Solara" (slc 460–61). As the girlfriend-then-wife governed by the whims of the abusive Michele ("He had taken everything of her, immediately, when she was almost a child. He had consumed her, crumpled her, and now that she was twenty-five he was used to her, he didn't even look at her anymore"; tlts 206) and second place in a competition her own man/master creates between her and Lila (tlts 208–9), Gigliola turns her life into a drama of jealousies, pretenses, and infidelities. In all likelihood, she is the one who sets fire to the photo panel that Lila recreates (snn 140; Wehling-Giorgi[4] 208). Both victim and victimizer, Gigliola represents the ambiguity of female aggression that defines the neighborhood.

Lila's powers of seduction fade too, she who was the most beautiful girl in the *rione*, a fact that underscores that both women are deluded—if in different ways—into thinking their youthful beauty equips them to navigate the patriarchal structure that actually exploits them. With unrelenting cruelty Elena describes the marks of old age, the traces of grief and loss on Lila's face and body:

> [. . .] she was permanently skin and bones. She had short hair that she cut herself; it was completely white, not by choice but from neglect. Her face was deeply lined, and increasingly recalled her father's. She laughed nervously, almost a shriek, and spoke too loudly. She was constantly gesturing, giving to each gesture such fierce determination that she seemed to want to slice in half the houses, the street, the passersby, me. (tlts 23)

Gigliola dies of a heart attack while walking down the street, but the cause of her death is deliberately put off so as to leave room for Elena's first suspicion. "At the time," Elena says, "we still didn't know that she had died of a heart attack, I thought she had been murdered" (slc 460). We do not learn the truth until the fourth volume (slc 459–61). In the opening pages of *Those Who Leave and Those Who Stay* the deliberate ambiguity as to the cause of Gigliola's death signals to readers that from here on out the quartet will be comprised of violent deaths. In fact, the scene in the gardens, which occurs when both friends are sixty-one, is only the last in a long line of murders and suicides: "How many who had been girls with us were no longer alive, had disappeared from the face of the earth because of illness, because their nervous systems had been unable to endure the sandpaper of torments, because their blood had been spilled" (tlts 24). Readers of the entire cycle encounter many images of death: the bloodstained pillow where the shattered head of Franco Mari rests, the gunshots that kill Bruno Soccavo and Gino (the neighborhood pharmacist), Alfonso's beaten body washed ashore in Coroglio, the train car where Lila's brother Rino is found dead of an overdose, the street on which the Solara brothers are taken out.

The grief that deforms Lila and Gigliola's bodies is mirrored by the metropolis, by the traces of violence in a space animated by a biology of bad moods (Wehling-Giorgi[4] 209):

> Dead, wounded. And shouts, blows, cherry bombs. The city seemed to harbor in its guts a fury that couldn't get out and therefore eroded it from the inside, or erupted in pustules on the surface, swollen with venom against everyone, children, adults, old people, visitors from other cities [. . .]. (tlts 27)

Elena reconstructs the arc of this "wounded urban topography" (Wehling-Giorgi[4] 207) snaking across her timeline and various settings: the skyscraper at the train station, the university classrooms, the swarm of the streets; during her adolescence in the *rione*, her oppressive homecomings from the Normale, her flight as an adult, her disenchantment in adulthood. Spaces and seasons are marked by cycles of violence that are of the *rione* yet transcend the *rione*, cycles that include Naples, Italy, Europe, and ultimately the whole world (cf. 4.9):

> Get away for good, far from the life we've lived since birth. Settle in well-organized lands where everything really is possible. I had fled, in fact. Only to discover, in the decades to come, that I had been wrong, that it was a chain with larger and larger links: the neighborhood was connected to the city, the city to Italy, Italy to Europe, Europe to the whole planet (tlts 28)

8. Disappearances

Disappearing is an extreme, two-pronged response by women to the sense of loss they experience because of male violence. The plunder and expropriation of oneself is a vacuum that generates another vacuum. Erasing oneself becomes "an aesthetic project" (slc 455), undertaken by Lila as it is by the protagonists of Ferrante's other novels. On the one hand, these feminine figures seem to have definitively succumbed to male violence, yet by making an abrupt exit they challenge the traditional structures of that violence, particularly the family structure. As Ferrante points out, "The disappearance of women should be interpreted not only as giving up the fight against the violence of the world but also as clear rejection. [. . .] 'Io non ci sto' [is literally a form that] means: I'm not here, in this place, before what you're suggesting" (fr 327). This form of "removing oneself from the picture," of "refusing to engage" (fr 339) in the sometimes explicit, sometimes underhanded game of violence can be deemed an "aesthetic project" because it allows women to reshape their lives and the lives of others.

It also shapes the narrative form. Indeed, the inconsistent consistency of Ferrante's storylines hinges on this radical gesture, and their knotty effects are often determined by the departure of feminine figures. *Troubling Love* is "the story of a disappearance" (fr 327) that operates on such an existential and aesthetic level: the mother's absence, while also being the mysterious cause that sets the thriller in motion, finally enables her daughter to understand her presence by rewriting the significance of their lives. Yet the mystery is never definitively resolved. Along with Delia, we can plausibly speculate that Amalia decided to disappear in the sea—chose, that is, to drown herself—but we can never be absolutely certain because at the moment of reckoning her daughter opts not to interrogate her mother's suitor, the one witness to the event (tl 135). The plot contracts and dissolves because of this disappearance, about which Delia feels she alone has the right to the last word: "I was the only possible source of the story," she says, "I couldn't nor did I want to search outside myself (tl 137).

In *The Days of Abandonment*, the *poverella*'s suicide is the most extreme act of protest available to this marginalized, humiliated, and offended woman. In *The Lost Daughter*, the original cause of Leda's unhappiness is a disappearance that took place many years earlier, when for three years she chose to abandon her own young daughters in the pursuit of a new life (ld 102). One can also sketch out a history of disappearances, since, behind Leda, one glimpses an oppressed mother who constantly elects to make an impossible escape ("In reality she was always there, in her words she was constantly disappearing from home"; ld 21). Moreover, the entire universe of Ferrante's writing is full of *frantumaglia*, a mass that revolves around the absence of identity produced by male colonization. If all the women on the covers of Ferrante's novels are faceless—their backs turned, their heads missing—that is "because they are engaged in looking for [their faces]" (Manetti[2]). Disappearance is, in short, a binary movement in which "being driven back" is countered with "driving oneself back." "Whenever a part of you emerges that's not consistent with the canonic female," Ferrante says, "you feel that that part causes uneasiness in you and in others, and you'd better get rid of it in a hurry" (fr 277).

There are various degrees of disappearance in the quartet, nesting dolls contained inside the most extreme, structural form: Lila's mysterious absence, which prompts Elena's writing, gives rise to the latter's hope of willing her friend back into existence by reconstructing their life and mutual bond (Maksimowicz 227–29). As in *Troubling Love,* here too construction implies deconstruction, because the disappearance of Lila becomes the emblem of a series of unfinished sequences about the incident, events that, however decisive, lack a clear cause. The first of these is the disappearance of Tina, Lila's beloved daughter, the lost child referred to in the title of the fourth volume whose name recalls the lost dolls with which the girls first forge their friendship (cf. 2.2, 2.4, 3.5, 4.5). The void remains inexpressible because those responsible for the hypothetical kidnapping or the possible car accident are never identified. This un-processable grief creates a dangerous rift:

> [Lila] had no lifeless body to cling to in despair, there was no one for whom to hold a funeral, she couldn't linger before a corpse that had walked, run, talked, hugged her, and had ended up a broken thing. (slc 339)

Lila's work on Naples disappears with her, and its disappearance is depicted as a vanishing of her body and the body of her lost daughter within the larger body of the city:

> Just at that moment the certainty sprang to mind that Lila, writing about Naples, would write about Tina, and the text—precisely because it was nourished by the effort of expressing an inexpressible grief—would be extraordinary. (slc 452)

Along with Lila's work vanishes Elena's excruciating fantasy of Lila's unique and unparalleled book that would have encapsulated Naples and, as Elena herself admits, definitively proven her own mediocrity as a writer (slc 461). Hence, disappearance is at the root of the story as well as the sabotaging of that story, not only because it dissolves the cause-and-effect relationships that would make the story cohere, but because it destroys the completion of a life and the immediacy of interiority in the quartet—the grand passions (cf. 1.2). The erasure of oneself is "a desire to disappear, to get lost, that calls into question every principle of melodramatic psychology precisely because in the end it crushes and negates those same passions that seemed sovereign and unassailable" (Donnarumma[1] 142).

In Lila's life this anarchic act precipitates many temporary deaths: the end of her comfortable marriage, the repudiation of the shoes she designed, the burning of *The Blue Fairy* at the factory, the end of her life as a laborer, the absorption of her creativity by abstract technology (cf. 7.5), the sale of Basic Sight, which she is in large part responsible for running aground. Finally, another loss, which occurs, significantly, at the same time as her daughter's disappearance, is that of language. Along with Tina, Lila's vibrant Italian, the language she always exhibited and wielded so well in her youth, vanishes, or at least becomes intermittent (cf. 5.5). Elena realizes that "a mutual communicative adjustment" (Alfonzetti 5) has become necessary for them:

> [Lila[resorted to Italian as if to a barrier; I tried to push her toward dialect, our language of candor. But while her Italian was translated from dialect, my dialect was increasingly translated from Italian, and we both spoke a false language. (slc 362)

The power of images to capture life can do little to stop this unstable dispersion. Like *Troubling Love*, the quartet abounds with ambiguous visions that seek in vain to contain Lila (Milkova[5] 167). The framed pictures of Lila's designs—those with which Stefano wants to celebrate his engagement to her—look like "precious relics" (mbf 250) taken off a cadaver. The image of Lila as a bride, the enlarged photo on which she justifiably unleashes her fury, is similarly macabre. Her need to elude all depictions of herself is affirmed in her first and final disappearance. In the prologue to *My Brilliant Friend*, "Eliminating the Traces," Lila removes her image from all the family photos, thus ritualizing her irreducibility (Milkova[5] 168-169).

9. Depicting Violence from a Woman's Point of View

Why is the subject of violence that emerges in Ferrante's writing so gripping? One answer is her *approach* to the subject, the expressive register she chooses, the angle of view from which she depicts the issue. In the first place, Ferrante refutes the "widespread conviction" that "conflict and violence in the domestic sphere and in all of life's most common contexts cannot be expressed other than via the modules that the male world defines as feminine" (fr 335). These expressive "modules" are the lament, victimhood, and mannered suffering. The repudiation of this colonized approach explains the particular rawness of Ferrante's descriptions of violence: gone are the pathetic haloes and facile oppositions between victims and victimizers. As in the scene of Lila's rape, the narrator focuses on the aggressor, allowing us to enter the consciousness of male violence and recognize its cultural roots. As with all widespread systematic abuse, the victims themselves can become victimizers. In *The Neapolitan Novels* the women of the *rione* are often accomplices and perpetuators of male violence.

Throughout the quartet, the abuse of women shapes identity: it reinforces the construction of masculinity as defined— in extremely different ways—by the tutelage and delegitimization of the other gender. This dynamic is put in the same language of physical oppression, which in Italian refers to "the forced manipulation of identity, to its cancellation" (fr 277). I'll bash your face in, I'll beat you beyond recognition: "Either you'll be the way I say or I'll change you by beating you till I kill you" (fr 277). When the bodies of women are transformed into images represented or re-created from a female point of view—as in the painting in *Troubling Love*, Lila's photo panel or Gigliola's body—they take on a new symbolic power able to draw a liminal line between the physical and the psychic, between old and new depictions of the feminine and maternal, as well as of time and space (Wehling-Giorgi[4] 210). Repositioning the power dynamics that propel violence on an aesthetic plane means employing a new paradigm of story-telling: depicting abuse from a female point of view also implies a different way of portraying content, of expressing creative resistance through literary forms. The disappearances, for example, are flights from the narrow confines of patriarchal violence as well as the disbanded forms of the thriller in *Troubling Love* or the fairy tale of the quartet. Like these dismantled structures, disappearance is a hybrid figure that weds destructive elements with creative elements: an apocalyptic escape from time yet also the tragic sense of ruptures in time; an act that protects the wholeness of the "I" yet also leads to its annihilation; a gaze blinded by a bright light yet the clear vision of an act that must be carried to completion. The words and images that delineate abuse, the various ways the two friends have pursued to defend themselves from middle- and underclass male violence, are turning points in the plot, just as they are in our imagination: they lie inside and outside the quartet. If Elena's first novel critiques the sexual repression that she hasn't fully come to terms with, and depicts the labyrinth of truth and lies in which the subordinate woman in the middle-class is both lost and found, Lila's photo panel is instead a fierce symbol of her provocative revolt against her world, her era, and her forms. In this day and age, women are in need of both.

CHAPTER SEVEN
History and Stories

1. Preliminary Investigation

I f you can't connect your story of the shoes with the story of the computers," Elena thinks as she argues with Lila, who is standing right in front of her, "it means only that you don't have the tools to do it" (slc 263). Elena makes the same silent, arrogant claim for her writing: that she has returned to live in the *rione* to conduct an "experiment in composition," that she knows how to "create order" where, according to her friend, there is no "coherence" (slc 262). Their quarrel is also with reality. Which of the two friends truly inhabits the age in which they live? Which of the two embodies it? The one with her vitality and entrepreneurial spirit, or the other with her books? Which of the two is capable of combining disparate facts in order to make a mark on the map of time? After long reflecting on the polyphony of the quartet in these chapters (cf. 1.5 and 2.6, for example), the only answer is both, and each thanks to the other. The scope of this chapter is to understand how the polyphony of these two subordinate women results in a set of values and prospects that makes depicting the vast world, and representing a large historical tableau spanning six decades, possible.

To understand how we as readers perceive time in the quartet, we should consider the words of Anna Banti, the author of major novels about Italian history including 1967's *Noi credevamo* (We Believed). "History," says Banti, "isn't all about the dates and biographies of conquering captains but about the truths that only through the careful meditation on heterogeneous elements, spoken in secret, are revealed" (Banti). Given the many nineteenth and twentieth-century novels (from De Roberto's *The Viceroys* to Lampedusa's *The Leopard* to Morante's *History*) that have depicted Italy's ahistorical chronology and that have questioned, at different times and in different ways, the rhetoric surrounding the country's national identity, Banti's statement may sound predictable. But it isn't. Because the temptation to commemorate events has to do with unsettled questions about Italy's private and public identity, and therefore this tendency resurfaces time and again in new forms and new guises. For example, the moment Italian writers attempt to engage with the years of protest and youth movements extending from 1968 to the end of the 1970s, many of them often come up against a tired rhetoric, thronged with the "conquering captains" that Banti mentions. In many novels inspired by this historical period, the cast of characters prominently features charismatic leaders or militants engaged in watershed moments that have by now become canonical (the Battle of Valle Giulia, the massacre in Piazza Fontana, the kidnapping and murder of Aldo Moro): "The overall effect is a kind of romance novel of remarkable public events that feeds off popular entertainment historicism, ultimately more misleading than the romance novel set forth by Elena Ferrante, which looks directly at ordinary life" (Donnarumma[1] 147). In these "romance novels," women often play secondary roles. Companions in life and activism, at times disturbing militant feminists, at others victims of political and/or sexual violence, they are almost always marginal to the plot. The male protagonists are positioned to experience political power as, in part, masculine power, and as its public voice: an element that closely connects them to their otherwise adversarial fathers.

Ferrante instead focuses at length on the subordination of young female activists in countless scenes that show how women continue to be repressed, especially linguistically, in the halls at the Normale and at the student movement gatherings before the explosion of the feminist movement (cf. 5.7). Still more innovative is the writer's adoption of a deliberately antiheroic perspective when feminism enters Elena's life. Even as it emerges as the most formative moment in the protagonist's life (cf. 7.4), it is depicted in muted tones, with a series of ordinary scenes. But the question of subordination and the new female centrality has to do not only with the chronological arc of the protests but with modernity *in toto*, as men find themselves reckoning—as they still do—with what Carla Lonzi, at the beginning of the 1970s, called "The Unpredictable Subject": women whose difference is generated by "having been left out of history for thousands of years" (Lonzi 47, 14–15). To create a form for this difference, Ferrante chooses a "lateral viewpoint with respect to Major Events," which is, at the same time, "a sign of her intelligence about the present" (Donnarumma[1] 147) and her ability to inhabit today's—so often bleak—world without seeking comfort in a fairy tale past. She does not nostalgically idealize, say, the sobering poverty of the postwar years or the political utopias of the 1960s and '70s, a period that was "[. . .] in reality very difficult and painful for those who started from a position of disadvantage"(fr 376), women most of all. To avoid the risk of nostalgia, the writer declares that she wants to reconstruct the past by conducting "a preliminary investigation," examining "trial exhibits":

[. . .] History and stories are written, and they are written from the balcony of the present, looking out on the electrical storm of the past; that is to say, there is nothing more unstable than the past. The past, in its indeterminacy, presents itself either through the filter of nostalgia or through the filter of [a preliminary investigation].[3] I don't love nostalgia; it leads us to ignore individual sufferings, large pockets of misery, cultural and civil poverty, widespread corruption, regression after minimal and illusory progress. I prefer [exhibits in the court record]. (fr 376)

The preliminary investigation metaphor is very intriguing, because it refers back to the idea of History, history that must neither be idealized nor courted but that, on the contrary, should be put on trial, examined with the cool eye of someone who seeks the truth, no matter how uncomfortable. Yet in Ferrante's metaphor, not only the term but the method of examining the "exhibits" is significant. Recounting events is associated with scrupulously gathering data at the scene of a crime, with inquests and fact-finding missions.

But why should the investigation and its cold, punctilious reconstruction of what happened be a preferred entry point into a plastic story about historical events? Why would that make room for the Unpredictable Subject's marginalized point of view? This courtroom method is in truth closely related to Ferrante's writing technique. In the quartet the "investigation" is a sweeping phenomenology of either ordinary scenes in which one or both friends are humiliated and silenced—scenes in which Elena and Lila often work together to formulate each other's discussion of inferiority (and therefore, in these cases, we must talk about self-humiliation and self-erasure; cf. 5.6–5.7 and 6.3–6.4)—or, conversely, of scenes in which both protagonists assert their objections and make their cries of revolt. This phenomenology manages to capture the great mobility and perennial metamorphosis of the Unpredictable Subject. With trial exhibits, she can reconstruct the numerous ways in which new female identities have experienced both conformity

---

[3] Translated as "preliminary impressions" in the first edition of *Frantumaglia* and corrected in subsequent editions.

and rebellion, experiencing the bogus equality of middle-class emancipation and Marxist revolutions and arriving at an understanding that "the oppression of women [. . .] is not resolved by equality but persists thanks to equality" (Lonzi 13).

Ever since their childhood, through their formative period and up through adulthood, the two protagonists are inhabited by a duplicate and divergent sense of time. On the one hand, they are driven backward to the static time of their mothers and the cave (cf. 3.3), to a world where women have been oppressed for thousands of years, while on the other, they are driven forward by the frenetic chronology of historical change:

> I felt as if Elena and Lila were alienated from History, with all its political, social, economic, cultural apparatus, and yet included in it almost without knowing it, in every word or act. (fr 283)

In Ferrante's narrative historical events are the fruit of these two temporalities and they result in a continuous exchange of glances, words, languages, and relationships: that universe of social psychology embodied by high and low dialect, by class and gender conflict, which shapes Elena and Lila and which they in turn try to shape. These are indistinct yet highly concrete elements of the relationship that map time:

> I wanted the historical period to be a faintly defined background and also to emerge from the changes that had an impact on the characters' lives, from their uncertainties, decisions, actions, language. (fr 283–84)

Because history becomes a story, explains Ferrante, it is necessary that "[. . .] the particularity of the era is caught in the workings of the text" (fr 79). The difference of this Unpredictable Subject, her capacity to speak to the "alienation-inclusion" margin and render it profoundly representative of those years, is what generates the pleasure of writing about historical time:

*

The historical period slipped naturally into the characters' gestures, thoughts, and choices about life, although it never imposed itself, settling outside them as a detailed background. [. . .] As for my distaste for politics and sociology I discovered that it was a screen, behind which lurked the pleasure—yes, I mean it—the pleasure of narrating a sort of female alienation-inclusion. (fr 283)

If the events of the quartet never ultimately achieve coherence, much less a final synthesis, that is because the subordinate figure sees and speaks from the edge of those events, seizing upon their irrationality more than their order, feeling estranged from them rather than involved in them. The meaning of events lies not in an emblematic era but in a viscous web of relationships (more often comprised of silences than words) or bodies (that seek pleasure, or else endure or accommodate male desires, which form and deform them). Female difference is the point of view that allows us to see this microhistory of slight miseries:

> It is like facing a mirror that not only reflects your image just as you are (and your blemishes and injuries and wrongs and hypocrisies and trivialities). It also reflects the exact image of your parents, friends, grandparents, girlfriends, colleagues, companions, sisters, brothers, acquaintances (and their blemishes, injuries, wrongs, hypocrisies, and trivialities). (Lo Moro)

2. Stories and Their Timelines

If stories and not history are what matter, then the tale cannot help but generate "an incongruous mixture of expressive registers, codes, and genres" (fr 368). For example, it has been rightly pointed out that there are at least four types of novels tucked into *Those Who Leave and Those Who Stay*: "the marriage plot, and later the affair plot, starring Elena; the nonfiction novel about the education of an intellectual (Elena again); the industrial novel about Lila's experience at Bruno Soccavo's factory; the historical novel about the workers' and students' revolts, the first feminist groups, the uprisings in public squares, and nascent terrorism" (Manetti[3]). The hybridity of the quartet's complex form and the "hyper-genre" construction of the narrative (cf 1.1)—recombining various forms in the mold of Morante's *Lies and Sorcery*—are largely due to the fact that human affairs outnumber history, and the compactness of emblematic eras is shattered into an endless array of minor events and microhistories. The hyper-genre is predicated on the idea that no one form can account for the lives of those years, because of an excess of life that often ends up spilling over into solitude. The steady beat of microhistories gives one the sense of each individual's inability to seize upon the significant possibilities that the years of the Italian economic miracle and the later uprisings afforded them. If, for example, Elena represents the conquests of social mobility in that era—in many ways unrepeatable today—she will be the one to shoulder the burden of failure, because "profound changes take generations; they must involve everybody. At times Elena herself feels that individual lives, even the most fortunate, are ultimately unsatisfactory and in many ways at fault" (fr 359).

But the hyper-genre also serves to make room for the Unpredictable Subject, who, excluded from history for millennia, has no public tradition and thus no literary tradition. The inclusion of many forms of the novel in one text signifies the need for a narrative voice to trespass; a narrative voice that, not having a stable place, begins many versions of the tale, trying to find a place that welcomes her, or at least a toehold in each. This story of national transformations, from the twentieth century until today, is a plastic proto-form within which many Italian women writers, in various ways, have negotiated and continue to negotiate the question of recognizing women in the literary and political arenas, giving rise to women as narrators and/or protagonists, ushering them from invisibility to visibility, from the margins to some kind of central position. One can map a clear constellation of women writers, from Elsa Morante to Goliarda Sapienza to Maria Rosa Cutrufelli, who reconstruct the national past "through a multitude of 'minimal' stories, strategically conceived of on the ridge of various literary genres" (Todesco 18).

The genesis of *The Neapolitan Novels'* historical tableau lies in a conflicting urge to conduct an investigation. On the one hand, the past must be reconstructed with absolute disenchantment, with cool detachment. On the other, the clear, brutal representation must be indirect: it must, so to speak, ooze from the characters' lives, because the changes are wrought on their flesh. It must never be told from a bird's-eye point of view, from the perspective of those who, at the end of the day, comprehend the intricate design. Instead it must adopt an on-the-ground angle that adheres to the confused and chaotic perception of those who live through an event in the moment, of those who live as subordinates in pursuit of emancipation.

Let's look at a few concrete examples of how the human stories destabilize History and confine it to the measure of minor events. *My Brilliant Friend*, which covers the years 1950 to 1961, is divided into an introduction ("Prologue: Eliminating All the Traces") and two sections that set in motion the actual narrative ("Childhood: The Story of Don Achille" and "Adolescence: The Story of the Shoes"). In the first section, "Childhood: The Story of Don Achille," Elena and Lila's school life is the one way to gauge time, yet this chronological compass is more often a means of losing one's way than a means to locate us in a specific time. While Chapter 13 touches on the tempestuous transition to middle school, which occurs when the two girls are "toward the end of fifth grade" (mbf 63) and therefore almost eleven years old (two-thirds of the way into the first volume we learn that both were born a week apart in August; mbf 226), Chapter 14, which features the two girls' famous interrogation of "the Ogre" Don Achille about the disappearance of their dolls, swings backward to two years earlier, because their age at the time of the adventure is given as "eight, almost nine" (mbf 34). However, their age does not appear in the chapter that describes the episode but in one of the first chapters (Chapter 3, mbf 34), and then it is almost buried in an aside. It is further obscured by the opening of Chapter 15 ("Gigliola Spagnuolo and I started going to the teacher's house to prepare for the admissions test"; mbf 67), which once again returns to the end of fifth grade and the girls' participation in the middle school admissions exam, which Lila is barred from taking.

This continual fragmentation of time shines a light on the magical time of childhood whose enchantment consists of two experiences connected to elementary school and friendship, while also underscoring the end of this period of time and symbiosis, once preparing for middle school and embarking on different paths becomes unavoidable. From then on, Lila will, formally speaking, belong to the majority of semiliterates in the *rione* who do not have more than an elementary school education. In this first part of the story we find no explicit references to World War II, which is later introduced in intense glimpses and associations charged with childhood anguish: "The oldest son of Don Achille—I had never seen him, and yet I seemed to remember him—had gone to war and died twice: drowned in the Pacific Ocean, then eaten by sharks" (mbf 32); "Our world was like that, full of words that killed: croup, tetanus, typhus, gas, war, lathe, rubble, work, bombardment, bomb, tuberculosis, infection" (mbf 33).

Another indirect but potent means of evoking historical drama, without having it appear explicitly but rather allowing its ghostly presence to loom over the scene, is the dislocation of imaginary or real objects. In this first category we can place Don Achille's black bag, the imaginary accessory in which, according to Elena and Lila, the omnivorous ogre has hidden the two dolls. "I imagined him with his mouth open," says Elena, "because of his long animal fangs, his body of glazed stone and poisonous grasses, always ready to pick up in an enormous black bag anything we dropped through the torn corners of the grate" (mbf 31). Elena is surprised to see Lila's impertinent accusation pains Don Achille. The ogre gleans from the little girl's innocent voice "confirmation of something he already knew" (mbf 67), which is to say—as we readers can deduce—that his notoriety as a "dealer in the black market, [a] loan shark" (as he is listed in the index of characters, starting with *The Story of a New Name*) who enriched himself by trading contraband during the war, has been conveyed to the children by their parents and nurtured in them fantasies of kidnapping.

To the second category belongs the object that terrifies Elena during her search for the dolls in the cellar ("I got scared by what seemed to me a soft face, with large glass eyes, that lengthened into a chin shaped like a box"; mbf 55). Lila calls it an "anti-gas mask" because "that's what her father called it" (mbf 56). Neither girl, therefore, understands its function or history. The key to interpreting these events, the ability of these objects to speak openly of the history that produced them, emerges only after another six years, when Pasquale—the Communist construction worker and son of a Communist grocer who died unjustly in prison—explains to a then-fourteen-year-old Lila the political forces in play between the war and postwar years. She immediately associates the ideologies with names and places:

> Fascism, Nazism, the war, the Allies, the monarchy, the repub-
> lic—she turned them into streets, houses, faces, Don Achille and
> the black market, Alfredo Peluso the Communist, the Camorrist

grandfather of the Solaras, the father, Silvio, a worse Fascist than Marcello and Michele, and her father, Fernando the shoemaker, and my father, all—all—in her eyes stained to the marrow by shadowy crimes, all hardened criminals or acquiescent accomplices, all bought for practically nothing. (mbf 154–55).

This "frenzy of absolute disclosure" (mbf 154) is not however the fury of an abstract ideological principle but rather a vocabulary that enables her to translate the enigmas of the lives in the *rione* and their mutual conflicts: "The apparently—and only apparently—abstract forces at work in the twentieth century, and that today seem handed down to us with labels void of meaning, have in the course of the narrative lives and bodies, ways of being in the world and of somehow abiding violence or opposing it, exploiting the poverty of others, robbing and loansharking—which is a form of theft—or else seeking redemption beyond the most basic hope" (Fortini).

The one date (aside from the so-to-speak mimetic date given in Donato Sarratore's inscription to Melina: "*To Melina who nurtured my poetry. Donato. Naples, 12 June 1958*"; mbf 129) explicitly stated in the entire first volume, December 31, 1958, ushers in the second section, "Adolescence: The Story of the Shoes," and chronicles the first episode of Lila's *smarginatura*. Our sense of time in *My Brilliant Friend* is gleaned by comparing this date to Elena's school cycles, the passing of seasons, and the anniversary of the friends' birthdays. For example, we learn that Elena is in her first year of high school when, "one Sunday in the middle of April" the following year (mbf 191), 1959, she takes a walk with her friends from the *rione*, which will lead to the fight with the boys from the nice neighborhoods in Naples (cf. 4.2). In the same scene we read that Lila (and therefore Elena) is fourteen (mbf 194); so, when Elena celebrates her birthday that August, we can determine that both girls are turning fifteen (mbf 226). Lila's wedding, celebrated in 1961, is reported in such a way that the date,

March 12th (mbf 275, 311), though frequently repeated, is never attached to the year, so much so that it becomes quite hard to distinguish how much time has elapsed between their wedding day and the time of their engagement (begun in 1959, though here too the specific date is missing). In short, it creates a hole in the time of their youth, marked more by the passing of the seasons than the change of one's marital status.

Like the black bag and the World War-II-era gas mask, two more objects, the television and cars—the Solaras' 1100 and Stefano's red sports car—are the objective correlatives of the economic boom. That both are associated with Lila's corruption—Marcello Solara gives the television to the Cerullo family while courting her, Stefano's car is a decisive factor in her decision (cf. 4.4) to accept his marriage proposal to guarantee her own wealth and that of her family—is a sign that the quartet is constantly critical of progress. Regarding the sea change wrought by the economic miracle, it is a *camorrista*, Marcello Solara, who makes the most staunch case for the ideology of social change characteristic of that time period, saying, "You begin with a cellar and from generation to generation you can go far" (mbf 201; Russo Bullaro 35).

3. Lives in the Age of Revolution

Only a few dates are ever given in the quartet. More importantly, they are spread out in such a manner as to foreground lived experience. When you attempt to identify or cite with greater precision the year in which an episode may have occurred—as this book does frequently for the sake of clarity—you are forced to carefully reconstruct the sequence of events. The quartet's downgrading of major historical events becomes even more troublesome as we reach the 1960s and '70s and the period of the workers' and student movements.

Provocatively, the official dates of *The Story of a New Name*, which covers the years 1961 to 1968, skim over the major protests, ignoring them completely. The now mythic spring of '68, consecrated in history by the May 1968 events in France, is mentioned merely in relation to the story of Gigliola's marriage to Michele Solara. "Either we marry by the spring of 1968," says Gigliola, "or I'm leaving and fuck him" (snn 419). The echo of the French protests reaches Elena through her politically conscious future sister-in-law, Mariarosa, who urges her to "take part in what she called *the unstoppable flow of events*" (tlts 62–63). But Elena's initial enthusiasm ("To go to Milan, and on to France, to arrive in Paris in revolt, face the brutality of the police, plunge with my whole personal history into the most incandescent magma of these months") is quickly quelled by the promotion of her first novel in Italy. "I left," says Elena, "but not for Paris" (tlts 63). The following autumn she is called upon to consider another marriage; this time it is Pietro who proposes to Elena, a proposal more businesslike than romantic:

> [. . .] Pietro remained serious, he had everything clear in his mind, he laid out his plan: two years to establish himself at the university and then he would marry me. He even set the date: September 1969. (snn 435)

In another instance, the date serves to establish the connection between a biological event and its social consequences. An ordinary "Sunday in the late autumn of 1963" (snn 349) becomes significant because it marks the moment when Lila, having just discovered that she is pregnant, decides to leave Stefano in order to live openly with Nino. In *The Story of a New Name* only one set of complete dates is recorded, when Elena returns to the *rione* from the Normale for Christmas vacation, on the cusp of 1965: "I stayed in the neighborhood for ten days, from December 24, 1964, to January 3, 1965, but

I never went to see Lila" (snn 377). This specific time period centers on the story of their friendship, its ups and downs and external features (in particular their competition for Nino) that either weaken or strengthen it. In this case, Elena willingly ignores her friend because both believe Nino is the father of Lila's newborn, and Elena would suffer unbearably to note the resemblance.

Another vague mention of time, connected to the mechanism of recognition and envy that binds the two friends together, is "the spring of 1966," during which Lila, "in a state of great agitation," entrusts Elena with "a metal box that contained eight notebooks" (snn 15). These secret diaries are, as we now know (1.5 and 2.3), the clearest evidence of Lila's brilliance, and therefore a source of torment that will drive Elena to throw them in the Arno a few months later. While the student protests explode in *Those Who Leave and Those Who Stay*—which spans from 1968 to 1976—the chronology is most concerned with celebrating Elena and Pietro's firstborn ("Our daughter was born on February 12, 1970, at five-twenty in the morning"; tlts 237). But the real driving force behind this troublesome private historiography is their marriage, the date and year of which is given ("I was married on May 17, 1969, in Florence; tlts 178), as is Elena's oncoming crisis. Once, with meticulous scruple, Elena reports the date that her husband forgets the manuscript of her second novel—given to him by her to read—under a pile of books; the rejection of the manuscript (by the publishing house her mother-in-law Adele recommends in the days that follow) makes her feel deeply failed: "The next day, July 30, 1973, I went to see if my husband had started reading: the typescript was under the books he had been working on for most of the night, it was clear that he hadn't even looked through it" (tlts 267). The failure of the book catalyzes time to the point that the cholera epidemic

in Naples is evoked—without providing the date of the outbreak (August 24, 1973)—only in connection with Lila's
reading and negative judgment of the novel (tlts 273). In
another circumstance, the soon-to-be adulteress remembers
the date when Nino, at her husband's invitation to dinner no
less, enters her home and her life, thus precipitating the end
of her marriage. "I remember the date precisely," says Elena,
"March 9, 1976" (tlts 355).

Mention is made of the coup d'état in Chile, on September
11, 1973, merely to foreground the climate of bourgeois patriarchy at home: "Once Dede wouldn't let [Pietro] watch the
news—it was right after the coup in Chile—and he spanked
her much too hard" (tlts 276). Then again, from Elena's perspective, the words of civic engagement always suffer from a
sense of alienation (cf 5.7); they are "sounds without sense"
that have, since her days at high school with Professor Galiani,
obliged her to toil her way through a cultural script:

> I would have to work even harder in order to be able to say
> to Nino, to Professor Galiani, to Carlo, to Armando: Yes, I
> understand, I know. The entire planet is threatened. Nuclear
> war. Colonialism, neocolonialism. The pieds-noirs, the O.A.S.
> and the National Liberation Front. The fury of mass slaughters.
> Gaullism, Fascism. France, Armée, Grandeur, Honneur. Sartre is
> a pessimist, but he counts on the Communist workers in Paris.
> The wrong direction taken by France, by Italy. Opening to the
> left. Saragat, Nenni. Fanfani in London, Macmillan. The
> Christian Democratic congress in our city. The followers of
> Fanfani, Moro, the Christian Democratic left. The socialists have
> ended up in the jaws of power. We will be Communists, we with
> our proletariat and our parliamentarians, to get the laws of the
> center left passed. (snn 158–59)

Things don't change with the arrival of 1968. For Elena the
year immediately becomes another arena to dominate as she
seeks to keep her anxiety about being a cultural parvenu at
bay. "Driving that decision to bring myself up to date by

forced marches was," Elena admits, "at least at first, I think, the old urgency to succeed" (tlts 52). Yet the language of protest remains a foreign language, a "wisp of smoke," stock phrases to memorize in order to make a space for herself during public debates and their rituals of recognition:

> (*The world is profoundly unjust and must be changed, but both the peaceful coexistence between American imperialism and the Stalinist bureaucracies, on the one hand, and the reformist politics of the European, and especially the Italian, workers' parties, on the other, are directed at keeping the proletariat in a subordinate wait-and-see situation that throws water on the fire of revolution, with the result that if the global stalemate wins, if social democracy wins, it will be capital that triumphs through the centuries and the working class will fall victim to enforced consumerism.*) (tlts 52)

The moment that her private affairs turn visceral, as when Elena finally makes love to Nino for the first time, in 1976, the public sphere and its watchwords immediately fade, and the body takes center stage:

> What did I care anymore about his political opinions, about Pasquale and Nadia, about the death of Ulrike Meinhof, the birth of the Socialist Republic of Vietnam, the electoral advances of the Communist Party? The world had retreated. I felt sunk inside myself, inside my flesh, which seemed to me not only the sole dwelling possible but also the only material for which it was worthwhile to struggle. (tlts 389)

But the map of time is more complex than it appears: the compelling game of the quartet is that of defending the relevance of minor lived events while endowing this existential sumptuousness with historic, if indirect, intensity. Two slices of life restore a particularly animated image of the times and transformations underway. The first is Lila's experience as a laborer (cf. 2.6), which is inserted into the contractual disputes of 1969. In perfect coherence with the story's anti-epic key, this historical period is never formally named during Elena's long account of her friend's experience, but it is brought to life concretely for the reader by way of a complicated storyline of personal relationships. The exchanges and conflicts between Lila and the workers and student committee on Via dei Tribunali ("[Lila] left in a daze, with the impression of having exposed herself too fully to people who, yes, were good-hearted but who, even if they understood it in the abstract, in the concrete couldn't understand a thing"; tlts 123); between Lila and the abstract middle-class fury of Nadia ("[Nadia] claimed that she was in the service of the workers, and yet, from her room in a house full of books and with a view of the sea, she wanted to command you, she wanted to tell you what you should do with your work, she decided for you, she had the solution ready even if you ended up in the street"; tlts 142); and between Lila and the factory workers ("They had all known one another a long time, they knew they were complicit victims, and they had no doubt about who the whistleblower was: she, the only one who behaved from the start as if the need to work didn't go hand in hand with the need to be humiliated"; tlts 126) effectively reconstruct a side of inchoate political life.

Among the many literary models that this tale of the working class draws from—Carlo Bernari's *Tre operai* (Three Workers), for example, or Vittorio Sereni's *Visita in fabbrica* (A Visit to the Factory)—the most convincing seems to be Morante's *History* and the anarchist Davide Segre's displacement in a factory (Fortini, Falotico 103–4). In this case, even though Lila's political consciousness conflicts with her sense of subproletarian disorientation, she can nevertheless claim an authenticity lacking in the speechifying bourgeois students:

> [Lila] said jokingly that she knew nothing about the working class. She said she knew only the workers, men and women, in the factory where she worked, people from whom there was absolutely nothing to learn except wretchedness. Can you imagine, she asked, what it means to spend eight hours a day standing

up to your waist in the mortadella cooking water? Can you imagine what it means to have your fingers covered with cuts from slicing the meat off animal bones? Can you imagine what it means to go in and out of refrigerated rooms at twenty degrees below zero, and get ten lire more an hour—ten lire—for cold compensation? If you imagine this, what do you think you can learn from people who are forced to live like that? [. . .] That is the situation in the factory where I work. The union has never gone in and the workers are nothing but poor victims of blackmail, dependent on the law of the owner, that is: I pay you and so I possess you and I possess your life, your family, and everything that surrounds you, and if you don't do as I say I'll ruin you. (tlts 121–22)

The trajectory of Franco Mari's life during those years is also eloquently narrated. We first meet him back at the Normale, then a benefactor who educates Elena about the sexual revolution in word and about the patriarchy in deed (cf. 6.3 and 6.4). We meet him again in a crowded classroom at the University of Milan, now a clear leader and passionate orator:

> He had stayed the same: the same warm and persuasive tone of voice, the same ability to organize a speech, moving from general statements that led, step by step, in a logical sequence to ordinary, everyday experiences, revealing their meaning. (tlts 72)

The home of Mariarosa also plays a part in Franco's political life. The house is a sort of commune with large crowded rooms, full of transitory lives and existential and erotic promiscuity. Aside from Franco, the student and political activist Silvia occupies another room with her son Mirko, the child she has just had with Nino (cf. 6.1). The Venezuelan painter Juan has his studio there; he will enter Elena's bed one night, a few hours after their having met, to make love, as if, she recalls, "it were a favor I owed him" (tlts 173). Even Elena gravitates to the house during the two years following the collapse of her marriage to Pietro. The escalation of political violence that comes to a head in the 1970s leaves a mark on Franco's body too. Beaten by fascists during a nighttime raid (the same in which Silvia is raped; cf. 6.1), he has to be taken to the hospital and loses an eye. Elena visits him in the ward: "He was as if shortened and distended, I can still see him in my mind's eye, because of the white bandages, the violet color of part of his face and neck" (tlts 289).

The last volume of the quartet, *The Story of the Lost Child*, spans a much longer arc of time, from 1976 to 2010. Its final section reaches the present day "as a precipice, the evaporating spray of a waterfall" (fr 346) and the volume opens with the signs of defeat. The indelible signs of violence are also the signs of a revolution in crisis; the failure of the revolution to launch leaves Franco increasingly disillusioned and depressed:

> We who wanted to enact the revolution were the ones who, even in the midst of chaos, were always inventing an order and pretending to know exactly how things were going. (slc 78)

The last chapter of Franco's life occurs one morning in 1979, when Elena, staying with her daughters as guests of the commune/house in Milan, finds a note on Franco's door asking her not to let the children in. Suspicious, Elena cautiously enters the room when her friend doesn't answer her knock. The body is lying inert on the bed, the pillow soaked with blood. Franco has killed himself.

> Franco had been a living material saturated with political culture, with generous purposes and hopes, with good manners. Now he offered a horrible spectacle of himself. He had rid himself so fiercely of memory, language, the capacity to find meaning that it seemed obvious the hatred he had for himself, for his own skin, for his moods, for his thoughts and words, for the brutal corner of the world that had enveloped him. [. . .] I thought for a long time about his note, the only one he left. It was addressed to me and in substance was saying: Don't let the children in, I don't want them to see me; but you can enter, you *must* see me. (slc 112)

Even more bitter is Franco's funeral, during which the gaze of Elena, always at heart an outsider to political engagement, cruelly studies the cortege of his companions: "a crowd of militants with weakly clenched fists" (slc 112).

4. Lives in the Age of Feminism

During her remarks to the collective of Via dei Tribunali, Lila also speaks about a dominant feature in the degrading life of a worker—the abuse that the women at her factory must endure from their colleagues and the factory owner, Bruno Soccavo:

> The women have to let their asses be groped by supervisors and colleagues without saying a word. If the owner feels the need, someone has to follow him into the seasoning room; his father used to ask for the same thing, maybe also his grandfather; and there, before he jumps all over you, that same owner makes you a tired little speech on how the odor of salami excites him. (tlts 122)

This part of her speech touches a nerve with Pasquale and Enzo, who—upon leaving the meeting—demand she give them an explanation, subtly remonstrating her for having spoken about it in public rather than in private to them. Lila's verbal reaction ("Fuck off [. . .] you and the working class") challenges the masculine need to separate class struggle from sexual exploitation and deprives them of taking out their vengeance privately. In short, Pasquale and Enzo see workplace harassment as a violation of honor, a code of respect among men that relies on the protection of the female body:

> You had to hide everything from men. They preferred not to know, they preferred to pretend that what happened at the hands of the boss miraculously didn't happen to the women important to them and that—this was the idea they had grown up with—

they had to protect her even at the risk of being killed. (tlts 123–24)

It is on this plane that Elena and Lila's now distinct stories converge. Lila's working-class novel and Elena's marriage novel mirror one another as soon as "the fault line of gender emerges and crosses the atavistic force of the social and cultural fault line" (Manetti[2]). The powerful reach of women's inequality is such that the two friends lead totally different yet similar lives: "Lila in her attempt to explain to her comrades that the servitude of workers is also sexual servitude, Elena in being swept away by a domestic and child-rearing life that even her cultured husband and revolutionary friends seem to accept as a fact of nature" (Manetti[2]). For Ferrante, "[getting] beyond the female gender" means liberating oneself from the image "that men have sewed onto us and that women attribute to themselves as if it were their true nature" (fr 324). In the quartet, crossing lines at the cost of feeling how deeply entrenched those lines are in the female "I," how much they have hollowed her out, is a crucial moment in Elena's experience.

A touchstone along the way to discovering this is Elena's encounter with the radical ideas of Carla Lonzi, the same feminist philosopher, scholar, and experimenter of the Unpredictable Subject referred to in the opening paragraph of this chapter. Lonzi's *Sputiamo su Hegel* (We Spit on Hegel)—published in 1970 and then in a revised edition in 1974—is a seminal text for Elena, providing her with a name for the humiliation she has felt all her life, her feelings of exclusion from all sense of self-worth and meaning. "To spit on Hegel" is to channel the immediacy of life toward a radical critique of all ideologies. Lonzi's polemic is specifically aimed at those "systems of thought"—like those of the German philosopher, expounder of dialectics, and champion of the idea that reality can be reduced to rationality—that "have maintained that woman is an accessory for human reproduction, a connection to the divine, or the gateway to the animal world; either private realm or pietas" sublimating "in metaphysics what was unjust or atrocious in the lives of women" (Lonzi 10). Elena sums up Lonzi's position thus:

> Spit on Hegel. Spit on the culture of men, spit on Marx, on Engels, on Lenin. And on historical materialism. And on Freud. And on psychoanalysis and penis envy. And on marriage, on family. And on Nazism, on Stalinism, on terrorism. And on war. And on the class struggle. And on the dictatorship of the proletariat. And on socialism. And on Communism. And on the trap of equality. (tlts 280)

In the writings of the feminist philosopher and activist, Elena finds Lonzi questioning the false equality both in the revolutionary movements and in the academic realm, where women are forced, for one, to apply the strictest discipline and protocols to emulate a male model that is, after all, structurally unattainable. The paradox of this mimetic mechanism is that the more the dominated parties seek to assimilate to the dominant parties and be recognized by them, the more they feel dominated (cf 5.7). The following passage, also from *We Spit on Hegel*, describes Elena's experience at the university, emblematic of the experience of so many other women like her (yesterday and today):

> For a girl, university is not the place where she will be liberated by culture but the place where her repression so well cultivated in the field of family is perfected. Her education consists of gradually injecting a poison that paralyzes her on the threshold of more responsible acts, of experiences that dilate the meaning of herself. (Lonzi 43)

In Lonzi's collection female inferiority is defined as a permanent yet plastic system of inequality. Even with its murky origins unearthed, this system is renewed throughout history through numerous forms of betrayal connected to the word. Its devices may change and expand over the centuries, yet they converge to achieve a common goal of not recognizing woman as a subject:

> Civilization defined us as inferior, the Church called us sex, psychoanalysis betrayed us, Marxism sold us off to its hypothetical revolution. We demand to know by what credentials thousands of years of philosophical thought have theorized about the inferiority of women. (Lonzi 9–10)

For Elena, the 1970s—perceived to be a vibrant period of experimentation and conflict—begin when she devours Lonzi's words outdoors, "under the gray sky of late winter," while—the image is significant—taking her two children to the public parks in Florence (at this point she is still a wife and mother of the Airota family). Lonzi's texts seem to have been written with Lila's brilliance, and, for the first time in her entire intellectual formation, rouse in Elena a sense of inferiority and displacement analogous to that which her friend has always felt: "I had come upon a female model of thinking that, given the obvious differences, provoked in me the same admiration, the same sense of inferiority that I felt toward her" (tlts 281). That model is one of exuberant thought: the idea of combining categories not by gathering them from books, or passively adopting cultural traditions, or practicing the discipline that has so cowed Elena, but on the contrary by systematically overturning them all:

> Every sentence struck me, every word, and above all the bold freedom of thought. [. . .] How is it possible, I wondered, that a woman knows how to think like that. I worked so hard on books, but I endured them, I never actually used them, I never turned them against themselves. This is thinking. This is thinking against. (tlts 280)

The parallels between Lonzi and Lila are all the more interesting because both the real-life person and the fictional character use disappearance as a form of existential and creative resistance. Lonzi controversially broke from the field of contemporary art criticism—of which she was for years an authoritative member—in 1969, a year before launching her feminist career, whereas, as we know, Lila attempts to avoid the marital status imposed on her by patriarchal marriage, first by reworking the enlarged photo of her in her wedding dress (cf. 6.6), and later, creatively, by adopting the abstract rationalism of information technology (cf. 7.5) until at last she withdraws from life itself (6.8).

Swept up in her enthusiasm over the discovery of this "counter-thought," Elena begins attending the nascent consciousness-raising women's groups. Yet somehow her own self-discipline, her own self-control, always distance her from them:

> I was fascinated by the way people talked, confronted each other—explicit to the point of being disagreeable. [. . .] What seduced me [. . .] was an urge for authenticity that I had never felt and that perhaps was not in my nature. I never said a single word, in that circle, that was equal to that urgency. But I felt that I should do something like that with Lila. (tlts 281–82)

Elena hopes to transport her consciousness through her friendship with Lila. Once again she tries to do so by having Lila shield her from the immediacy of experience, from the risk of failure. But when Lila is consulted about her hypothesis and asked to join a group reading of Lonzi's work on counter-sexuality, she reacts with profound sarcasm: "'What the fuck are you talking about, Lenù, pleasure, pussy, we've got plenty of problems here already, you're crazy'" (tlts 282). This solitude, this necessity to have to go it alone without her friend's acknowledgment, drives Elena to take the crucial step of showing up during one of the consciousness-raising evenings at Mariarosa's house in Milan. Here Elena homes in on a crucial moment in her relationship with Franco during their years at the Normale:

> For Franco, I said, I was an opportunity for him to expand

into the feminine, to take possession of it: I constituted the proof of his omnipotence, the demonstration that he knew how to be not only a man in the right way but also a woman. And today when he no longer senses me as part of himself, he feels betrayed. (tlts 352)

In the wake of this intuition, and at the encouragement of Mariarosa, Elena decides to write an essay on "men who fabricate women" (tlts 361) in which she compares her private experiences with those that have emerged from consciousness-raising. In fact, during group meetings there often emerges a sense that alienation, the feeling of being completely absorbed by the other, and colonized, is intrinsic to female identity:

[. . .] although we were all women [. . .] we struggled to understand what a woman was. Our every move or thought or conversation or dream, once analyzed in depth, seemed not to belong to us. (tlts 351)

Elena chooses to study theology—the one appearance of transcendence in the quartet—by rewriting the creation story of Adam and Eve in order to locate the root of misogyny within the story of Genesis (cf. 5.7). This secular rethinking of the biblical origins of inferiority seems to allude to the actual feminist studies of theology of that period. One crucial work is the Norwegian writer Kari Børresen's *Subordination and Equivalence*, a pioneering dissertation first published in France in 1968. Interpreting feminism as an epistemological revolution, the scholar lays the groundwork for questioning theological "andro-centrism" (Børresen 8). From this perspective Elena traces the archetypal signs of Franco's dream and the dreams of many other men—their need to reduce women to an extension of themselves—back to the two episodes of creation. Adam is in fact born in God's image, Eve later fashioned from male material—and therefore derived from man. In Elena's reconstruction of the passage in Genesis 2:23, the situation prompts the first man to say the following:

> This thing is not, like the army of all that has been created, *other* than me, but is flesh of *my* flesh, bone of *my* bones. God produced it from me. He made me fertile with the breath of life and extracted it from *my* body. I am Ish and she is Isha'h. In the word above all, in the word that names her, she derives from me. I am in the image of the divine spirit. I carry within me his Word. (tlts 364)

Elena's book is developed and published while her marriage is falling apart and her relationship with Nino heating up. In fact, she is in part motivated to write by a need to "make a good impression" on Nino, who will be the first to read the manuscript (tlts 370). It is no coincidence that the story underscores the connection between her feminist book and the recognition of a man who will turn out to be one of the most zealous manufacturers of "female automatons created by men" (tlts 354). Its impure origin doesn't diminish the value of her study; on the contrary, it is enriched by it, because in the quartet the ultimate meaning of feminism lies in its offering itself as concrete experience that fuels the critique of all ideologies, as an analytical tool for revealing the contradictions in, and deconstructing the false transparency of, identities.

In keeping with her anti-essentialist perspective, Ferrante has always emphasized her affinity with feminism while also expressing her need to practice it eclectically ("I don't write to illustrate an ideology—I write to tell without distortions what I know"; fr 302) and not fret about whether her literary tale is orthodox. One piece of evidence of the writer's interpretive freedom is the way Elena confronts her newfound fame among the (now international) elite after the publication of her book. Her public appearances show that the authenticity she observed in the consciousness-raising groups did not free her from reciting the intellectual's script nor from taking mainstream positions. Her speech is still inspired by the "power of the false" (cf. 6.4)—that blend of truth and lies that is a core tenet of her assimilation into the middle class:

> I had a natural ability to transform small private events into public reflection. Every night I improvised successfully, starting from my own experience. [. . .] I discovered in myself an unsuspected capacity to summarize disagreement and agreement, choosing in the meantime a role as mediator. I was good at saying in a convincing way: *That isn't exactly what I meant.* (slc 56, 77).

The fact that Elena resorts to conventional male rhetoric and public discourses, presenting a false portrait of herself, does not disprove the questions posed by Lonzi's theories about the feminism of difference, but rather raises them again. One of the many public events for Elena's book takes place in Ferrara, roughly a month after the murder, on May 9, 1978, of Aldo Moro—yet another political tragedy of the era that has little impact on the lives of the characters in the quartet. The public, in large part composed of exponents of the far left, lambast her for calling Moro's killers "murderers": "'Murderers' didn't sit well with the audience—*the fascists are murderers*—and I was attacked, criticized, jeered." As soon as she becomes unable to calibrate her words "according to the current usage of the radical left" (slc 87) and states an evident yet controversial truth, Elena immediately feels as if she is falling into the mother's cave:

> How I suffered in situations where approval suddenly vanished: I lost confidence, I felt dragged down to my origins, I felt politically incapable, I felt I was a woman who would have been better off not opening her mouth, and for a while I avoided every occasion of public confrontation. (slc 87)

Paradoxically, the narrator's unsparing description of her own scattered, approval-seeking rhetoric proves to be a genuine story of the (sometimes) inescapable fictions that a subjugated party must tell in order to hold court. The scene does not detract from her authenticity nor from her personal experiments—leaving her husband, living with Nino, finally combining households in the *rione* with Lila (herself a bold experimenter)—nor from her writing experiments, however tainted by existential disturbances.

The narrative deliberately stresses the impure origins of her study (as partially a ploy to seduce perhaps the biggest misogynist in the entire quartet) and the mendacity of her language. The weakness, vulnerability, opportunism, and inadequacy that visibly mark Elena's public appearances are the practical depiction of how men have dominated and colonized women's identities for millennia. Elena's contradictory emancipation is a key passage of the new yet necessarily discontinuous sense of time that emerges from her experiences of feminism. In the quartet this collective metamorphosis is recounted not only as "the first political moment in history to critique family and society" but also, and above all, as an opportunity to "operate on another plane" (Lonzi 8, 42), gradually inventing female otherness. More than the content, the form of *The Neapolitan Novels* springs from the controversial modes by which this difference has changed the Unexpected Subject's relationship to the other and therefore with psychic and social space, producing the story's polyphony (cf. Introduction and 1.5, 2.6).

5. Lives in the Age of Computer Programming and Terrorism

According to Ferrante, Elena and Lila's wavering relationship is attributable to the different ways they inhabit their historical period. "While Lena," says Ferrante, "is the tormented omega of the old system, Lila embodies the crisis and, in a certain sense, a possible future" (fr 371). The uncertainty of the present and almost painful, premature birth of a new age are already felt in the two friends' encounter at the factory in 1967 (cf. 2.6). Before burning *The Blue Fairy*, the symbol of her former creative ambitions, Lila tells Elena that she has begun studying computer programming, a new language, one "not for writing novels" (snn 465). By her heroic effort—studying with Enzo at night, after their work shifts, when both are exhausted—Lila does not intend to carve out a place for herself in an institution with a pre-established hierarchy, like the Normale her friend attends. Elena's college education represents a means of social mobility that up until a few decades ago was considered traditional and plausible in Italy. For Lila, studying computer programming is instead "the manifestation of a permanent anxiety about intelligence, a necessity imposed by the relentlessly chaotic circumstances of life, a tool of daily struggle" (fr 371). This unprecedented experiment enables her to blaze another trail on her way to emancipation and gain a raft of resources, foreshadowing the most creative flank of today's modern global precariat. That her choice isn't a fall-back but a vital necessity is revealed when she remarks to Elena, in her "dismissive tone," that "[they're] not languages for writing novels". In fact, Lila is drawn to computer programming by a profound psychic need to fit chaos into a "form that could be controlled" (snn 343), that could rein in her ever-resurgent *smarginatura*. Lila's need for a language as objective as programming, one that can group together worlds separate in appearance only, that can reduce "everything to the alternative true-false" (snn 465), stems from her reaction to the feelings of extreme vulnerability that she experienced in the years prior, the long period during which Stefano raped and beat her. Leafing through her notebooks a year before their encounter at the factory, Elena finds to her great surprise numerous descriptions of women who were murdered and disemboweled by men, of accounts of femicide she finds in crime reports:

And she added details that the newspapers didn't report: eyes dug out of their sockets, injuries caused by a knife to the throat or internal organs, the blade that pierced a breast, nipples cut off, the stomach ripped open from the bellybutton down, the blade that scraped across the genitals. (snn 343)

With their scrupulous lexicon these anatomical studies serve to arrest the dismembering anguish of *smarginatura* triggered in Lila by the high probability that Stefano will discover her relationship with Nino and murder her.

In this light, the language of programming becomes a powerful tool to control reality, releasing Lila from the condition of helpless victim and propelling her into the active role of archivist and cataloger of an endless inventory. Programming is a frenzy "to reduce the entire wretched world [. . .] to the truth of 0s and 1s" (tlts 114), to jettison the constant indeterminacy of reality, to control actions and shoehorn them into a binary system (Carvalho):

> [Enzo and Lila] preferred to dull their senses by competing with block diagrams as if they were equipment for gymnastics.
> "Let's do the diagram of the door opening," Lila said.
> "Let's do the diagram of knotting the tie," Enzo said.
> [. . .] From the simplest actions to the most complicated, they racked their brains to diagram daily life [. . .]. (tlts 114)

Besides having the power to rid the "I" of complexity and relegate it to an algorithm ("*The day will come when I reduce myself to diagrams, I'll become a perforated tape and you won't find me anymore*"; tlts 345) in keeping with her desire to disappear, a desire Lila associates with the collage-work done to her photo panel ("*You remember what we did with my wedding picture? I want to continue on that path*"; tlts 345; cf. 6.6 and 6.8), abstract technology is also the divine attribute of a demiurge:

[Enzo] dominated all that material like a god, he manipulated the vocabulary and the substance inside a large room with big air-conditioners, a hero who could make the machine do everything that people did. (tlts 262)

Like scripture, computer code is only understood by technological priests. It baffles most people, even highly educated people like Elena.

[. . .] [Lila] began updating me on the computer story, bewildering me with an incomprehensible jargon. [. . .] She talked to me about ferrite cores, rings traversed by an electrical cable whose tension determined the rotation, 0 or 1, and a ring was a bit, and the total of eight rings could represent a byte, that is a character. (tlts 261–62)

In 1967, Elena views with disbelief the idea of opening a computing center, the first of its kind in Italy, in Naples.

I still remember her voice, as it tried to erase San Giovanni, the salami, the odor of the factory, her situation, by citing with false expertise abbreviations like: Cybernetics Center of the State University of Milan, Soviet Center for the Application of Computer Science to the Social Sciences. She wanted to make me believe that a center of that type would soon be established even in Naples. I had thought: in Milan maybe, certainly in the Soviet Union, but here no, here it is the folly of your uncontrollable mind [. . .]. (tlts 27–8)

Yet in 1978, after working for decades as system engineers, crisscrossing the map of modernized Southern Italy (from an underwear factory fifty kilometers from Naples, another in Nola with three hundred technical workers, and a data-processing center in Acerra), Enzo and Lila open their own computer company, Basic Sight. They even install their office in the old neighborhood. The exotic English name, necessary for attracting an international clientele ("[. . .] *otherwise they don't take you seriously*"; slc 126), is soon Neapolitanized to *"basissit"* (slc 271).

The new company promptly delivers on the promise of its name, or so it seems, establishing itself as a company with an essential, objective vision that provides immediate returns.

Soon the entrepreneurial project turns Lila into a guardian saint, the benefactor of the *rione*, and—from a national and international perspective—a figure who has outdone the great utopias of the protest years and become the first to seize upon "the explosiveness of the digital revolution" (Fusillo 152). The excitement over this new age is enshrined in a scene in which Lila teaches Elena how to use the first word-processing program in 1984:

> Lila began to type on the keyboard, I was speechless. It was in no way comparable to a typewriter, even an electric one. [. . .] What was in her head, attached to who knows what cortex of the brain, seemed to pour out miraculously and fix itself on the void of the screen. It was power that, although passing for act, remained power, an electrochemical stimulus that was instantly transformed into light. It seemed to me like the writing of God as it must have been on Sinai at the time of the Commandments, impalpable and tremendous, but with a concrete effect of purity. Magnificent, I said. I'll teach you, she said. (slc 311)

But underneath the magic of the nascent Information Age, traumatic transformations are lurking. Pietro intuits them as early as 1974, while talking to Enzo, when he foresees the risk of rationalizing production systems that will dramatically reduce the need for workers and lead to layoffs and social strife (tlts 299). A few years later Enzo himself admits that the illusory order of computers actually serves to "transform the filth of exploitation into the tidiness of programming" (slc 126). If "abstraction" is the key word that explains why Lila is attracted to this new language, with its promise of "abstract linearity" that she hopes will "assure her a restful tidiness" (tlts 114), during those years the same word reemerges to describe her suspected involvement in a terror campaign. During the summer of 1974, a series of fishy interactions with Lila (extraordinarily, she asks Elena to look after her son Rino with the excuse of starting a new programming job, though it turns out—as Enzo accidentally reveals—that she works there only part-time; tlts 298) leads Elena to suspect that her friend may be behind a string of political executions (Bruno Soccavo, the pharmacist Gino) and other acts of terrorism performed by Pasquale and Nadia. In the meantime, the latter two go on the lam. While never accusing Lila directly, many years later Nadia names Enzo as a coconspirator; he is arrested in 1988 and later exonerated in 1990 (slc 426). As with computer programming, Lila may have hatched the terrorist plots because she is drawn to "abstract purity," which can render impersonal the material and moods of life:

[. . .] she would be able to give murderous intentions an abstract purity, she knew how to remove human substance from bodies and blood, she would have no scruples and no remorse, she would kill and feel that she was in the right. (tlts 312–13)

Paradoxically, the language of abstraction winds up becoming a bloody, homicidal language, one of human lives cut short, which makes for much more convincing reading than Elena's fiction:

[. . .] she would reappear triumphant, admired for her achievements, in the guise of a revolutionary leader, to tell me: You wanted to write novels, I created a novel with real people, with real blood, in reality. (tlts 313)

The Information Age is a vast system made up of two interdependent universes: a chilling dimension of algorithms contains an abyss of hatred, violence, and painful metamorphoses—and their opposite. The hidden connection between hyper-rationalism and violence can be seen as the infinite complementarity of two poles that fuel one another in radical, obscure, and uncontrollable ways as much as they purport to keep them drastically separate.

6. Lives in the Age of Dissolved Rationality

The destructive plot is caused by the hierarchy and subordination imposed *on* the symmetrical and emotional logic of human experience *by* the rational and asymmetrical logic of human experience. To understand the function of these two logics we can examine what happens to Alfonso during the Information Age. His metamorphosis and tragic character arc speak to this same form of subordination, upon which an asymmetrical will to control reality generates increasingly uncontrolled symmetrical instances of dissolving boundaries. *Smarginatura* may be compared to the vast system of the subconscious, to dreams and emotions (Carvalho). In such a complex and boundless area of human experience, the rational logic of asymmetry—according to which A can never be B—does not apply; what applies is a symmetrical logic according to which A *is* B (Matte Blanco). If we consider Alfonso's transition to a *femminiello*, his having felt *"blurry, without clear outlines"* (tlts 345), his "brittle" sexual identity (slc 187), and finally his desire to win Michele—the most smugly virile man in the quartet—by accentuating his resemblance to Lila as far as possible, we see that this symmetrical logic operates in a twofold manner. First, the term *femminiello* refers to a man who is also a woman (cf. 4.8), and second, for Michele this male/female is the sexual double of Lila, the object of his obsession. A (a man, Alfonso) can therefore be B (a woman, Lila) in both the broader context of gender identity as well as the narrower context of an erotic relationship.

But the infinite and indivisible symmetrical space of equivalences that is *smarginatura* (Carvalho) is constantly channeled by Lila within the asymmetric dimension of an obsessive control over reality. Alfonso's metamorphosis is in fact aimed at weakening Michele's identity, which leads Lila to deceive herself into thinking that she can control and extort the *camorrista* power of the Solaras:

> Michele thought he was who knows what, and yet all I had to do was find his boundary line and pull, oh, oh, oh, I broke it, I broke his cotton thread and tangled it with Alfonso's, male material inside male material, the fabric that I weave by day is unraveled by night, the head finds a way. (slc 177–78)

Not by accident, Elena makes the shocking discovery of Alfonso and Michele's relationship in the place that embodies this increasingly boundaryless and boundary-breaking rationality: Basic Sight, whose logo—"a swirl around a vertical line" (slc 126)—was created by Lila in 1978 and seems to allude to the strange interdependence of warps and wefts in a fabric that keeps on being woven and unwoven. Toward the end of 1980, in a company side room, Elena encounters what for all intents and purposes is a couple, seeing as Michele has thrown his wife and children out of their beautiful house in Posillipo and is living with Alfonso. However cagey he is about it, he tells her, "'[P]eople have to do what they feel like, otherwise they get sick'" (slc 188). The hyper-rationality behind Michele and Alfonso's arrangement generates even more extreme and irreversible forms of *smarginatura*. In 1983, when Michele realizes that Lila has been trying to manipulate him and that he will never vicariously satisfy his erotic obsession with her, he brutally rejects Alfonso ("Michele [. . .] began to punch and kick him, then he grabbed the pole that was used to lower the shutter and beat him methodically, for a long time"; slc 277). A traumatized Alfonso will regress unstoppably into a virile man. Now marginalized from his own desires, vulnerable in body and spirit (on more than one occasion he shows the signs of breaking up), Alfonso becomes the emblematic victim of homophobia. In 1984 he is found beaten to death on the shores of Coroglio (cf. 4.8), a fate foreshadowed by the recovery of a dead body in a tunnel in the *rione*: "The person [. . .] looked like a woman but was a man: there was so much blood in the body that it flowed all the way down to the gas pump" (slc 272).

On other occasions, too, this muddle of experimentation—now cynical, now desperate—and hangovers from the past comes to define Basic Sight, leading Elena to realize that Lila "was doing new work but totally immersed in our old world" (slc 273) and that, rather than "some sort of meteorite that had fallen from outer space," the computer company is actually "the unexpected product of poverty, violence, and blight" (slc 271). In fact, Basic Sight's "swarm" of clients is made up of "small provincial entrepreneurs, big luxury cars, clothes of a vulgar wealth, heavy bodies that moved sometimes aggressively, sometimes with servile manners" (slc 273). This braid of order and chaos, modernity and corruption, and abstraction and visceral experience defines the new world of computer programming and anticipates our own murky present that hovers between the archaic and ultramodern. As with present-day globalization, the "small" stories of the quartet shatter the order of modernity, impede it from resolving into a tidy landscape of big events and linear progress, make it a blur of progression and regression, civility and savagery—a continuous metamorphosis of time.

7. The Past and the Present

Stunned by life, human beings almost always perceive time as inchoate and confusing, even as it formulates many of their destinies. According to the philosopher Paul Ricœur, narrative time—the time literary fiction presents us with—is the one chronological experience that people can grasp. Paradoxically, the only possibility of rendering time perceptible in a clear, and thus human, way, is articulated not in the real world but in the fantastic world of literature. However imaginary, literature has the power to reveal the "virtual experience of being-in-the-world" (Ricœur 100). From this perspective, what potential form of existence does Ferrante propose with the quartet and its sophisticated temporal structure? What does she mean to tell us by systematically downplaying major events, by willfully wringing them of rhetoric and glorification, by ensnaring them in the tangled net of life? Reading her long narrative, we experience time as a blur, a viscous flow or endless sequence, as we are immersed in the sometimes confused, sometimes desperate, sometimes euphoric or even omnipotent lives of two friends. The preliminary investigation, this method stripped of illusions, has the integrity to narrate a small, ordinary story nevertheless capable of becoming epic: the story of two women and two friends. We inherit from Elena and Lila a lucid and visionary sense of time, the same that prompted Carla Lonzi to say, "We are the dark past of the world, we make the present" (Lonzi 48).

Elena Ferrante and the Power of Storytelling in the Age of Globalization

1. Storytelling and Underground Realism

At the end of this long journey through the labyrinth of Ferrante's work, I would like to summarize my overarching argument by returning to the words with which the Introduction of this book begins. The words belong not to me but to Jonathan Franzen, one of the great writers of our age. I would like to think back on the admiration for Ferrante's work that Franzen expresses in the documentary *Ferrante Fever* and connect it to a feeling that, at a certain point in the film, overwhelms the American writer.

During his interview, Franzen becomes emotional as he recalls a scene in *My Brilliant Friend* that he describes as "one of [his] favorite moments in any novel in the longest time, one of [his] top twenty moments." It is the moment when Lila, contemplating her dress on the morning of her wedding, and catching a glimpse of the unhappy fate ahead of her, urges Elena to study, to be better than all the rest, because she is her "brilliant friend." At this point in the film, Franzen's voice cracks. For a few seconds he loses his composure. He is reliving his reaction—"the first moment I cried reading these books"—to the surprising revelation that the brilliant friend of the title is not Lila but Elena. That revelation, says Franzen, "hits us as it hits her."

Franzen's reaction conveys to viewers the emotional and conceptual power of Ferrante's storytelling. For Ferrante, that power "isn't very far from political power . . . the power to bring order to the chaos of the real under our own sign" (fer[6]).

At this point in the documentary, every one of us understands the force of the story that the quartet has to tell, its brilliant and popular gift—as I say in Chapter One—for portraying a wide array of characters, relationships, and social classes. Not only has the intensity of Ferrante's story led more than ten millions readers to be moved by the lives of her characters and devour her fictional world, to inhabit that world as if it were real, it has also helped them to extrapolate from it a value system, a way of being, and a code with which to interpret the present day.

Is that *all* Ferrante's realism is? A means of cultivating empathy? Of *merely* ensnaring readers in an emotional web through the illusion of an utterly transparent and plausible fictional universe? Not in my opinion. It is that, but that isn't all it is. Ferrante's realism is powerful because it is both realistic and experimental. This dichotomous realism presents us with a concrete world and, at the same time, with its disintegration from the inside out, prompting readers both to empathize with it and to lose their way in its labyrinth. Hers is an underground realism: a form of writing that, in order to dig below the surface, opens with "what we have forced inside the uniform of the ordinary" (fer[7]), and even dares to begin with the stereotype of the "ordinary" (what could be more unoriginal and overdone, more "neorealist," than a story about poor girls in Naples in the 1950s?). The story's point of view explodes its realistic effects: only by bridging the gaps that have been multiplied by our technologically-advanced and media-saturated world, only by taking on an extremely intimate perspective, does the ordinary become interesting, does the commonplace produce a feeling that can move a reader as astute as Franzen, first while reading to himself, and then again on camera for all to see.

This point of view plunges readers into the world of two subaltern girls and their linguistic and symbolic polyphony.

Elena's polyphonic narration turns the frozen surface of the everyday into a fluid liquid, revealing its true depths, which rise to form a wave and pull the reader under, making them feel the physical "impact" (fr 233) of its content, giving them a bottom-up view of the world, a view from the deeps of their ancestry. Indeed, Ferrante's central metaphor speaks to this subterranean world: with every crisis of *frantumaglia*, the emancipated daughters risk falling into these "caves." (Such is the fate of all the author's female characters.) These daughters, firmly "anchored . . . to the computer" they use to write, are forced to situate themselves "among [their] single-celled ancestors, among the quarrelsome or terrorized muttering (. . .), among the female divinities expelled into the darkness of the earth" (fr 107–8).

For the daughter, grief disrupts her sense of time as sequential. Instead, she perceives time as synchronous: the victories of progress blur with an ancient maternal heritage, with the humiliations suffered by mythical queens and goddesses (cf 3.3). Ferrante's striking image of female ancestors and divinities "expelled into the darkness of the earth" evokes an age-old genealogy of women who have been dominated, silenced, and ultimately erased by being caged in a hidden subterranean space—a form of archetypal female repression to this day directed by patriarchal domination.

Polyphony is the umbilical cord of *The Neapolitan Novels*, connecting the realistic surface to the truth of the cave, and nourishing both. Polyphony catches both the objective and indefinite aspects of reality. In Chapters One and Two the word polyphony is defined as the speech of a marginalized female "I" (Elena) who tells the story of another marginalized female "I" (Lila), as an assertive and supportive language that seeks to conquer new historical frontiers. This speech is also murky, derived from the depths of the cave and a heritage that is feminine and maternal yet also complicit with patriarchal violence and domination. Social opportunism, the assimilation of patriarchal violence, matrophobia and matricide, envy, competition, and, ultimately, a rivalry that verges on the murderous: based on what emerges in Chapters Two and Three, these are the shock waves of underground realism recorded by the seismograph on the surface of the world depicted. Female abjection—"what is formidable about women" (fr 151)—overlays the social abjection of Neapolitan "plebs," constantly unleashing a surge of emotion in the quartet that consists of echoes of dialect in the Italian text. By a mix of insertions, para-dialectical rhythms, and rare outbursts, dialect reverberates throughout the neutral Italian prose, bearing with it a sense of subalternity, violence, and belonging (cf. Chapters Four and Five).

2. Uncanny Realism

This experimental underground realism is also a form of uncanny realism, set in motion by the subterranean erosion of each character's solid boundaries. As a result, the writing operates on two simultaneous and coinciding planes: For Ferrante, to write means "to make something *present*, to place something before the eyes of readers, to make it immediate" (fer[8]). At the same time, to write also means to "leave abysses, construct bridges and not finish them, force the reader to establish the flow" (slc 169). *Smarginatura* is a dark well that "escapes the narrative order" (fr 312) and makes the real motivations behind characters' actions impenetrable, even when their behavior is, on the surface, melodramatic. *Smarginatura* is the unreliable way in which the narrator, Elena, claims she is writing to will her friend back into existence. *Smarginatura* is the transsexual metamorphosis of Alfonso until he vanishes and resurfaces in his original male body. It is the bewitching energy that inspires Lila to make copper pots explode, set fire to her enlarged photograph, and speculate that a hermaphroditic creature murdered Don Achille. *Smarginatura* is the deep and abiding love of Michele—a man who contemptuously wields his power over women—for Lila's intelligence and bravery.

But—as comes to light in Chapters One to Six—the uncanny charge of *smarginatura* also acts as the main story-telling technique, dissolving the story by withholding from readers important parts of the plot and never clearing the air of mystery and suspense. Indeed, six decades of lives and stories revolve around five inexplicable disappearances that translate to ellipses in the narrative and black holes in the plot. The dolls disappear for almost the entire story, and readers will know nothing about their theft, or the joint liability for their theft, over the course of six decades. The dolls do not resurface until the end of the quartet, thereby closing *and* dissolving the circle (cf. Chapter 1). Then there are the eight notebooks Lila gives to Elena in the spring of 1966, which disappear when, several months later, Elena throws them in the Arno in a fit of jealousy—a "clearly metaphorical murder" (Turchetta 109). The reader never has access to the notebooks that can confirm Lila is the superior artist. Tina disappears and, after that, Lila's phantom book about Naples, a book that, for the obsessed Elena, would have reembodied the girl and the narrative brilliance of her friend. Finally, Lila vanishes, mirroring the uncanny fates of her daughter and the dolls, and leaving the reader with no idea of the cause nor positive closure.

The intensity of uncanny underground realism—closely linked to the bewitching realism of Elsa Morante's first, extraordinary novel *House of Liars*—spreads out in another direction too. The real author's choice to remain absent and reinvent herself as the pseudonymous Elena Ferrante, inviting us to speculate about her identity and distancing herself from the mediaverse, harkens back to the concept of absent presence. Absence/presence is, first of all, an act of resistance that Ferrante has practiced consistently for almost three decades, rejecting our demands for access to an author's identity—a demand, as I argue in the Introduction, made particularly of women writers—and refusing to diminish her work by parading her life and posting her image in the media.

Yet the author's split and oxymoronic position as an absent presence is also a powerful creative act, because it strengthens the realistic effect of the novel and makes Ferrante immediately present for readers. Committing this self-erasure to the work, portraying it as an "aesthetic project" (slc 455), the writing becomes charged with intensity and stands out as an authentic artifice. In Chapter Six, I emphasized that all the main characters in Ferrante's novels are variously affected—defined, even—by forms of disappearance, some more, some less radical. Therefore, for many readers, Ferrante's entire narrative has been seen as one long fictional memoir, the work constantly attributed to the life, the traits of the characters endlessly ascribed to her pseudonym (cf. Introduction), which often turns into a kind of hyper-heteronym, a stand-in for all the fictional female characters created by the author. However, this magical system of equating the life with the writing does not stem from a cult of the "I," but, on the contrary, from the novels themselves. In other words, we do not speculate about Ferrante's identity *and therefore* read her books; we speculate about her identity *because* we have read her books. The pseudonym is made authentic by the truth of the fiction.

3. Reality Hunger

By revivifying realism (Kurnick) Ferrante taps into the "reality hunger" (Shields) at the heart of our collective imagination today. The "return of the real" and "the referential"

(Foster XVII, 168) derive from a renewed sense of trauma: the rise of a threat so brutal that it hovers between the "unthought known" (Bollas) and one of its earlier, painstaking metabolizations. Indeed, this return to the materiality and social roots of identity appears in an inchoate and contradictory form because it springs from the painful tension between images in the media and the real transformations going on in the world. This tension relates, for example, to the conflicted reception of Ferrante's absent/present position in the contemporary imagination. On the one hand, Ferrante's position has been supported by a wide-ranging global feminine avatar made up of figures and social and international phenomena connected to the translations of the quartet into other languages and other media (the visibility of her English translator Ann Goldstein, the practice among women of buying the quartet together, the consensus among scholars from different cultures and languages, the birth of blogs and seminars about Ferrante's art, and the faces of the actresses who play Elena and Lila in the TV series directed by Saverio Costanzo). These phenomena have gradually filled the void left by the author (Milkova[1], Pinto). However, the author's decision has been derailed by some as a sham, a "drawing board" invention, a cynical post-truth strategy to promote works actually made by a pair or trio or quartet, etc., of authors.

As we shuttle from media images of reality to urgent social truths, from repression to awareness, our perception becomes social, volcanic, disorderly, fragmented. Yet reality is no longer primarily determined, as it was in postmodern culture, by language and its endless combinatorial arrangements for building or deconstructing the world and the "I." Instead, language is determined by the traumatic collision of the subject with the material, thereby making artistic representation multiple yet limited, volcanic yet always circumscribed by its social system and context. The directions of new materialism, a new and vast area spearheaded by quantum physicist and feminist philosopher Karen Barad, are establishing a new paradigm of reality based on "entanglements," or "the mutual constitution of entangled agencies" (Barad 33) that constantly redefine the conditions of time and what is possible. Today, postmodern and deconstructionist language has been eclipsed by a discursive-material scenario in which the subject constantly interacts with the object until the two are indistinguishable: the frame from the painting, the method of analysis from the data.

As has already been pointed out (Ferrara), *frantumaglia* and *smarginatura*—the dissolution of the "I" into "a tangle," "a crowd of others," and "heterogenous fragments" (fr 366, 368)—along with the quartet's narrative devices—the unreliable polyphonic narrative voice, the opaque characters, the disappearing structure—are plainly in concert with the new poetics of trauma and the fluid, hybrid, liminal materiality now being investigated by new materialism. This form of "traumatic realism" (Foster 130) is born at the sunset of postmodernism. It simultaneously descends from and moves beyond that ironic and/or relativist interpretation of modern trauma found in the multiplicity of images in Pop Art, in the primacy of style and experimental play with functionality, in the rejection of the aesthetic manners of, and allusions to, the canon, and, finally, in the endless deconstruction and denial of identities (Huber 21–50).

The "new shared frameworks of reality" (Timmer 361) are instead the current enterprise of international artists in search of new ways of experimenting with language in order to reconstruct the story of the "I." Like Ferrante's uncanny underground realism, these "frameworks" are subterranean, and by way of epiphanies, ellipses, and dislocations in time, they generate a sense of a world facing imminent (ecological, migratory, and economic) crises.

The perception of a fractured age under attack also infuses

the narrative mechanism of the quartet. As shown in Chapter Six, the entire plot can be boiled down to the following dynamic: every time the two women encroach on the public sphere, men react with violence or by expropriation. The dilated time of the narrative further serves to show the profound cyclical reoccurrences of this mechanism in a narrative arc that spans the 1950s to the start of the new millennium. This form of storytelling not only speaks to our past but to our dire future: recent multigenerational novels are also dystopias about an age of violence and regression, narratives haunted by ghosts, eerie apparitions, and nightmares.

4. Storytelling and the Global Novel

In transnational writing today, the traumatic cry of reality gives identities a new liminal texture, as manifest in eyewitness reports or survivor stories that blur the lines between historical, photographic, or journalistic texts, creative nonfiction (literary journalism, for example, or, in certain respects, memoirs), and autofiction. The latter two genres have been firmly established in Italy for three decades, resulting in a "hyper-modernity" that goes beyond postmodernism and finds an important model in Roberto Saviano's work of investigative journalism, *Gomorrah*, published in 2006 (Donnarumma[2] 190–95).

However, the story of problematic (yet not relativistically fragmented) individuals is also at the root of what Ferrante calls the return of "the great foundational novels" (fr 269). The nineteenth-century plot—which postmodernist writers, and many modernist writers, dismissed as obsolete and mystifying—is now being revisited in original ways gleaned from the modern experimental canon. Just as in the great nineteenth-century tradition, storytelling and the pleasure taken in stories have regained importance, so has the development of characters to lend gravity to daily life and the multiple arcs of human destinies.

Restoring and greatly exacerbating certain traits of nine-teenth-century capitalism and widespread inequality (Steger 105), neoliberalism now has the dizzying and devastating abil-ity to bring cultures into contact with one another and set them at odds. Faced with increasingly clear, opposing, and contem-poraneous identity-related phenomena, faced with the division between global subjects in a liminal state of transformation and those in a state of inflexible narrow-mindedness, writers are restoring the nineteenth-century plot to the center of represen-tation and narrative truth: its development, its complex web of characters, and its capacity for combining genres and forms for both experimental and communicative purposes. If the novel has returned to being an emblematic story, to presenting us with a social repertoire and shared vocabulary, that is because today cohabitation with the Other, the traumatic speed of social transformations, and the decline of major ideologies are now urgently compelling a "discursive negotiation" (Calabrese 47) that depends on our ability to make sense of reality through stories.

Through her eclectic, didactic, and psychological concept of storytelling, Ferrante has tapped into this profound need of our collective imagination and honed a powerful tool, in the form of *The Neapolitan Novels*, for ordering and interpreting reality. On the one hand, the quartet presents itself as a "hyper-genre" work (Porciani 89, cf. Chapter One). It imbues the written word with emotional intensity through its mix of high and low, revisiting both "the classics" and the "cellar of writ-ing" piled high with "stories in women's magazines" and "the trash about love and betrayal" (fr 64). It also makes informal and anti-intellectual use of the materials of everyday life. On the other hand, style in the narrative cycle is a means of estab-lishing a form for "the very personal store of urgent things

[. . .] to tell." "The more powerful" the style, writes Ferrante, "the more material it holds for comprehensive life lessons." (fer[9]). There is nothing moralizing about her didactic story-telling, no appeal to fashions. Educational storytelling pro-motes awareness and generates an emotion that "changes us inwardly—dramatically, even—under the impact of words that are true and charged with feeling" (fer[9]): it cannot overlook the narrative form in which it is told.

Practitioners of this new fictional realism known as the global novel form an international canon of authors that includes Chimamanda Ngozi Adichie (*Americanah* 2013), Margaret Atwood (*Oryx and Crake* 2003), Amitav Ghosh (*The Hungry Tide* 2004), Haruki Murakami (*1Q84* 2009–2010), Jonathan Franzen (*The Corrections* 2001) and Zadie Smith (*White Teeth* 2000), to name just a few. Since the late 1990s, the galaxy of the transnational novel has proven extremely diverse. And yet, broadly speaking and with exceptions, its authors' heterogeneous writing practices are bound by a few common threads: a continuous translation of, and tension between, different languages and conceptions of the "glocal," which is to say the numerous changes of the global and local (Robertson 226); a plot containing multiple settings (from peripheries to hubs) and synchronous intertwined timelines (from the archaic to the ultramodern); a focus on character that flies in the face of postmodernism and is inspired by new subjectivities who are diasporic yet grounded, disoriented yet altogether coherent (due to the straitened circumstances that have, in part, shaped them); a text about trauma connected to urgent issues of our age concerning migration, ecology, terror-ism, and feminism (Ganguly).

The quartet is considered a central and highly innovative global novel (Kirsch 92–103) because the international success of this sweeping narrative cycle is rooted in a "glocal" lan-guage, space, and imaginary created by the author. Indeed, at the heart of the story lies an oxymoronic *rione* of the soul, radically defined and incarnated: a place both metaphorical and particular—an expression of the larger Global South and of an Italian story that has no equivalent—that acts as the linchpin for a plot scattered across Italy and Europe and that ultimately shapes identities that are hybrid and local. Lila and (increasingly so) Elena experience an "estrangement of the familiar," a perennial sense of the "unhomely" (Bhabha 11). Yet they are also hounded—even in the apparently neutral and translatable context of the Italian language—by their origins and dialect, which they feel are an "extension of the body" (fr 65), a "burned skin" that they must tear off (ld 88).

5. Magical Spaces and Objects

In many cases, the global novel repurposes the postcolonial tradition of magical realism, stripping it of exoticism and setting it, so to speak, in the heart of the empire. This holds true for American writer Alice Sebold's 2002 bestseller *The Lovely Bones*, which tells the story of a teenage girl's otherworldly life as if it were a plausible fact, one intrinsic to the plot, after her rape and murder (Calabrese 191, Pennacchio 40). The most authoritative representatives of the magical realist strain in the global novel are Salman Rushdie's *Fury* (2001), and Mohsin Hamid's *Exit West* (2017), whereas a significant line of contemporary North American novels hinges on the fantastic (Huber). Fantasy and magic build bridges and passageways between the diverse and otherwise incompatible temporalities of contemporary subjectivities who increasingly constitute figures of "incessant *dis*patriots" (Calabrese 51) at a far remove from the momentous migrations of our day, whose identities hover between their origins and new (geographical, ideological, and cultural) homelands, whose borders are dissolved by a daily existence that constantly blurs the archaic and ultramodern.

In the global world, whose painful transformations we have yet to process, the return to magic and fantasy serves, once again, to reckon with the trauma of a modernity that has failed to deliver freedom and with a progress that has not redeemed western democracies but, on the contrary, produced a "primordialist bug" (Appadurai 143) within them. The quartet's uncanny underground realism is related to these two modes of expression. As Ferrante points out, the "caves" are a magical and transitional space, a time capsule where "the past [is] not to be overcome but to be redeemed, precisely as a storehouse of sufferings, of rejected ways of being" (fr 107); a space where the daughter, like Elena, brings her computer and uses it to tell her story; a space where Melina's drama is reflected in the dramas of Ariadne and Dido, and Delia's search for the truth in *Troubling Love* is shadowed by the story of Demeter and Persephone; a space where linear progress is ultimately eroded.

Like Leda's stolen doll in *The Lost Daughter* and the missing doll in *The Beach at Night*, Elena and Lila's dolls are liminal objects in the plot, caught between the world above and the world below, between realistic cohesion and the mysterious dissolution of the storyline, because—as I stated in my discussion of disappearance (cf. part 2, paragraph 2)—they turn out to be both points of strength in the story *and* a means of deconstructing the story. The narrative ellipsis surrounding the disappearance of the dolls is, furthermore, a symbolic ellipsis that bears more than one meaning, given that their disappearance and reemergence recall the various and constitutively intertwined temporalities of women's social erasure and survival (cf 6.8, 6.9), as well as the way the women are modeled after the dolls: hybrid figures caught between the feminine and maternal. Like other objects in the quartet (Lila's shoe designs, enlarged photograph, and notebooks, as well as the notebooks of Signora Solara), the dolls emerge on the stage as "anchors of the novelistic world but then, like household items shaking loose in an earthquake, become enchanted—with the result that we longer know quite what the real is, or how to feel about it" (Kurnick).

6. Feminist Storytelling

The enigma of the dolls—the way that for women they stand as metaphorical and liminal symbols exemplifying both erasure and survival, matrophobia and redemption—throws another feature of Ferrante's experimental realism in stark relief: her distinct feminist matrix. In the act of storytelling, a wide array of feminist theories and ideas is brought to life and transformed into a creative, eclectic, and universally shared logic; thus the realism of the quartet takes on new political meaning. As I say in the book's introduction, Elena and Lila's survival should be understood as "living above" (Pigliaru), or rather, beyond, trauma. However, that entails having first lived through trauma. Indeed, it entails having repeatedly fallen prey to it. The characteristic downward trajectory in Ferrante's work is, in this sense, crucial: The dolls are *cast down* into the cellar. Lila's notebooks *sink* to the bottom of the Arno. In Elena's essay, daughters find themselves down in the caves. The writer herself trespasses into the "cellar of writing" to rummage for marginalized writing (cf. part 1, paragraph 6).

Survival is therefore the arc not of exemplary subjectivities but subjectivities who are, by necessity, ambiguous and contradictory, purveyors of the underground world able to accommodate that subterranean space and tell a different story: a story not of victimhood, and that is therefore always vital. Women today are now looking to the eclectic yet clear truth of the feminist story, to its universal power, in a world in which an international, anti-feminist, homophobic, and xenophobic fundamentalism is taking shape that women readers counter with the international force of Ferrante's storytelling.

Still, at various events in Italy and abroad, I have heard many women voice concerns that the quartet is ultimately a negative tale, that the final balance of Elena and Lila's lives is bitter, or excessively bitter. But the point is that every person's development and self-individuation is *also* a form of solitude, and at least partially destructive. If anything, what remains difficult to process is that this existential hardship, which men have long experienced and symbolized, pertains to women too, and women can render it interesting and imbue it with meaning.

In addition to its supposed negativity, the quartet's depiction of friendship showcases Elena and Lila's private and public adventures in the world (both characters' pregnancies, Elena's education and writing, Lila's small-scale and managerial entrepreneurship, Lila's class struggle and technological vision) alongside their undeniable ability to relish new forms of existence and bravely invent new types of relationships. At times it can be difficult to grasp how powerful this breakthrough is, in part because Ferrante's portrayal of the new era of Elena and Lila is extremely understated. The last chapter of *Elena Ferrante's Key Words* speaks to this shadowy aspect of the quartet's chronology, rooted in the fact that *The Neapolitan Novels* reconstruct a female way of inhabiting time, downplaying the myths of History and ideologies that continue to be central to male discussions of engagement.

Uncanny underground realism's focus on the static and invisible space of the dominated means major historical events overlap in a completely incidental manner with the characters' private dramas. Yet a series of momentous historical and political circumstances make it so that Elena and Lila go from being excluded to included, from marginal "Unpredictable Subjects" (Lonzi 47) to figures at the heart of History. That explains why it is possible to feel, through them, the euphoria of the trials and tribulations of modern times. If it is up to Lila to intuit the future, to exhaust it in a euphoric and destructive spiral of gains and losses, introducing words like "heroin," "IBM," and "Chernobyl" (Kurnick) into the narrative and into the old-fashioned *rione*, it is Elena's job to survey the gray zones: the shortcomings of her education, the patriarchal and linguistic violence in the democratic school systems, the deceptions of her own creativity and intellectual commitment, and the decline of Lila's bold technological project, swallowed up by power dynamics and the bullying tactics of organized crime in Southern Italy.

Polyphony—the mutual *smarginatura* of "Lila's model" with "Elena's model" (Micali)—is also a labyrinth of timelines, where the two friends must realize that the archaic and modern are not opposing elements, that time cannot simply be understood as the contrast between a premodern, unsophisticated southern *rione* and a progressive Italian consumerist society. On the contrary, in the labyrinth, the archaic is embedded in modernity. The labyrinth is a return to "primordialism" (Appadurai 139) that women readers around the world fear they see in store for them: the looming, sweeping, and crosssectional threat of a return to the old order of nationalism, identity politics, misogyny, and racist fundamentalism—even in the West. Ferrante's storytelling is a compass in this new and pervasive war on today's unpredictable subjects, a guide for occupying the complex border now being drawn in the world, a traumatic line where the lives of millions of men and women risk being even more violently beholden to external influences and relegated to the margins of History.

BIBLIOGRAPHY

WORKS BY ELENA FERRANTE[4]

ban—2016. *The Beach at Night*. Translated by Ann Goldstein. New York: Europa Editions

doa—2005. *The Days of Abandonment*. Translated by Ann Goldstein. New York: Europa Editions

fer[1]—"Se l'amore è furioso." *La Repubblica*, November 30, 2007. http://ricercarepubblica.it/repubblica/archivio/repubblica/2007/11/30/se-amore-furioso.html

fer[2]—"The Experience of Writing a Diary Transformed Me into a Fiction Writer." Translated by Ann Goldstein. *The Guardian*, February 3, 2018. https://www.theguardian.com/books/2018/feb/03/elena-ferrante-on-writing-a-diary

fer[3]—"I'm Tired of Fiction, I No Longer See a Reason to Go Hunting for Anecdotes." Translated by Ann Goldstein. *The Guardian*, February 17, 2018. https://www.theguardian.com/lifeandstyle/2018/feb/17/elena-ferrante-im-tired-of-fiction-i-no-longer-see-the-reason-to-go-hunting-for-anecdotes

fer[4]—*"La mia amica che va in TV."* Interview with Valentina De Salvo. *La Repubblica/Robinson*, July 3, 2017. http://www.repubblica.it-/cultura/2017/07/03/news/elena_ferrante_la_mia_amica_che_va_in_tv_-169813940/?ref=search

---

[4] Works by Elena Ferrante cited in the volume are listed in alphabetical order according to their abbreviation.

fer[5]—"Yes, I'm Italian but I'm Not Loud, I Don't Gesticulate and I'm Not Good with Pizza." Translated by Ann Goldstein. *The Guardian*, February 24, 2018. https://www.theguardian.com/lifeandstyle/2018/feb/24/elena-ferrante-on-italian-language-identity

fer[6]—"A Power of Our Own." Translated by Ann Goldstein. *The New York Times*, May 17, 2019. https://www.nytimes.com/2019/05/17/opinion/elena-ferrante-on-women-power.html

fer[7]—"I Insist on Writing Things I Think I Would Never Put in Writing," Translated by Ann Goldstein. *The Guardian*, May 5, 2018. https://www.theguardian.com/lifeandstyle/2018/may/05/elena-ferrante-insist-on-writing-things-never-put-in-writing

fer[8]—"My Brilliant Friend: PW Talks with Elena Ferrante." Interview with Martha Schulman. *Publishers Weekly*, November 30, 2012. https://www.publishersweekly.com/pw/by-topic/authors/ interviews/article/54949-my-brilliant-friend-pw-talks-with-elena-ferrante.html

fer[9]—"A Writer's Talent Is Like a Fishing Net, Catching Daily Experiences that Can Educate." Translated by Ann Goldstein. *The Guardian*, January 5, 2019. https://www.theguardian.com/lifeandstyle/2019/jan/05/elena-ferrante-one-of-the-purposes-of-a-text-is-to-instruct

fr—2016. *Frantumaglia*. Translated by Ann Goldstein. New York: Europa Editions.

ld—2008. *The Lost Daughter*. Translated by Ann Goldstein. New York: Europa Editions.

mbf—2012. *My Brilliant Friend*. Translated by Ann Goldstein. New York: Europa Editions.

slc—2016. *The Story of the Lost Child*. Translated by Ann Goldstein. New York: Europa Editions.

snn—2013. *The Story of a New Name*. Translated by Ann Goldstein. New York: Europa Editions.

tl—2006. *Troubling Love*. Translated by Ann Goldstein. New York: Europa Editions.

tlts—2014. *Those Who Leave and Those Who Stay*. Translated by Ann Goldstein. New York: Europa Editions.

GENERAL WORKS[5]

Arendt, Hannah. 1970. *On Violence*. New York: Harcourt, Brace and Company.

Appadurai, Arjun. 1996. "Life after Primordialism." In *Modernity at Large*. Minneapolis: University of Minnesota Press, 139-57.

Audet, Élaine. 2000. *Le Cœur Pensant. Courtepointe de l'amitié entre femmes*. Québec: Le Loup de Gouttière.

Barad, Karen. 2007. *Meeting the Universe Halfway: Quantum Physics and the Entanglement of Matter and Meaning*. Durham: Duke University Press.

Barbetta, Pietro. 2017. "Lingua materna e memoria ferita." *Doppio Zero*, June 17. Accessed May 19, 2019. www.doppi-ozero.com/materiali/lingua-materna-e-memoria-ferita.

Beck, Ulrich. 2002. "The Cosmopolitan Society and Its Enemies." *Theory, Culture & Society* 19, no. 1–2, 17–44.

Belmonte, Thomas. 2005. *The Broken Fountain: Twenty-fifth Anniversary Edition*. New York: Columbia University Press.

Bhabha, Homi K. 2004. *The Location of Culture*. London: Routledge Classics.

Bollas, Christopher. 1987. *The Shadow of the Object: Psychoanalysis of the Unthought Known*. New York: Columbia University Press.

---

[5] When more than one work by an author is referred to, the work in question is indicated with a number. For example: Bourdieu[1] refers to the first work cited, Bourdieu[2] to the second, etc. In the bibliography, works are listed in the order they appear in this book, not in chronological order.

Bourdieu, Pierre. 1999. "The Contradictions of Inheritance." In *The Weight of the World: Social Suffering in Contemporary Society*, edited by Pierre Bourdieu et al., 507–13. Stanford, CA: Stanford University Press.

—. 1986. "The Forms of Capital." In *Handbook of Theory and Research for the Sociology of Education*, edited by J. Richardson, 241–58. Westport, CT: Greenwood.

—. 2002. *Masculine Domination.* Stanford, CA: Stanford University Press.

—. 1977. *Outline of a Theory of Practice.* Cambridge, UK: Cambridge University Press.

Børresen, Elisabeth Kari. 1968. *Subordination et équivalence. Nature et rôle de la femme d'après Augustin et Thomas d'Aquin.* Paris: Maison Mame.

Bourke, Joanna. 2007. *Rape: Sex, Violence, History.* Berkeley: Counterpoint.

Buchanan, Laurie. 1993. "'Island' of Peace: Female Friendships in Victorian Literature." In *Communication and Women's Friendships: Parallels and Intersections in Literature and Life*, edited by Janet Doubler Ward and Johana Stephens Mink, 77–96. Bowling Green: University Popular Press.

Calabrese, Stefano. 2005. *www.lettura.global: Il romanzo dopo il postmoderno.* Turin: Einaudi.

Calef, Victor, and Edward M. Weinshel. 1981. "Some Clinical Consequences of Introjection: Gaslighting." *Psychoanalytic Quarterly*, Vol. 50, Issue 1, 44–46.

D'Agostino, Gabriella. 2013. "I femminielli napoletani: alcune riflessioni antropologiche." In *Genere: Femminielli. Esplorazioni antropologiche e psicologiche*, edited by Eugenio Zito and Paolo Valerio, 75–90. Naples: Dante & Descartes.

Danna, Daniela. 2007. *Genocidio. La violenza contro le donne nell'era globale.* Milan: Elèuthera.

de Certeau, Michel. 1984. *The Practice of Everyday Life, Volume 1.* Translated by Steven Rendall. Berkeley: University of California Press.

Deleuze, Gilles. 1989. *Cinema II.* Minneapolis: University of Minnesota Press.

Deleuze, Gilles, and Felix Guattari. 1986. *Kafka: Toward a Minor Literature.* Minneapolis: University of Minneapolis Press.

De Mauro, Tullio. 2017. *Storia linguistica dell'Italia unita.* Rome: Laterza.

—. 2014. *Storia linguistica dell'Italia repubblicana. Dal 1946 ai nostri giorni.* Rome: Laterza.

Didi-Huberman, Georges. 2016. *The Surviving Image. Phantoms of Time and Time of Phantoms: Aby Warburg's History of Art.* Translated by Harvey L. Mendelsohn. University Park, Pennsylvania: Penn State University Press.

—. 2000. *Devant le temps: Histoire de l'art et anachronisme des images.* Paris: Editions de Minuit.

Fanon, Franz. 2008. *Black Skin, White Masks.* New York: Grove Press.

Foster, Hal. 1996. *The Return of the Real: The Avant-Garde at the End of the Century.* Cambridge: The MIT Press.

Foucault, Michel. 1998. *Aesthetics , Method, and Epistemology.* Translated by Robert Hurley and others. New York: The New Press.

Freud, Sigmund. 1997. *Sexuality and the Psychology of Love.* New York: Touchstone Books.

Ganguly, Debjani. 2016. *This Thing Called the World: The Contemporary Novel as Global Form.* Durham: Duke University Press.

Grosz, Elizabeth. 1999. "Bodies-Cities." In *Feminist Theory and the Body: A Reader*, edited by Janet Price and Margrit Shildrick, 381–87. New York: Routledge.

Hamon, Phillippe. 1992. *Expositions: Literature and Architecture in Nineteenth-Century France.* Berkeley, CA: University of California Press.

Huber, Irmtraud. 2014. "Tracing Shifts." In *Literature after Postmodernism. Reconstructive Fantasies.* 21–78. New York: Palgrave.

Huggan, Graham. 2001. *The Post-Colonial Exotic: Marketing the Margins.* London: Routledge.

Irigaray, Luce. 1993. "Body against Body: In Relation to the Mother." In *Sexes and Genealogies.* Translated by Gillian C. Gill, 7–22. New York: Columbia University Press.

Jung, Carl Gustav. 1969. *The Archetypes and the Collective Unconscious.* Princeton: Princeton University Press.

—. 1976. "The Transformation of Libido." In *Collected Works of C.G. Jung vol. 5*, edited by Gerhard Adler et al., 222–58. New York: Princeton University Press.

Klein, Melanie. 1975. "Envy and Gratitude." In *Envy and Gratitude, and Other Works*, 176–235. New York: The Free Press.

—. 1975. "Some Reflections on 'The Oresteia.'" In *Envy and Gratitude, And Other Works: 1946-1963*, 275–99. New York: The Free Press.

Kristeva, Julia. 1982. *Powers of Horror: An Essay on Abjection.* New York: Columbia University Press.

Lonzi, Carla. 2010. *Sputiamo su Hegel. E altri scritti.* Milan: Et al.

Marcus, Sharon. 2007. *Between Women. Friendship, Desire and Marriage in Victorian England.* Princeton: Princeton University Press.

Matte Blanco, Ignacio. 1981. *The Unconscious as Infinite Sets.* Abingdon-on-Thames: Routledge.

Melandri, Lea. 2011. *Amore e violenza. Il fattore molesto della civiltà.* Turin: Bollati Boringhieri.

Moe, Nelson. 2006. *The View from Vesuvius: Italian Culture and the Southern Question.* Berkeley: University of California Press.

Moretti, Franco. 1997. *La letteratura vista da lontano.* Turin: Einaudi.

Muraro, Luisa. 1991. *L'ordine simbolico della madre.* Rome: Editori Riuniti.

Nussbaum, Martha C. 2013. *Political Emotions.* Cambridge, MA: Belknap Press of Harvard University Press.

Pennacchio, Filippo. 2018. *Il Romanzo Global*. Milan: Biblion.

Pfirsch, Thomas. 2016. "La città frammentata. Geografia sociale di una metropoli in crisi." *Napoli Monitor*. Accessed May 17, 2019. http://sdc.napolimonitor.it/la-societa/2-abitare/la-citta-frammentata-geografia-sociale-di-una-metropoli-in-crisi/.

Ramondino, Fabrizia. 1977. "Introduzione." In *Napoli: I disoccupati organizzati. I protagonisti si raccontano*, edited by Fabrizia Ramondino. Milan: Feltrinelli.

Raymond, Janice. 2001. *A Passion for Friends: Towards a Philosophy of Female Affection*. North Melbourne: Spinifex Press.

Rich, Adrienne. 1995. *Of Woman Born: Motherhood as Experience and Institution*. New York: W.W. Norton and Company.

Ricœur, Paul. 1985. *Time and Narrative, vol. 2*. Chicago: University of Chicago Press.

Robertson, Roland. 1992. *Globalization: Social Theory and Global Culture*. Thousand Oaks, CA: SAGE.

Said, Edward. 2000. *Reflections on Exile and Other Essays*. Cambridge, MA: Harvard University Press.

Shields, David. 2010. *Reality Hunger: A Manifesto*. New York: Alfred A. Knopf.

Spivak, Gayatri. 2010. *Can the Subaltern Speak?: Reflections on the History of an Idea*. New York: Columbia University Press.

Steger, Manfred B. 2003. *Globalization: A Very Short Introduction*. Oxford: Oxford University Press.

Timmer, Nicoline. 2010. *Do you Feel it Too? The Post-Postmodern Syndrome in American Fiction at the Turn of the Millennium*. 21–51. Amsterdam: Rodopi.

Turner, Victor, and Edward Bruner, eds. 1985. *The Anthropology of Experience*. Champaign, IL: University of Illinois Press.

Winnicott, D.W. 1999. *The Family and Individual Development*. London: Routledge.

Woolf, Virginia. 1929. *A Room of One's Own*. New York: Harcourt, Brace and Company.

LITERARY CRITICISM[6]
(ON ELENA FERRANTE AND OTHERS)

Alfano, Barbara. 2018. "The Fact of the Matter: Ethics and Materiality in Elena Ferrante's Neapolitan Novels." *Italian Quarterly*, 52.

Alfano, Giancarlo. 2010. "Un 'vivere pieno di radici.' Il modello spaziale di Napoli nel secondo Novecento." In *Paesaggi mappe tracciati. Cinque studi su letteratura e geografia*, 91–150. Naples: Liguori.

Alfonzetti, Giovanna. 2018. "Il dialetto 'molesto' in Elena Ferrante." In *Dialetto e società*, edited by Gianna Marcatto. Padua: Cleup.

Alsop, Elizabeth. 2014. "Femmes Fatales: La Fascinazione di morte in Elena Ferrante's 'L'amore molesto' and 'I giorni dell'abbandono.'" *Italica: Journal of the Americas Association of Teachers of Italian* 22: 466–485.

Banti, Anna. Interview with Anna Banti. Radio3Suite. Transcribed by Serena Todesco. *Tracce a Margine*, 43.

Benedetti, Laura. 2012. "Il linguaggio dell'amicizia e della città." *Quaderni di Italianistica* 2: 171–88.

—. 2007. *The Tigress in the Snow: Motherhood and Literature in Twentieth-Century Italy.* Toronto: University of Toronto Press.

Benini, Annalena. 2013. "Le amiche geniali." *Il Foglio*, December 9. https://www.ilfoglio.it/articoli/2013/12/09/news/le-amiche-geniali-55886/

Blau, Rachel DuPlessis. 1985. "To Bear My Mother's Name: Künstlerromane by Women Writers." In *Writing Beyond the*

---

[6] When more than one work by an author is referred to, the work in question is indicated with a number. For example: Brogi[1] refers to the first work cited, Brogi[2] to the second, etc. In the bibliography, works are listed in the order they appear in this book, not in chronological order.

Ending. Narrative Strategies of Twentieth Century Women Writers, 84–104. Bloomington: Indiana University Press.

Brogi, Daniela. 2013. "Sé come un'altra. Su 'L'amica geniale' di Elena Ferrante." *Le Parole e le Cose,* December 8. Accessed June 30, 2019. http://www.leparoleelecose. it/? p=13515.

—. 2015. "Esiste una scrittura maschile?" *Nazione Indiana*, June 21. https://www.nazioneindiana.com/2015/06/21/esiste-una-scrittura-maschile/

—. 2005. "'Pubblico grosso' e 'pubblico fino'. Strategie di lettura dei 'Promessi sposi'." In *Il genere proscritto. Manzoni e la scelta del romanzo*, 204–22. Pisa: Giardini.

—. 2018. "Lei chi è? Forme e fantasmi del femminile nelle narrazioni novecentesche." In *Scritture del corpo*, edited by Marina Paino, Maria Rizzarelli and Antonio Sichera. Pisa: ETS.

Cardone, Lucia. 2015. "Sensibili differenze. 'L'amore molesto' da Ferrante a Martone." In *Filmare il femminismo. Studi sulle donne nel cinema e nei media,* edited by Lucia Cardone and Sara Filippelli, 95–104. Pisa: ETS.

Carvalho, Richard. 2018. "Smarginatura and Spiragli: Uses of Infinity in Ferrante's Neapolitan Quartet." *Allegoria* 77: 94–111.

Cavanaugh, Jillian R. 2016. "Indexicalities of Language in Ferrante's Neapolitan Novels: Dialect and Italian as Markers of Social Value and Difference." In *The Works of Elena Ferrante: Reconfiguring the Margins*, edited by Grace Russo Bullaro and Stephanie Love, 45–70. New York: Palgrave Macmillan.

Cavarero, Adriana. 2017. "Filosofia della narrazione e scrittura del sé: primi appunti sulla scrittura di Elena Ferrante." *Testo & Senso.* Accessed May 30, 2019. www.testoesenso.it.

—. 2011. "L'altra necessaria." In *Tu che mi guardi, tu che mi racconti. Filosofia della narrazione*, 105–20. Milan: Feltrinelli.

—. 2007. *Orrorismo, ovvero della violenza sull'inerme.* Milan: Feltrinelli.

Clark, Alex. 2016. "Sister Act: Female Friendship in Fiction from Woolf to Ferrante and Zadie Smith." *The Guardian,* August 6. Accessed June 28, 2019. https://www.the guardian.com/books/2016/aug/06/women-friendship-world-ferrante-zadie-smith-fiction-alex-clark.

Conti, Eleonora. 2015. "Abiti madri e figlie ne 'L'amore molesto' di Elena Ferrante." *Lettera Zero* 1: 103–13.

Crispino, Maria Anna. 2015. "Luna e l'altra." *Leggendaria.* http://www.leggendaria.it/2015/01/primopiano-elena-ferrante-2/

De Caprio, Chiara. 2017. "Spazi, suoni e lingue nel romanzo 'di Napoli.'" *Nazione Indiana,* December 16. Accessed May 9, 2019. https://www.nazioneindiana.com/2017/12spazi-suoni-lingue-nel-romanzo-napoli/.

de Rogatis, Tiziana. 2017. "Cerimoniale iniziatico e strutture rituali ne 'L'amore molesto', 'I giorni dell'abbandono' e 'La figlia oscura' di Elena Ferrante." In *Nel nome della madre. Ripensare le figure della maternità*, edited by Daniela Brogi, Tiziana de Rogatis, Franco Cristiana and Lucinda Spera, 71–92. Bracciano: Del Vecchio.

—. 2018. "'L'amore molesto,' 'I giorni dell'abbandono' e 'La figlia oscura' di Elena Ferrante: riti di passaggio, cerimoniali iniziatici e nuove soggettività." In *Femminismo e femminismi nella scrittura italiana dall'Ottocento al XXI secolo*, edited by Sandra Parmeggiani and Michela Prevedello, 99–120. Florence: SEI.

—. 2014. "'L'amore molesto' di Elena Ferrante. Mito classico, riti di iniziazione e identità femminile." *Allegoria* 69–70: 273–308.

—. 2016. "Elena Ferrante e il Made in Italy. La costruzione di un immaginario femminile e napoletano." In *Made in Italy e cultura*, edited by Daniele Balicco, 288–317. Palermo: Palumbo.

—. 2016. "Metamorfosi del tempo. Il ciclo dell'Amica geniale." *Allegoria* 73: 123–37.

Donnarumma, Raffaele. 2016. "Il melodramma, l'antimelodramma, la Storia: sull''Amica geniale' di Elena Ferrante." *Allegoria* 73: 138–47.

—. 2014. *Ipermodernità. Dove va la narrative contemporanea.* Bologna: Il Mulino.

Elwell, Leslie. 2016. "Breaking Bonds: Refiguring Maternity in Elena Ferrante's 'The Lost Daughter'." In *The Works of Elena Ferrante: Reconfiguring the Margins*, edited by Grace Russo Bullaro and Stephanie Love, 237–69. New York: Palgrave Macmillan.

Falkoff, Rebecca. 2016. "To Translate Is to Betray: On the Elena Ferrante Phenomenon in Italy and the United States." *The Guardian,* October 5. Accessed June 30, 2019. https://www.theguardian.com/books/2016/oct/05/to-translate-is-to-betray-the-elena-ferrante-phenomenon-in-italy-and-the-us.

Falotico, Caterina. 2015. "Elena Ferrante: Il ciclo dell''Amica geniale' tra autobiografia, storia e lettura." *Forum Italicum* 49: 92–118.

Ferrara, Enrica Maria. 2016. "Performative Realism and Post-Humanism in 'The Days of Abandonment'." In *The Works of Elena Ferrante: Reconfiguring the Margins*, edited by Grace Russo Bullaro and Stephanie Love, 129–58. New York: Palgrave Macmillan.

—. 2017. "Elena Ferrante e la questione dell'identità". *Oblio* 26–27: 47–55.

Fortini, Laura. 2012. "Due ragazze del secolo scorso raccontate da Ferrante". *il manifesto*, October 31. Accessed June 2, 2019. https://www.edizionieo.it/review/2699.

Fusillo, Massimo. 2016. "Sulla smarginatura. Tre punti chiave per Elena Ferrante." *Allegoria* 73: 148–53.

Gambaro, Elisa. 2016. "Splendori e miserie di una duplice affabulazione." *Allegoria* 73: 154–65.

—. 2014. "Il fascino del regresso. Note su 'L'amica geniale' di Elena Ferrante." *Enthymema* 11: 168–77.

Giorgio, Adalgisa. 2002. "The Passion for the Mother: Conflicts and Idealizations in Contemporary Italian Narratives by Women." In *Writing Mothers and Daughters: Renegotiating the Mother in Western European Narratives by Women*, edited by Adalgisa Giorgio, 119–54. New York: Berghahn Books.

Guglielmi, Marina. 2017. "Gli spazi della sorellanza. Le stanze di Valeria Parrella e Valeria Comencini." In *Sorelle e sorellanza nella letteratura e nelle arti*, edited by Claudia Cao and Guglielmi Marina, 335–55. Florence: Cesati.

Jesurum, Costanza. 2017. "Memorie di una lettrice perbene. Su 'L'amica geniale' di Elena Ferrante." *bei zauberei,* August 16. Accessed June 29, 2019. https://beizauberei.word-press.com/2017/08/16.

Kirsch, Adam. 2016. "Starting from Home: Elena Ferrante's Neapolitan Novels." In *The Global Novel: Writing the World in the 21st Century*, 92–103. New York: Columbia Global Reports.

Kurnick, D. 2015. "Ferrante, in History." *Public Books*. https://www.publicbooks.org/ferrante-in-history.

La Capria, Raffaele. 2014. "Il labirinto nero di Elena Ferrrante. A Napoli la vita è un rione infetto." *Corriere della Sera*, December 30. http://www.corriere.it/cultura/16_marzo_12/elena-ferrante-napoli-rione-romanzo-o-4a76b44c-e855-11e5-9492-dcf601b6eeea6.html

Lagioia, Nicola. *In Spite of Everything: Answers to questions from Nicola Lagioia*, interview with Elena Ferrante in fr, 364–84.

Librandi, Rita. 2018. "Una lingua silenziosa: immaginare il dialetto negli scritti di Elena Ferrante." In *Dal dialogo al polilogo: l'Italia nel mondo. Lingue, letterature e culture in contatto*, edited by Elzbieta Jamrozik and Anna Tylusinska-Kowalska. Warsaw: Atti del Convegno.

Lombardi, Giancarlo. 1999. "Scambi d'identità: il recupero del corpo materno ne 'L'amore molesto.'" *Romance Languages Annual* 10: 228–91.

Lo Moro, Viola. n.d. Correspondence with the author.

Love, Stephanie. 2016. "'An Educated Identity': The School as a Modernist Chronotope in Ferrante's Neapolitan Novels." In *The Works of Elena Ferrante: Reconfiguring the Margins*, edited by Grace Russo Bullaro and Stephanie Love, 71–97. New York: Palgrave Macmillan.

Lucamante, Stefania. 2018. "For Sista Only? Smarginare l'eredità delle sorelle Morante e Ramondino, ovvero i limiti e la forza del post-femminismo di Elena Ferrante." In *Sorelle e sorellanza nella letteratura e nelle arti*, edited by Claudia Cao and Marina Guglielmi, 315–34. Florence: Franco Cesati Editore.

—. 2008. "Writing Is Always Playing with the Mother's Body: Mother's Rewrites." In *A Multitude of Women: The Challenges of the Contemporary Italian Novel*, 28–108. Toronto: University of Toronto Press.

Maksimowicz, Christine. 2016. "Maternal Failure and its Bequest: Toxic Attachment in the Neapolitan Novels." In *The Works of Elena Ferrante: Reconfiguring the Margins*, edited by Grace Russo Bullaro and Stephanie Love, 207–37. New York: Palgrave Macmillan.

Manetti, Beatrice. 2012. "Le donne e la città." *L'Indice dei Libri del Mese* 29: 28.

—. 2014. "Le confessioni di un'italiana." *L'Indice dei Libri del Mese* 21: 18.

—. 2014. "Guardami finché non mi addormento." *L'Indice dei Libri del Mese* 31: 19.

Micali, Simona. 2014. "La scrittura e la vita." *L'Indice dei Libri del Mese* 21: 18.

Milkova, Stiliana. 2016. "The Translator's Visibility or the Ferrante-Goldstein Phenomenon" *Allegoria* 73: 166–73.

—. 2013. "Mothers, Daughters, Dolls: On Disgust in Elena Ferrante's La Figlia oscura." *Italian Culture* 31: 91–109.

—. 2017. "Spazio liminale, labirinto urbano e città femminile ne 'L'amica geniale' di Elena Ferrante." *Contemporanea* 15: 77–78

—. 2016. "Artistic Tradition and Feminine Legacy in Elena Ferrante's 'L'amore molesto.'" *California Italian Studies*, 6: 1–15.

—. 2016. "Elena Ferrante's Visual Poetics: Ekphrasis in 'Troubling Love,' 'My Brilliant Friend,' and 'The Story of a New Name'." In *The Works of Elena Ferrante. Reconfiguring the Margins*, edited by Grace Russo Bullaro and Stephanie Love, 159–82. New York: Palgrave Macmillan.

Palermo, Massimo. n.d. Correspondence with the author.

Pezzella, Mario. 2017. "La nitidezza e il gorgo. Sulla 'Frantumaglia' di Elena Ferrante." *Tysm,* October 30. Accessed April 30, 2019. http://tysm.org/la-nitidezza-e-il-gorgo-sulla-frantumaglia-di-elena-ferrante/.

Pigliaru, Alessandra. 2019. *Presentation of "Elena Ferrante. Parole chiave."* Libreria delle Donne di Milano, February 9, 2019. http://www.glibbo.it/IT/news/video/19841/

Pinto, Isabella. 2019. *Poetiche e politiche nella scrittura del sé di Elena Ferrante*. Dissertation, Università degli studi Roma Tor Vergata.

Porciani, Elena. 2013. "La scelta di Don Chisciotte. Sulle tracce del familienromance di Elsa Morante." *Contemporanea* 11: 85–96.

Rea, Domenico. 2005. "Le due Napoli." In *Opere*, edited by Francesco Durante, 1333–51. Milan: Mondadori.

Russo Bullaro, Grace. 2016. "The Era of the 'Economic Miracle' and the Force of Context in Elena Ferrante's 'My Brilliant Friend.'" In *The Works of Elena Ferrante: Reconfiguring the Margins*, edited by Grace Russo Bullaro and Stephanie Love, 15–44. New York: Palgrave Macmillan.

Sambuco, Patrizia. 2012. *Corporeal Bonds: The Daughter-*

Mother Relationship in Twentieth-Century Italian Women's Writing. Toronto: University of Toronto Press.

Santovetti, Olivia. 2018. "Melodrama or Metafiction? Elena Ferrante's Neapolitan Novels." *Modern Languages Review* 113: 502–20.

—. 2016. "Lettura, scrittura e autoriflessione nel ciclo dell'Amica geniale di Elena Ferrante." *Allegoria* 73: 179–92.

Scarinci, Viviana, 2014. "Elena Ferrante." *Doppiozero* (epub).

Sellitti, Ottavio. n.d. *Where Is Elena Ferrante. The Life in the Rione.* Accessed May 17, 2019. https://osellitti.com/where-elena-ferrante-the-life-in-the-rione/.

Setti, Nadia. 2016. "Il genio dell'ambivalenza". In *Dell'ambivalenza. Dinamiche della narrazione di Elena Ferrante, Julie Ossuka e Goliarda Sapienza*, edited by Anna Maria Crispino and Serena Vitale, 105-19. Guidonia: Iacobelli.

—. 2018. "Dal/del Sud: dis/locazioni." In *Donne e Sud. Percorsi nella cultura italiana contemporanea*, edited by Manuela Spinelli and Ramona Onnis. Florence: Cesati.

Small, Pauline. 1999. "Mario Martone's 'L'amore molesto': Desperately Seeking Delia." *The Italianist* 19: 299–317.

Todesco, Serena. 2017. *Tracce a margine. Scritture a firma femminile nella narrativa storica siciliana contemporanea.* Gioiosa Marea: Pungitopo.

Tortorici, Dayne. 2016. "Those Like Us: On Elena Ferrante." *n+1* 22. https://nplusonemag.com/issue-22/reviews/those-like-us/

Turchetta, Gianni. 2016. "Dal rione al mainstream. 'L'amica geniale' di Elena Ferrante." In *Tirature '16. Un mondo da tradurre*, edited by Vittorio Spinazzola, 104–11. Milan: Mondadori.

Van Ness, Emma. 2016. "Dixit Mater: The Significance of the Maternal Voice in Ferrante's Neapolitan Novels." In *The Works of Elena Ferrante: Reconfiguring the Margins*, edited by Grace Russo Bullaro and Stephanie Love, 293–312. New York: Palgrave Macmillan.

Villarini, Andrea. 2016. "Riflessioni sociolinguistiche a margine de 'L'amica geniale' di Elena Ferrante." *Allegoria* 73: 193–203.

Wehling-Giorgi, Katrin. 2018. "Picturing the Fragmented Maternal Body: Rethinking Constructs of Maternity in the Novels of Elena Ferrante and Alice Sebold." *Women. A Cultural Review* 2.

—. 2017. "Ero separata da me: Memory, Selfhood, and Mother-Tongue in Goliarda Sapienza and Elena Ferrante." In *Goliarda Sapienza in Context: Intertextual Relationships with Italian and European Culture*, edited by Alberica Bazzoni, Emma Bond, and Katrin Wehling-Giorgi, 215–29. Madison-Teaneck, NJ: Fairleigh Dickinson University Press.

—. 2017. "Playing with the Maternal Body: Violence, Mutilation, and the Emergence of the Female Subject in Ferrante's Novels." *California Italian Studies* 7: 1–15.

—. 2016. "Elena Ferrante's Neapolitan Novels: Writing Liminality." *Allegoria* 73: 204–10.

Wood, James. 2013. "Women on the Verge: The Fiction of Elena Ferrante." *The New Yorker.* https://www.newyorker.com/magazine/2013/01/21/women-on-the-verge.

ABOUT THE AUTHOR

Born in Naples, Tiziana de Rogatis is currently an associate professor of Comparative
Literature at the University for Foreigners of
Siena. Her recent work analyzes modern
constructions of the feminine interpreted in
an anthropological manner via the reemergence of classical myths. She has written and
lectured widely on Elena Ferrante in Italy
and elsewhere in Europe, Asia and the
United States. She lives in Rome.